Preparing for Life

The Complete Guide for Transitioning to Adulthood for those with Autism and Asperger's Syndrome

Dr. Jed Baker

Preparing for Life

The Complete Guide for Transitioning to Adulthood for those with Autism and Asperger's Syndrome

All marketing and publishing rights guaranteed to and reserved by

FUTURE HORIZONS™ INC.

721 W. Abram Street
Arlington, Texas 76013
800-489-0727
817-277-0727
817-277-2270 (fax)
E-mail: info@FHautism.com
www.FHautism.com

Cover design and book layout: Matt Mitchell, www.mattmitchelldesign.com

ISBN 1-932565-33-7

Acknowledgments

I wish to thank all the students, their families, teachers, and employers who have taught me what skills are important to teach in preparation for adult life. Their needs and goals guided the content of this book.

I also want to thank my colleagues who made crucial contributions to the work. Rick Blumberg, Ph.D., wrote Chapter 4, which in many ways is the centerpiece of the book. Daphne Gregory, M.A. was inspirational in detailing her transition model and expressing her constant enthusiasm for preparing her students for adulthood. Kenwin Nancoo, LPC, NCC, CNLP, M.S. made significant contributions to the dating sections as only an eligible bachelor can do. Ilana Levitt, M.A., M.Ed., LPC, offered extremely helpful suggestions to me regarding the employment section.

At some point, it felt like *Preparing for Life* might take a lifetime to complete as several parts were rewritten to make it a better work. I wish to thank Kelly Gilpin for her endless patience in editing and reediting through this process.

Last but not least, thank you to my wife Beth and our children, Jake and Lindsay, for continually trying to prepare me for adulthood and putting up with me as I squeeze every extra hour into writing skill lessons.

—Jed Baker, Ph.D.

Table of Contents

• **Money Matters**

• **Preparing for Emergencies**

• **Transportation**

Chapter One
Asperger's, Autism Spectrum Disorders and the need for life skills training

I recently was asked to create a life skills training curriculum for two teens in a special high school program for students with Asperger's Syndrome (AS). Although many students with AS remain in mainstream high school settings, these very bright young men had long histories of behavioral and academic difficulties in their previous school settings that led them to this specialized program. I was told they needed help with their social skills, but might not be open to receiving such help. After years of social rejection, they wanted to be accepted for who they were rather than to be told they need to change. How then could I motivate them to want to learn new social behaviors without suggesting that there was something problematic about their current social functioning?

I thought it might be interesting to have them participate in teaching others about social skills rather than convincing them that they needed to learn new skills. I arranged for them to be paid for their participation in the making of a new social skill picture book that demonstrated the "right" and "wrong" ways to enact a variety of skills. Although we selected skills that I knew they needed to work on, I presented the activity as a project primarily to help others. One student took to the activity with some enthusiasm. He posed for pictures, sequenced pictures together on the computer and added text to create a story.

The other student was more reluctant to participate. I decided to show him an example of a picture skill so he could get a better idea of the project. I showed him the skill for greeting people "appropriately" since *he* typically greeted others with the phrase "death to all." His reaction was honest and thought provoking, "I will not participate. Your depictions of 'right' and 'wrong' are typical psychological propaganda." I had to admire his insight and wit. He was right. Who was I to tell others how to behave in a socially appropriate manner? As my wife will attest, I am certainly not the model of social grace and style.

This young man reminds us that there is no one person who can dictate what is appropriate social behavior. However, there are certainly behaviors that, depending on the situation, will facilitate or get in the way of reaching individuals' goals. This young man has entertained the notion of getting a graphic design degree at some point. Saying "death to all" to greet a college admissions officer might not be a very practical approach to reaching his goal. In contrast, saying, "death to all" to those who know and accept his sarcastic wit might even help maintain friendships by bringing humor to his interactions.

It is my philosophy that the skills in this book and others do not represent a model of social correctness. They are, however, ideas about how to behave that may help students reach their own goals. People with Asperger's need acceptance, not judgments that how they behave is "incorrect." The skill lessons in this book can be thought of as ways to expand social repertoires to reach personal goals rather than change "faulty" behaviors. The message is, don't alter the uniqueness that makes you special in so many great ways—just add to what you can do.

Asperger's Syndrome and Autism Spectrum Disorders

Autism spectrum disorders (also know as pervasive developmental disorders) refer to a wide range of symptoms that span across an individual's sensory, cognitive, motor, language, and social-emotional development. Asperger's Syndrome, autism, and Pervasive Developmental Disorder - Not Otherwise Specified (PDD-NOS) are some of the most common autism spectrum disorders.

The autism spectrum is considered a "spectrum" because individuals vary greatly from each other. Intellectually, some fall in the mentally retarded range while others clearly fall in the superior intellectual range. Asperger's Syndrome and High Functioning Autism involve, by definition, individuals with average to above-average intellectual ability and better communication skills than those with more "classic" autism who tend to have lower intellectual functioning and more communication difficulties. Those who have symptoms of an autism spectrum disorder, but do not meet the full criteria for a specific diagnosis like autism or Asperger's Syndrome are typically given the diagnosis of Pervasive Developmental Disorder – Not Otherwise Specified (PDD-NOS). This actually represents the largest category of individuals on the spectrum, which means that although we can identify individuals on the spectrum, we are not that good at making specific differential diagnoses among autistic spectrum disorders.

Current diagnostic criteria describe autism spectrum disorders as involving difficulties in three general areas: (a) qualitative impairment in social interactions (e.g., impairment in responding to or initiating interactions with others, or failure to form peer relationships), (b) qualitative impairment in verbal and nonverbal communication (e.g., no mode of communication, or impairment in the ability to initiate or sustain conversations), and (c) restricted, repetitive, and stereotyped patterns of behavior, interests or activities (e.g., preoccupation with restricted patterns of interest, or inflexible adherence to nonfunctional routines or rituals) (American Psychiatric Association, 1994).

Problems with social interaction can include difficulties initiating or responding to conversation, difficulties using or responding to nonverbal gestures (e.g., pointing out objects), lack of or inconsistent eye contact, impairments in responding to others' feelings, difficulties working cooperatively with peers, and subsequent failure to develop peer relationships. Understanding what to do or say in social situations is a core concern for autistic individuals.

Communication problems range from no ability to communicate and use language to more subtle difficulties with the flow of conversation and social communication (pragmatic language). Some classically autistic individuals may have difficulties understanding the meanings of most words and may show little spontaneous language communication. In contrast, those with High Functioning Autism and Asperger's may appear to have excellent command of language in terms of their ability to express themselves and understand others, yet they may have great trouble with the flow of social conversation, talking *at* people instead of *with* people, relaying factual information or phrases memorized from TV shows without responding to what their listener is saying or doing. Thus individuals with Asperger's may have extensive vocabularies, but difficulty using them in a fluid way to make conversation in social situations.

Repetitive and ritualistic behaviors reflect a preference for sameness and repetition with regards to interests, daily routine, and body movements. Many youngsters with autism develop a fascination with a particular area of interest and elaborate on that interest to the exclusion of learning about new things. For example, I knew a youngster who became obsessed with vacuum cleaners and was reluctant to attend to or talk about anything else. Many autistic individuals also exhibit non-functional routines that appear superstitious in nature. One individual I worked with had to hang every picture in the house at a crooked angle before he could use the toilet. Other students may not have non-functional routines, but prefer that their daily routines occur the same way all the time and may become very anxious or upset when changes or transitions are introduced. Youngsters may also demonstrate repetition in their use of language (repeating the same phrase over and over) or in their physical movements (e.g., repetitive hand flapping, body rocking, or twirling around and around).

Because of the difficulties individuals with ASD have in negotiating social situations and handling changes in their environment, many students experience stress, frustration and anxiety on an almost constant basis (Kim, Szatmari, Bryson, Streiner, & Wilson, 2000; Myles & Southwick, 1999). Wanting to interact with another student but not knowing how, not understanding the change in teacher directions for a new challenging task, hearing other students laugh around them and not knowing whether they are the target of the joke—these are all stressful situations that youths with AS experience daily.

Despite this level of stress, it is important to point out the emotional variability among students with autism spectrum disorders. Some students rarely seem to get upset, as they may handle their stress by withdrawal and go virtually unnoticed. Others present additional anxiety disorders (e.g., Obsessive-Compulsive Disorder, Social Phobia, or Panic Disorder). Some students seem to be constantly frustrated, impulsive, and have frequent tantrums. Many of these individuals may also get diagnosed with Attention Deficit Disorder or a Mood disorder (e.g., Bipolar disorder). Although students may react to and cope with the stresses in their lives quite differently, they may share a similar reason for experiencing high levels of stress, as described below.

Given the variety of symptoms and intellectual functioning among individuals with autistic spectrum disorders, a number of researchers have theorized about the core underlying problem within the disorders. Three, perhaps related, theories have received the most attention:

1. Frith (1989) suggests that autistic individuals lack the ability to simultaneously integrate multiple linguistic, social and emotional messages typically present in social situations. Something about their neurological functioning makes it difficult to assimilate and organize all the pertinent information. Since most social situations have multiple levels of sensory input, autistic individuals do not always fully grasp what is happening or how to respond. Instead, they may attend to and process only a fragment of the social experience, resulting in repetitive and atypical social behavior.

2. Baron-Cohen (1995) suggests that the core problem is the inability to understand the thoughts and feelings of others, a process termed "theory of mind." Thus, autistic individuals have difficulty taking other people's perspectives.

3. Hobson (1996) suggests that autism involves the inability to perceive and understand emotional expressions. This would then lead to difficulties in perspective taking and subsequent problems in social interaction.

These three theories can be considered complementary. Both Baron-Cohen and Hobson's theories suggest that autistic individuals cannot easily empathize with or understand another person's view of the world. Frith's theory helps explain why. The inability to simultaneously integrate information about what is happening in a social situation makes it difficult to imagine what others might be thinking and feeling. To take another's perspective, one has to synthesize information about the other person (e.g., the person's recent past experiences and preferences), along with what is happening to the person.

Most social skills rely on the ability to mentally adopt another person's perspective. For example, knowing why to say hello when you greet someone is based on understanding how others might think or feel if you ignore them rather than greet them. Knowing when to stop talking, take turns, respond to others' initiations, compromise, help others, or share, all come naturally when a person can easily take another's perspective. However, these social skills do not come naturally to autistic individuals, and must be taught explicitly if they are going to be mastered. The Social Skills Lessons laid out in Chapter 9 attempt to do just that—to break down social skills into their components and make explicit what to do and say in social situations and why.

What Life Skill Lessons are Relevant for Students on the Spectrum

As described above, individuals on the spectrum may have difficulties with: (a) perspective taking and empathy, (b) the use of nonverbal communication, (c) conversation skills, and (d) handling frustrations and anxiety. The skill lessons in Chapter 9 try to address these issues across a variety of situations (e.g., with peers, parents, educators, and employers). The life lessons outlined are primarily social skill lessons as they impact on how individuals will interact with others.

Perspective-taking and empathy: All the skill lessons in Chapter 9 address the issue of perspective taking in that every lesson gives some information about the impact of one's behavior on others. Each lesson begins with a "rationale" that includes a description of how the particular skill influences others' perception of the student. For example, a skill like "Don't impose rules on others" involves information about how others will feel and react if a student tells them what to do too much. In addition to the perspective-taking that pervades every skill lesson, the issue of showing empathy for others when they are upset is specifically addressed in lessons on empathic listening and showing understanding for others' feelings.

Nonverbal communication: Since many social skills rely on the accurate understanding and expression of nonverbal behaviors, some crucial nonverbal skills are outlined in the beginning of Chapter 9. Unlike many authors writing on this subject, I do not necessarily think it is relevant (or even possible) to teach how to accurately read all emotions and nonverbal communications.

Instead, I have tried to present information on those nonverbal cues that are relevant to most social interactions. A crucial nonverbal issue that cuts across many skills is the ability to read and express interest (versus disinterest), a welcoming attitude (versus unwelcoming behaviors) and sincere emotional expression (versus sarcasm). These distinctions help students know when to continue to pursue a social interaction and how to express a desire for others to continue to interact with them. If someone looks bored, unwelcoming, or teases sarcastically, then this may be time to back off, while others' interest, welcoming attitude and genuine positive expressions are reasons to continue to interact. For those readers interested in more information about identifying various emotional expressions, they may find the Mind Reading software developed by Simon Baron-Cohen (Baron-Cohen, 2002) and colleagues to be helpful.

Conversation Skills: A large proportion of lessons is devoted to the conversation area as these skills are crucial for most social interactions. Working cooperatively with others in school and employment settings, making friends, meeting, and developing intimate relationships all rely heavily on effective conversation. Skills here focus on the ability to initiate, respond to, and manage the flow of conversation with sensitivity to one's partner.

Anger/Frustration and anxiety: Chapter 9 has two sections of skill lessons devoted to managing one's own emotions; one for managing anger/frustration and the other for managing anxiety. Intense frustration or anxiety can make a student unavailable for learning. Thus for those whose anxieties or frustrations interfere significantly with functioning, these skill areas often have to be targeted first.

Chapter Two
The transition process and the law

Research over the past 25 years has shown that many young adults with disabilities who graduated from high school remain unemployed, socially isolated, or in trouble with the criminal justice system (Mcafee & Mann, 1982; Patton & Dunn, 1998; Wagner, Balckorby, Cameto, Hebbeler, & Newman, 1993). As a result, many special education advocates pushed for changes in the law to assure better planning for the transition from high school to adult life. The Individuals with Disabilities Education Act (IDEA) (P.L. 10 1-476) and the 1997 Amendments (P.L. 105-17) mandate secondary schools to create transition plans for each student with a disability to help them successfully move on to post-school activities like college, vocational training, employment, independent living and participation in the community. The IDEA 1997 Transition Regulations defines transition services as:

"a coordinated set of activities for a student with a disability that

1. Is designed within an outcome-oriented process that promotes movement from school to post-school activities including postsecondary education, vocational training, integrated employment (including supported employment), continuing and adult education, adult services, independent living, or community participation;

2. Is based on the individual student's needs, taking into account the student's preferences and interests; and

3. Includes:
   I. Instruction
   II. Related Services
   III. Community experiences
   IV. The development of employment and other post-school adult living objectives
   V. If appropriate, acquisition of daily living skills and functional vocational evaluation."

The law requires schools to develop, and update annually, a student's transition plan by age fourteen focusing on the student's course of study (e.g., advanced placement courses or vocational education program) and by age sixteen to establish a transition plan detailing any interagency responsibilities or needed linkages (e.g., links to the department of vocational rehabilitation or to employer sponsored internship or paid work programs).

The transition plan is based on an evaluation of the student's needs, as well as the student's preferences and interests. Thus it is crucial that the student, the student's family, and the school have a clear understanding of the student's strengths (and possible interests) and challenges (and related compensatory strategies or plans to remedy those areas). The assessment section of this book describes a form (Appendix A in the back of Chapter 3) to summarize the results of educational, vocational, and psychological evaluations and help map out assets and challenges. This form is not a substitute for these evaluations, but rather a convenient form to summarize the results of such evaluations.

Daphne Gregory, founder and president of the New Jersey Transition Coordinators Network, has developed a model program for transition services at Millburn High School in New Jersey. Her program has set the standards that lawmakers have used to create many of the laws governing how transition services should be provided. Her model takes students through several stages as they participate in transition group meetings that meet every month:

Stage 1: Self-awareness. In 9th grade, students begin to assess their assets and challenges. They develop information about their disability, needed modifications or training, and talents and interests.

Stage 2: Self-advocacy. Based on their self-awareness, students learn to advocate for themselves. They learn to express their interests and preferences, to develop their own goals, participate in their IEP and eventually run their IEP meetings, and educate others about their disability.

Stage 3: Career awareness. By their Junior year, students begin career assessments to determine their career interests, and match their strengths and weakness to career goals. A crucial component of this is the development of appropriate internship experiences to try out different employment/career options. This allows for what the law above describes as a "functional vocational assessment," which is an ongoing assessment of the skills needed to perform while in a particular work environment. By actually working in a real work environment, it is possible to assess what skills the student still needs to learn and to have real opportunities to generalize those new skills in the actual work setting. To this end, frequent feedback from employers and supervisors is crucial to inform further targets for skill development. For more information on Daphne Gregory's program, see Hunsberger (2001).

Social skills training is a crucial component of every aspect of Transition Services. To advocate for oneself in an IEP meeting or later in college, to gain and maintain employment, and to negotiate the community and live independently all require successful social interactions. Consistent with Daphne Gregory's model, we begin the process of social skills training with self-awareness. Self-awareness is a crucial part of what drives the motivation to learn social skills as described in the next chapter.

Chapter Three
Self-awareness and moving beyond denial

Self-awareness

Before one can learn social skills, or any skills for that matter, it is crucial that the learner is motivated. Motivation may come from an individual's insight into his or her own pattern of assets and challenges. From such insight, one may desire to alter behavior and learn more skills in order to achieve desired social or vocational goals. For example, an individual who knows he has a fine motor problem affecting his handwriting may desire to learn keyboarding skills if he wants to get an office related job. Similarly, an individual who is aware of her difficulties starting and maintaining conversations with others and desperately wants to make friends may desire to learn conversational skills to achieve her social goals.

Not only does accurate self-awareness help motivate the learning process, but it also leads to more efficient self-advocacy. With accurate knowledge one can plan better how to deal with otherwise frustrating situations. For example, the individual with fine-motor problems can ask for a laptop computer rather than get frustrated trying to deal with handwriting tasks. An individual with conversation skill difficulties might decide not to put herself in situations with high conversational demands, but opt instead for quieter environments to work or socialize.

Having a student evaluated

Getting information about a student's pattern of strengths and challenges typically begins with a review of past and current educational, vocational, psychological, social, and psychiatric evaluations. Students identified as having special needs are entitled to such a comprehensive evaluation free of charge by their public school's special education team. Students who are not recognized by their school system as having special education needs (because of good academic functioning) yet are experiencing many social difficulties may benefit from an evaluation by a qualified mental health professional (e.g., a psychologist, neurologist, or psychiatrist) experienced with autistic spectrum disorders or related social-communication difficulties. Such an evaluation should result in a report of diagnostic impressions and treatment recommendations targeting social or emotional supports. A variety of local and national autism organizations may be helpful in securing referrals to experienced clinicians.

A therapist, counselor, or thoughtful parent can review the results of past and current evaluations to help a student develop awareness of assets and challenges. This must be done with sensitivity to the student's self-esteem, highlighting more assets than challenges, and detailing ways to compensate or remedy weaker areas. I have developed a form to summarize assets and challenges and plan ways to capitalize on strengths and compensate or remedy any challenges (see Appendix A in the back of this chapter). As described earlier, this form is not a substitute for thorough evaluations, but rather a convenient form to summarize the results of such evaluations.

Should a student be told their diagnosis?

Sometimes self-awareness involves the use of a diagnostic label. We might help the student understand that their particular pattern of assets and challenges is consistent with Asperger's Syndrome, Autism, Pervasive Developmental Disorder-Not Otherwise Specified, or a related disorder. There are pros and cons to giving the diagnosis.

An accurate diagnosis has legal, financial, and personal advantages. Legally, the diagnosis may entitle the student to needed services through schools or compensation for treatment services through the family's insurance company. Personally, the diagnostic label helps the student access information about the diagnosis, useful treatment options, and a community of individuals with similar disorders. Discovering there is a name for what you have and that past social difficulties were a result of this neurological disorder can free the student from self-blame and begin a path to self-acceptance. When confronted with other individuals who have the disorder and who model self-acceptance and successful futures, students can begin to accept themselves. It has been my experience that students with similar diagnoses have found great relief in talking with each other and have developed truly reciprocal friendships as they share experiences and interests.

Alternatively, some students have great difficulty accepting the notion of a disorder, perceiving it as an immutable defect causing unending social difficulty and unhappiness. Moreover, they may have received many conflicting diagnoses from different clinicians in the past. The diagnosis of Autistic Spectrum disorders, particularly for those with good intellectual ability, is often fraught with ambiguity. For example, professionals disagree as to whether Asperger's can be distinguished from High Functioning Autism (see Klin and Volkmar, 2000, for a discussion of this issue). Similarly, the boundaries are not always clear between Asperger's Syndrome, "normal" eccentricity, schizoid personality disorder, and social phobia. As a result, many students lose faith in the diagnosticians and resent being told what is "wrong" with them. Rather than force acceptance of a diagnosis, I would much prefer to focus on their pattern of assets and challenges. This acceptance is crucial for their growth. They must accept their talents to maintain self-esteem and understand their difficulties so they know how to navigate around them or get help. For example, you do not need an official diagnostic label to realize that you may need more practice with a desired sport if you have athletic coordination problems. Similarly, it is not a requirement to have a diagnosis to realize that you may need to work on interview skills to get a job you want.

At some point, awareness of a diagnostic label will be helpful to students when advocating for themselves with schools, employment settings, and insurance companies. Even if they do not accept the diagnosis, it is useful to know they could qualify for that diagnosis if they want to use it to get services that they may need.

Getting past denial and resistance

Table 1 outlines a number of approaches to motivate students to address their needs for training or related services.

TABLE 1: Motivating students to address their needs

1. Link needed training or services to meeting their own goals
2. Make training or services enjoyable
3. Use external rewards if intrinsic motivation is missing
4. Shore up assets and strengths before addressing any challenges
5. Testimonials from successful individuals with autism spectrum disorders
6. Helping to teach others

Link needed training or services to meeting their own goals

If students express some future goals, it always makes sense to first link needed training or services (including social skills training) to the students' own goals. If students want friends, a job, good grades, or to be able to engage in an activity (sports, clubs, or a special event), then teaching crucial skills can be linked to these goals. For example, many adolescents who never wanted to learn social skills suddenly develop motivation to learn certain skills in an effort to help them find a date.

Make training or services enjoyable

If services and training are fun and enjoyable, then this certainly increases the probability that students will accept those services. Chapter 6 outlines many strategies to keep social skills training fun and engaging.

Use external rewards if intrinsic motivation is missing

When students do not express any particular goals and show no intrinsic desire to address a particular challenge, external rewards can be considered. For example, students can be paid for attending a job training session so that they can eventually get a paying job. Similarly, students can be offered access to certain privileges (e.g., a ride to the movies, a trip to their favorite restaurant, or access to certain video games) for attending social skills training or other helpful services. If such external rewards are going to be motivating, they must in part be chosen by the student and varied so that the student does not become bored by any one particular reward. The long term goal of using an external reward is to get the student to attend the needed services long enough to improve some aspect of their life such that the student now sees the benefit of the service and no longer requires external rewards to attend.

Emphasize assets and strengths before addressing any challenges

Strategies cannot be so straightforward for the student who seems to have no goals, has become depressed and is withdrawing from the social world entirely. Many students with special needs deny or otherwise resist any mention of weakness or difficulty. It takes a modicum of self-esteem to tolerate thinking about what difficulties you have. Many students who have had many academic and social difficulties are in no position to tolerate any critical feedback about their behavior. Without being able to tolerate such feedback, personal growth is stymied. For example, the young man who greets others with the phrase "death to all" most likely needs to alter or expand his greeting repertoire if he wants to get into college or get a job. If we point out the need to greet others differently, he perceives it as a personal attack on his personality and either asserts that he no longer wants to go to college and get a job, or that the college admissions officers and employers should just learn to accept his greeting style.

Students who show this kind of denial or blaming of others cannot be forced to look directly at their challenges nor can they be asked to willingly learn new skills. Before this can happen, they may need to be convinced of their strengths. It is only in a position of some positive self-worth that they can tolerate hearing critical feedback about their behavior. So how can we improve a student's self-esteem so they can tolerate constructive criticism so necessary for personal growth?

Individual counseling to map out assets and challenges

One way is through counseling that allows them to explore and experience their talents and strengths. For most students, it is helpful to have someone else point out two to three assets for every challenge that is highlighted. The student can be asked directly what talents and challenges they have and then the counselor can add or refine that list of strengths before delving into areas in need of improvement. Counselors and students can use results of educational, psychological, and vocational testing to identify assets and challenges and summarize them on the form in Appendix A in the back of this chapter. Because testing often highlights areas of weakness more than strengths, testing results must be filtered by a counselor or other adult to help the student identify a pattern in which more assets than challenges are described.

I have found it helpful to represent this pattern of assets and challenges graphically using the form in Figure 1. Figure 2 shows an example of this form filled out for a particular student. Several areas are highlighted that depict where the student is "well above average," and a lesser number of areas are identified in which the student may need some improvement. Those challenging areas may dictate what skill areas we may first target for training and generalization.

Figure 1

Blank Graph of Assets and Challenges

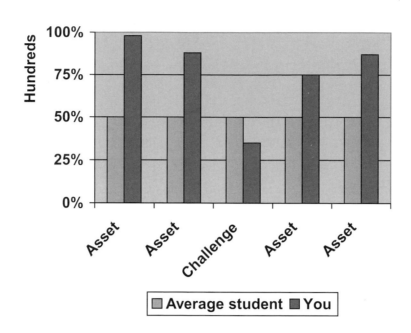

Figure 2

Sample Graph of Assets and Challenges for a Student

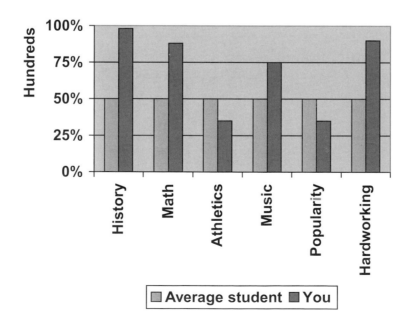

Any discussion of challenges must be *constructive* in that it focuses on how to remedy the problem or compensate for it. Statements of challenges without any practical ways to handle the challenge are useless. For example, if a counselor wanted a student to understand that being on the basketball team might be difficult given visual-motor difficulties, constructive feedback should be offered on how to cope with that, such as outlining a way to over-practice those basketball skills until they improve, or to pursue other activities that tap natural strengths such as becoming the statistician for the sports teams, the sports announcer or joining another club that matches their interests.

Effective "self-esteem" counseling is not just talking about their strengths, but also includes real experiences in the sessions that demonstrate their abilities and leave them feeling successful. Through activities that allow the therapist to comment positively about the students' strengths (e.g., journal writing, art, trivia games, spelling bees, geography challenges, composing or playing music, creating photos or films) students can begin to recognize their own competence.

Planning successful experiences outside the counseling office

Nothing is more self-esteem enhancing as real-life experiences in which the student is succeeding. For adults, finding appropriate employment builds self-esteem more than any amount of therapy could ever provide. Feeling that others value what you do, or "need" your services, is crucial for self-worth for most adults.

For high school and college students, academic and social demands may need to be modified to allow the student to experience success in their daily routines. For academic classes, this may include alternative classes, reduced homework, tutoring and any myriad of modifications stemming from a good evaluation of academic functioning (see Appendix A for areas in which modifications may be needed). Social modifications may include limiting the social demand by creating quieter and more structured environments instead of the typical noisy, unstructured social scenes in a high school or college cafeteria. In high schools, staff members may help facilitate lunch-time or after-school groups to teach social skills and create a supportive peer group. In college, special considerations may be made in dormitory living arrangements to assure the student is not isolated. These might include: pairing with dorm–mates who have similar interests, having the residential director check in regularly with the student to help encourage participation in dorm activities and meal-times, and to establish social support groups through the student counseling centers.

Once a student has experienced some success, then they can begin looking at possible challenges along with their strengths. Then they can plan for what kinds of help or accommodations they may want or need.

Testimonials from successful individuals with autism spectrum disorders

Hearing from successful individuals with autism spectrum disorders is an extremely powerful way to build self-esteem and better tolerate feedback about weaknesses. In Millburn High School, students with learning or social difficulties entering the 9th grade hear presentations from older classmen who have successfully managed their disabilities and gone off to successful internships and other academic experiences. This sets the stage for the new students to begin their journey to self-awareness of their strengths and learning challenges.

When live speakers are not available, learning and reading about highly successful individuals, both present and historical figures, can be helpful. Resources include autobiographies by individuals with autism spectrum disorders and biographies written about historical figures suspected of having an autism spectrum disorder (see Ledgin, 2001).

Helping to teach others

One way to reduce resistance to learning new skills is to have students participate in ways to teach others various skills. Through creating picture books, videos or live skits, students can demonstrate the skills to others. As such, they can learn a skill without having to acknowledge that they themselves needed to learn it. Chapter 6 outlines a number of these strategies to motivate participation in skills training activities.

Appendix A

Mapping assets and challenges: A form to summarize results of educational, vocational and psychological evaluations

Name:_____   Date:_____

Next to each item, indicate if it is a strength or a challenge. For strengths, indicate how you might capitalize on that talent. For challenging areas, indicate how to compensate or improve in that area.

A. Academic

    1. Knowledge base and interests

       Assets: What can I do with this strength?

       _____

       Challenges: How will I compensate or improve?

       _____

    2. Verbal skills

       A. Expressive—oral not written

          1. Vocabulary

             Assets: What can I do with this strength?

             _____

             Challenges: How will I compensate or improve?

             _____

          2. Fluidity

             Assets: What can I do with this strength?

             _____

Challenges: How will I compensate or improve?

_____

B. Receptive/Comprehension

Assets: What can I do with this strength?

_____

Challenges: How will I compensate or improve?

_____

C. Verbal abstract reasoning

Assets: How will I use that strength?

_____

Challenges: How will I compensate or improve?

_____

3. Calculation skills

Assets: What can I do with that strength?

_____

Challenge: How will I compensate or improve?

_____

4. Visual-spatial skills

A. Mechanical ability

Asset: What can I do with that strength?

_____

Challenge: How will I compensate or improve?

_____

B. Reasoning

    Asset: What can I do with that strength?

_____

    Challenge: How will I compensate or improve?

5. Written Expression

    A. Generating ideas

        Asset: What can I do with that strength?

_____

        Challenge: How will I compensate or improve?

_____

    B. Organizing ideas

        Asset: How will I use that strength?

_____

        Challenge: How will I compensate or improve?

_____

    C. Connecting ideas

        Asset: How will I use that strength?

_____

        Challenge: How will I compensate or improve?

_____

B. Behavioral/Emotional

1. Attention and concentration

    Asset: How will I use that strength?

_____

Challenge: How will I compensate or improve?

_____

2. Impulse control: ability to wait for what you want, not interrupt, listen to all directions before starting a project.

Asset: What will I do with that strength?

_____

Challenge: How will I compensate or improve?

_____

3. Frustration control: ability to tolerate mistakes, challenging work, correction, teasing, stopping a favored activity.

Asset: What can I do with that strength?

_____

Challenge: How will I compensate or improve?

_____

4. Acceptance of authority: ability to assert yourself in a non-aggressive way, desire (not ability) to cooperate.

Asset: How will I use that strength?

_____

Challenge: How will I compensate or improve?

_____

5. Anxiety Issues: willingness to assert yourself rather than remain passive, willingness to initiate interactions with others, willingness to respond to others' initiations; obsessive-compulsive symptoms; general phobias, panic attacks with or without agoraphobia.

Asset: How can I use that strength?

_____

Challenge: How will I compensate or improve?

_____

6. Depression issues: general mood, general self-esteem, hopefulness for self, world and the future, ability to sleep, eat and concentrate.

Asset: How can I use that strength?

_____

Challenge: How will I compensate or improve?

_____

C. Sensory Issues—sensitivities or need to seek out stimulation

1. Noise   2. Light   3. Smells   4. Taste   5. Touch

Asset: How will I use that strength?

_____

Challenge: How will I compensate or improve?

_____

D. Motor Issues

1. Fine motor problems

Asset: How will I use that strength?

_____

Challenge: How will I compensate or improve?

_____

2. Gross motor problems

Asset: How will I use that strength?

_____

Challenge: How will I compensate or improve?

_____

E. Social Issues

1. Generally I do too much of: _____

2. Generally I do too little of: _____

3. Fill out Social Skill Menu indicating which skills I need to work on.

Social Skill Menu

Name:_____   Date:_____

Circle those items that may be a challenge for the student.

- **Nonverbal cues/Body language**

    1. Expressing and reading welcoming versus unwelcoming social cues

    2. Interest versus boredom social cues

    3. Sarcasm versus genuine expressions

    4. Attending to others

    5. Respecting personal space and belongings

    6. Personal hygiene

    7. Dealing with odd motor mannerisms

- **Dealing with anger/frustration**

    8. Understanding your anger

    9. Identifying triggers to your anger

    10. Altering or avoiding the triggers to your anger

    11. Better ways to think about and deal with the triggers to your anger

    12. Calming yourself when angry

    13. Talking versus acting out your feelings

    14. Using the Daily Anger Record

- **Dealing with anxiety**

    15. Dealing with anxiety and fear—understanding the alarm reaction

    16. Dealing with unpleasant, intrusive thoughts and compulsive behaviors

    17. Dealing with social fears

18. Dealing with new feared situations

• **Conversation**

19. Saying hello's and goodbye's

20. Introductions

21. Politely interrupting

22. Maintaining and joining a conversation

23. Starting conversations with people you know

24. Getting to know someone new

25. POSTER: Summary of Starting and Maintaining Conversations

26. Conversation repair strategies

27. Politely changing topics

28. Being sensitive to the listener's interests

29. Politely ending conversations

30. Answering the telephone and taking messages

31. Calling friends on the telephone

• **Building and maintaining friendships (and dealing with roommates)**

32. Where to find friends

33. Don't try too hard too soon

34. Sharing friends

35. Avoiding touchy subjects and insults

36. Complimenting

37. Respecting others' views

38. Don't impose rules on others (minding your own business)

39. Avoid bragging

40. Dealing with peer pressure and avoiding setups

41. Empathic listening

42. Showing caring for others' feelings through supportive statements

43. Deepening relationships—sharing personal information

44. Conflict resolution/Assertiveness

45. Dealing with teasing

46. Showing good sportsmanship

47. Getting attention in positive ways

• **Dating**

48. Where to find a date and how and when to ask someone on a date

49. Asking someone out on a date

50. Reading the signals—when to pursue a romantic relationship

51. Sexual harassment

52. Do's and Don'ts on a date

53. Communicating clearly to meet each other's needs

• **Dealing with school and family demands**

54. Asking for reasonable modifications

55. Dealing with frustrating work

56. Accepting no or waiting for what you want

57. Asking nicely for what you want

58. Working cooperatively in groups

59. Dealing with mistakes and correction

60. How to respectfully disagree with teachers, parents, or supervisors

61. Dealing with stressful living situations

• **Employment skills**

62. Choosing job/career directions

63. Conducting a job search

64. Writing a resume and cover letters

65. Scripts for networking with friends, relatives, and potential employers

66. Interview skills (and whether to disclose a disability)

67. Handling rejection

68. Do's and Don'ts to maintain a job

69. Responding to criticism, accusations or complaints on the job

70. Exiting a job

• **Money Matters**

71. Managing money

• **Preparing for Emergencies**

72. Dealing with emergencies and emergency workers
    (such as police or hospital workers)

• **Transportation**

73. Negotiating transportation

Chapter Four

College, Career and Residential Options Beyond High School: What parents can do to prepare their son or daughter
by Rick Blumberg, Ph.D.

The first step in preparing your son or daughter for life after school is to develop a vision for the life you'd like them to have. To do this, it's important to understand that *everything is possible given the right types of support.*

Where will he live? In an apartment, his own home, or some type of supported living arrangement? What type of work will she do? What type of supports will she need to get and keep a good job? Will she require some kind of post-secondary education or training to have the career she wants? What will he do for leisure and recreation? What kinds of support or skills training does he need to develop and maintain a vital social network?

Once you have developed a vision for the type of lifestyle and career that matches your child's interests and preferences, you can think about the types of education, training, experiences, and supports he'll need to be successful.

A few words about supports: Everyone needs supports to be successful in life. This isn't unique to youths with autism or Asperger's Syndrome. The important thing to know is the amount and type of supports your son or daughter wants and needs. This is determined by your knowledge of their abilities, skills, interests and preferences. There are three basic types of support that individuals use; people, materials, and services. For example, she might need a person (to help manage her household budget, or think through a problem); she might need materials to perform a task (calculator or computer) or a service (job development or coaching) to find, learn and maintain a job.

The intent of this chapter is to introduce concepts, strategies, tools and resources you will need to ensure that your son or daughter has a successful, meaningful and enjoyable life after high school.

Preparing for the future

I have known too many families that experience a sense of panic as their child's last year of high school begins. They clearly sense the urgency of having only one more year of school to prepare for life after high school. They are facing the end of the security of the entitlement to services that IDEA provides. Ahead is a confusing array of government agencies, eligibility criteria, and veritable mountains of paperwork. There is a way to avoid the confusion and uncertainty—begin the process of planning, research, networking, accessing resources and developing supports early, no later than the first year of high school.

Table 1. Provides an overview of some of the educational, financial, career and residential options that parents and students should consider, and the activities that will help prepare students for them.

Table 1.

College	1. By age 14: Transition statement should include preference to attend college or not, and course and sequence that provide opportunity to do so should be laid out.
	2. By end of freshman year: Review whether college is still part of vision. Does student understand their IEP? Consider requests for PSAT accommodations if needed, and the need for foreign language courses.
	3. By end of sophomore year: Does vision still include college? Does student understand his/her disability and need for accommodations, and can they take a lead in IEP meeting? Can student discuss needs with teachers and request SAT accommodations if needed?
	4. By end of junior year: Has student visited colleges? Has student communicated accommodation needs, taken SAT, begun considering financial aid for college?
	5. By end of senior year: Pass the HSPA, enough credits to graduate, college acceptance, current testing documenting disability done within two years of graduating, can student take leadership role in obtaining educational needs.
	6. Request accommodations in college as early as possible and supply documentation of disability.

Supplemental Income	1. By the end of freshman year, ensure the student has applied for and received a social security number and card.
	2. By the end of sophomore year, investigate the eligibility criteria and required documentation to apply for SSI and SSDI benefits. Obtain required medical and other documentation for eligibility determination
	3. By senior year, and/or prior to age 18, apply for SSI or SSDI benefits. Apply for Medicaid health benefits.
	4. By senior year, investigate work incentive programs available through the Social Security Administration.
Employment	1. Begin planning for your child's future employment and career beginning no later than freshman year of HS. If your vision includes post-school employment, follow the steps below.
	2. By freshman year, or by age 14, ensure that your child's IEP contains plans for career exploration and vocational preparation.
	3. By the end of sophomore year, ensure that your child's IEP contains plans for conducting a *Functional Vocational Assessment.*
	4. By the end of sophomore year, ensure that your child's IEP includes plans for career exploration including such activities as job shadowing, job sampling and/or internships.
	5. At the beginning of junior year, apply for Vocational Rehabilitation services, and if your child is found eligible, request a technical consultation with a VR counselor.
	6. By senior year, ensure that your child's IEP has specific employment goals, including part-time employment during senior year, vocational training, internships, employment development and/or job search activities.
Residential	1. During freshman year, or by age 14, ensure that your child's IEP contains plans to evaluate his/her independent living skills. If your child is likely to have complex support needs, consider person-centered planning.

	2. By freshman year, apply for eligibility through your state division of developmental disability services. Obtain any documentation necessary to determine eligibility.
	3. By junior year, ensure your child's IEP includes plans to explore appropriate residential options such as group homes, supervised apartments and supported living programs.

Planning

Some young people and families know exactly what they want and need to be successful and happy. I haven't met too many of these individuals, so for most readers, developing a vision of an ideal future for their son or daughter is an important first step. Because there are many things to consider and questions to answer, I find it's helpful to have a process to use that guides your thinking and helps you to find good answers to difficult and often complex questions. One such process is called *Person-Centered Planning.*

Person-Centered Planning is an umbrella term used to describe several approaches to developing goals for the future and identifying the supports and resources a person may need to achieve his/her goals. What these planning processes have in common is that they:

- are based on the perspectives of people who know the young person well

- make use of both traditional systems (governmental and private service providing agencies) and natural supports (family members, friends, church groups)

- begin with how the person wants to live or work today, as a starting point for thinking about the future

- ensure that the person with a disability is heard, regardless of the severity of their disability

To learn more about Person-Centered Planning, explore these websites:

www.elp.net

www.allenshea.com

www.capacityworks.com

Post-Secondary Education

The process of thinking about post-secondary education should begin no later than your son/daughter's freshman year. As early as possible, schedule a meeting with his guidance counselor to discuss his post-secondary goals, and review the information about his disability and its impact on learning and academic achievement. Discuss the high school courses and credits your child will need for college admission, as well as the schedule of tests he will need to take. Each year, your child's IEP should include the activities and coursework necessary to prepare her to meet her post-secondary goals. Discuss the accommodations and adaptations that will help your child be successful in coursework, testing and extra-curricular activities.

Youths with autism and Asperger's Syndrome often possess the ability to perform well in academic coursework. However, many young people we know require specific types of support and accommodations to be successful in academic and social environments. After high school, the entitlement for students with disabilities to a free and appropriate public education ends. However, there is federal legislation that mandates the right of your child to accommodations and supports in post-secondary institutions. Because it is the responsibility of the student to know his/her rights, and to request reasonable accommodations, it is important for you and your child to be familiar with these laws and their implications for your son or daughter's post-secondary education.

Section 504 of the Rehabilitation Act was designed to ensure that post-secondary programs do not discriminate against students on the basis of a disability. Section 504 requires any program (college or school) that receives federal funding to provide accommodations for qualified students. Most colleges and schools receive federal funding. That means that if you can document that your son or daughter is a person with a disability and that they are otherwise qualified to attend the program (e.g., have finished high school and/or have taken the appropriate coursework), the program must provide him/her with reasonable accommodations, or the supports that will enable him/her to succeed.

The *Americans with Disabilities Act* (ADA) requires that people with disabilities be provided with equal access to public programs and services. The ADA adds to the rights of students with disabilities protected by Section 504 by requiring post-secondary programs to make their physical sites accessible for example, providing ramps on buildings and reserved spaces in parking lots. The ADA also requires that programs make information about their programs and communications about goods and services accessible. That means that if a program uses the internet for communication, the web-site must be accessible for students using adaptive technology. Informational materials and software for coursework must also be accessible.

So, what is an *accommodation?*

An accommodation is a legally required modification or service that gives a student with a disability an equal opportunity to benefit from education or training. Some examples of accommodations include:

- Changes to the classroom environment or task

- Removal of physical barriers

- Changes to policies, practices and procedures

- Provision of aids and services

- Other adaptations or modifications that enable students to enjoy equal access to the benefits and privileges of the programs services and activities

Section 504 and the ADA require post-secondary programs to make reasonable accommodations for students with disabilities without changing their academic standards. Some reasonable accommodations include but are not limited to:

- Testing accommodations (more time, alternative formats)

- Adaptive technology services

- Other supports such as interpreters, note-takers, scribes and readers

Post-secondary programs are not required to provide personal devices such as wheelchairs, hearing aids or glasses, or personal services such as assistance with eating, toileting, dressing, etc.

Develop a post-secondary portfolio. This will be useful for admissions and for your son/daughter to document his/her need for reasonable accommodations in college. Here are some of things you should include in your child's portfolio:

- Child study team records including evaluation reports and copies of his/her IEPs

- A copy of his/her WAIS-R (Weschler Adult Scales of Intelligence) or other similar testing that yields valid information about cognitive functioning

- A Functional Vocational Assessment

- Copies of high school transcripts, High School Proficiency Test (HSPT) and SAT scores.

- Information and materials describing extracurricular activities, clubs, sports, service learning.

- Examples of best academic work, papers, projects, etc.

Disability services on college campuses

Four-year colleges and universities and community colleges are required to have an office that coordinates services for students with disabilities. They are often called by different names like the Disability Services Office, Office of Differing Ability Services, etc. The important difference between the services and supports available in high school and the supports that post-secondary schools are required to provide, is that your son or daughter *must apply and be found eligible for them*. Another important difference is that he/she must be able to effectively advocate for the supports he/she needs to be successful.

Selecting a college

There are many options for youths with autism and Asperger's Syndrome when considering college. Here are some things you should consider to assist your child to explore post-secondary programs:

- Course of study: Can he get the preparation at this school for the kind of work he wants to do?

- Location: How far is it from home? Will she commute or live on campus?

- Admission requirements: Does he have the coursework and grades to be admitted to this school?

- Cost: Can she afford to attend? What types of Financial Aid are available and does he qualify?

- Campus life: Is this the kind of school she wants to attend. How accessible is the campus? Are there other students with disabilities attending this school? Are there activities she can attend?

- Disability Services: What types of services are offered? How knowledgeable and responsive is the Disability Services office? (If they are not responsive now, it's unlikely they will be once your son/daughter begins attending the school)

Resources for income supports, employment and residential services

Individuals with autism or Asperger's Syndrome may be eligible for a variety of disability-related services and supports. These include, but are not limited to, income supports, employment services, and residential services. The type of services available and eligibility criteria vary from state to state. We will briefly describe some of the resources you should become familiar with.

Income supports

The Social Security Administration administers two federally funded programs that provide financial supports for eligible individuals with disabilities. You should begin researching application procedures, and eligibility criteria no later than your child's first year of high school. These programs can provide income support and other resources your child may need.

Supplemental Security Income (SSI)

SSI benefits may be paid to persons who have a documented disability and who have little or no income. SSI provides cash to meet the basic needs of food, clothing and shelter.

Individuals who are over 18 are considered eligible for SSI if they have a medically determined physical or mental impairment that precludes "substantial gainful activity" (in other words, the person is unable to support him/herself due to a disability). Once your child turns 18, your family income is not taken into account. After 18, only your child's income is considered for eligibility determination and benefits.

Social Security Disability Insurance (SSDI)

SSDI is an income assistance program that provides cash payments to individuals who have a disability. To be eligible, a person must have worked and paid taxes for about five years, or be the adult child of a person who has worked and paid taxes.

To learn more about income supports provided by the Social Security Administration:

1-800-772-1213

www.socialsecurity.gov

Employment supports

Preparing your child for a meaningful career that enables him/her to be self-supporting should begin no later than the first year of high school. It is essential that your child's IEP includes annual goals that; 1) involve him/her in career exploration and awareness, 2) allow him/her to sample different jobs through tours, job shadowing and internships, and 3) connects your child with employers and agencies that can help him/her find employment prior to graduation.

An important first step in preparing your child for work and a career is to ensure that his/her IEP contains a *functional vocational assessment*. The purpose of this assessment is to identify his/her interests, preferences, abilities, and aptitudes. Functional vocational assessments involve both written and hands-on assessments of your child. Many schools have personnel trained to conduct these, but if they do not, you should request that the school contract with an individual or agency that is qualified to conduct the assessment.

The functional vocational assessment will provide information that may guide the planning of coursework and activities that should be included in your child's IEP. The following are some of the activities that may be useful in your child's vocational preparation:

Career fairs and job tours: Many high schools conduct annual career fairs that provide opportunities for students to become aware of employment and career opportunities in their community. If your school does not sponsor such an event, discuss the development of such an activity with them. Local community colleges also sponsor career days/fairs. Job tours are another way for your son or daughter to explore work and career opportunities. These are typically less formal opportunities for individuals or small groups of students to visit local industries and businesses to observe what is done there, and to talk with employers and workers about particular jobs.

Community Asset Mapping: This is a useful activity that can be conducted as a classroom activity or homework assignment. To complete a community asset map, a student makes a list of employers in their community, and the types of jobs available. This can be done by consulting the yellow pages, newspapers and conducting web searches. Family members, friends and church members are also good sources for this information. The community asset map can serve as a resource for identifying opportunities for job shadowing and internships.

Job shadowing and internships: Job shadowing involves a student spending some time with a person who does a job that the young person has some interest in. Job shadowing is usually a short term activity, from one to a few visits. Internships are a more formal and long term activity, typically involving a student working part time in an employment setting each week for a semester or school year. Job shadowing should occur in freshman and/or sophomore years, and internships in the junior and senior years.

Supported Employment: Is an approach that involves the provision of individualized supports to help young people with significant disabilities get and maintain competitive employment. Many schools provide supported employment services, or contract with an adult service agency to provide them. Depending on the goals and needs of the student, supported employment services may be provided as early as the sophomore year as part of a student's Individual Education Program. Supported Employment services may be provided in the following ways:

Group placement model: This involves a full-time instructor working with a small group of students in an integrated employment setting. This model enables students to learn a particular job in depth. The student works alongside peers with instructor support.

Mobile crew: A full-time instructor works with small group of students in multiple work sites in various community settings. This approach enables students to sample a variety of jobs with instructor support.

Entrepreneurial business model: A private business, typically retail or manufacturing, employs students with disabilities, and provides competitive employment opportunities as well as contact with the general public. Many schools have developed their own small businesses in order to provide such experiences for students. For example, one school we know operates a bakery/delicatessen. The business is located in a shopping mall and people with disabilities work alongside non-disabled co-workers.

Individual Placement Model: In this approach, students are assisted to obtain competitive employment in an integrated setting. Initial training and on-going support are provided by an instructor or job coach. Natural supports, such as co-worker support, are utilized.

Department of Vocational Rehabilitation

Vocational Rehabilitation (VR) is a nationwide, federal and state funded program to assist eligible individuals to identify employment goals, and to obtain education, training and other supports needed to become employed. Each state has a central VR agency with local offices. You must apply for Vocational Rehabilitation services and your child must be found eligible based upon documentation of his/her disability. You should apply for VR services no later than the beginning of your child's junior year of high school. If your child is found eligible, and becomes a client of VR, rehabilitation counselors will provide technical consultation to you, so that appropriate services may begin following graduation.

One-Stop Career Centers

The federal Department of Labor, in partnership with the states, has created a network of local One-Stop Career Centers. These Centers provide a variety of employment related services, including career counseling, job listings, and referrals to job training programs. To learn more about One-Stop Career Centers:

1-877-348-050

www.careeronestop.org

Residential supports

Most young people with autism and Asperger's Syndrome can live independently following high school. However, some young people require residential supports to be safe, healthy and have a quality lifestyle. The level of support a young person needs is determined individually, and can range from intermittent and occasional, to intensive and ongoing support. Depending on the level of support your son or daughter needs, you should know about some agencies that can help you plan and develop appropriate supports.

Residential services are formal supports provided by service providers who are paid to support your son or daughter. Residential services can be expensive, and usually require that you apply for government funds to help you to pay for the services you receive. You may be required to pay some of the cost of these services. There are a range of residential services that you can choose from. Let's briefly discuss some of the choices available to you.

- Group homes are owned and operated by service providing agencies. In a group home, your son/daughter will live with other people and be supported all day, every day, by agency staff. Agency staff members are trained to keep him/her safe and healthy, and to provide recreational and learning activities. For example, if he doesn't know how to prepare meals, group home staff can prepare meals for him, assist him, or teach him to prepare meals. If she takes medications, group home staff will make sure she takes the right dose at the right time. If she has a particular problem, they may help her solve it. Food and other household items are provided and household bills are paid by the agency.

In a group home your son will have roommates that he generally doesn't get to choose. He may not have very much privacy, and there are generally rules that he will have to follow. Support staff members are hired by the service providing agency and you generally don't get to decide who supports your child.

- Supervised apartments are living arrangements where your son/daughter may live with a roommate and have 24-hour staff to help him. Members of support staff live nearby. They can help him to do things that may be difficult for him, like paying bills, and making sure he has the right food to eat. They can help him in an emergency.

If your daughter chooses this option, she may have more privacy and independence. However, she may not be able to choose her roommate. The service-providing agency decides who her support staff will be.

- In foster or sponsor families, your son may live with a family or a trained support provider. He can receive care and assistance from that person 24 hours a day. He can have some privacy, but will be living with a family and, as in other families, there are rules, shared space, etc.

- Supported living programs are designed to provide just as much support as a person needs and wants in the living arrangement of their choice. In this option, your daughter can choose where and with whom she lives, though her support staff may still be hired by the agency providing supports.

Funding and supports for residential services (State Developmental Disabilities Agencies)

Each state has a central office that administers services and supports for people with developmental disabilities. To be eligible for DD services, individuals must apply and then meet the state agency's eligibility criteria. Services and eligibility criteria vary from state to state. Your state DD agency develops standards for and oversees a broad array of community services, including residential services.

State DD offices typically provide some funds to pay for residential services for eligible individuals. Most state DD agencies also provide some funding for employment and other services.

To learn more about your state office for Developmental Disabilities:

www.Disabilityresources.org/DD.html

Centers for Independent Living

Centers for Independent Living (CILs) are federally funded agencies run by people with disabilities. They are regional non-profit agencies that provide information and advocacy for individuals with disabilities who wish to live independently. Centers for Independent Living work to assure that individuals with disabilities have access to housing, transportation, community resources, recreation, health and social services. These Centers can be an invaluable source of information and referral. To learn more about CILs: www.ilusa.com/links/ilcenters.htm

Greg's Story

My first experience with the planning of residential supports for a young person with autism was the case of a young man we'll call Greg. Greg's mother had contacted me because he was engaging in various problem behaviors in the group home he was living in. Greg was 23 years old and had lived in his mothers home until after graduation from high school. He was diagnosed with autism and has a visual impairment. His mother was experiencing serious health problems and had placed Greg in the group home at the recommendation of a social worker.

Greg began to experience problems soon after he moved into the group home and these gradually worsened. It seems that Greg was having frequent temper outbursts, during which he would scream, throw items and hit walls and furniture. When the group home staff intervened, Greg would sometimes hit them. Greg did not appear happy in his living arrangement and the group home staff was becoming afraid of him.

I asked an ex-teacher of Greg's to conduct a Personal Futures Planning meeting for Greg at his Mom's house. Personal Futures Planning is a form of person-centered planning that draws upon the knowledge, resources and contributions of a group of people who know the person with a disability well, and who are committed to supporting his/her dreams for the future.

Greg's mother invited other family members to attend, as well as his social worker, the pastor from his church, and another former teacher. At the meeting, the facilitator asked the group some simple, straightforward questions, to develop a vision of an ideal living arrangement for Greg, and to begin to brainstorm for ways to make this vision a reality.

These are the questions she asked and the answers the group was able to generate:

- What are our dreams for Greg?

- What are his talents and strengths?

- What seems to work for Greg in a living arrangement?

- What would not work or be difficult for him?

- What types of support would he need to be successful in this living arrangement?

- What steps can we take to make this vision a reality?

Greg's Personal Futures Plan

Dreams:

- Greg lives with a family that cares about him

- Greg visits his mother often

- Greg has privacy and a place to play his electric piano

- Greg has a pet

Strengths:

- Greg can do many things to care for himself, like getting dressed and feeding himself

- Greg can be a good friend

- Greg likes music. He likes to sing with other people and has a good voice.

What works:

- Living with one or two people

- Privacy and quiet

- His environment (what's around him) and his schedule (when he does things) staying pretty much the same from day to day

- Pets

What doesn't work:

- Lots of people and noise

- Not having privacy

- Talking to Greg in a loud voice

- Changes in his environment (what's around him) and his schedule (when he does things)

Support needs:

- Help with showering, shopping, cooking, laundry, doctor's visits and money

- Transportation to work and to visit his mom

- Help to solve problems that come up

Next steps:

- Identify a foster or sponsor family or individual Greg can live with.

- Help family to learn about supporting Greg

- Continue to meet with the family and support Greg's new living arrangement

Based on the information generated by the planning process, the group agreed that recruiting a foster family was the next step. We decided to make up a flyer that described what we were looking for, and distribute the flyer. Greg's sister volunteered to design the flyer; other people volunteered to put the flyers up around town.

Greg's pastor offered to ask his congregation for help in getting the word out. Flyers were posted at the local community college, an adult service agency, a local Y, the town's community center, and several local churches and temples.

Two weeks later, someone from one of the local churches called to say that a member of her church might make a good foster family for Greg. This woman lived in a quiet rural area with her son, who was about Greg's age. They had an extra bedroom in their house, and a basement space where Greg could play his electric piano. The woman thought she and her son could provide the home and supports Greg wanted, and she and her son could use the extra income they would make by being a foster family.

Greg and his mom visited the home and met the woman and her son. Greg didn't say much, but he seemed comfortable. He held the family cat and even fed it. Greg's mom thought the arrangement was worth giving a try. Greg's social worker assisted the woman to become a foster care provider.

The lessons of Greg's story

Greg's story underscores the importance of early planning for life after high school, and the usefulness of person-centered planning and circles of support. Greg and his family should have received assistance with planning and developing his residential supports while he was still in high school. The plan should have been based on knowledge of Greg's disability, interests, and preferences. If this type of planning and development had occurred early on, he and his family could have avoided a very unpleasant experience with the group home.

Moving forward

Putting these concepts and strategies into practice will require effective collaboration with school, government and adult agency personnel. This requires that you be knowledgeable about the roles and responsibilities of the different professionals you will be collaborating with. In our experience it may mean that you, the parent, are facilitating collaborations that have not existed previously. You may likely find yourself in the position of educating the professionals about how your son's or daughter's disability affects him/her, and given this understanding, what supports would be most helpful.

Youths with autism and Asperger's Syndrome benefit from repeated practice of new skills in natural settings. For this reason, early exposure to the demands of future work and living environments is vital to future success. Social skills training is essential for vocational success, independent and supported living. Ongoing social skills training should be interwoven with job training and the skills of residential/community living.

Our experience with many young people and their families confirms that given early individualized planning, and appropriate skills instruction, youths with autism and Asperger's Syndrome can successfully transition from high school to adult living, and achieve meaningful, satisfying lifestyles.

References (for Chapter 4):

Roberson, K., Blumberg, R., & Baker, D. (2005) *Keeping It Real: How to Get the Help You Need for the Life You Want.* The Elizabeth M. Boggs Center on Developmental Disabilities. Center for Medicaid Services, U.S. Department of Health and Human Services.

The New Jersey Partnership for Transition (1997) *How About College?: Guidelines for Students with Disabilities.* U.S. Department of Education, Office of Special Education and Rehabilitation Services, H158A30013-97CFDA84.158A

Blumberg, R. & Camuso, A. (2003) *Introduction to Supported Employment.* New Brunswick, NJ. The Elizabeth M. Boggs Center on developmental Disabilities, University of Medicine and Dentistry of New Jersey, Robert Wood Johnson Medical School

Chapter Five

Assessment of Skill Needs: Deciding what skills to target and where to teach them

In assessing a student for social skills training, there are two essential questions that need to be answered:

1. What skills does this student need to be taught?

2. Where should skill instruction be conducted, in group or in individual sessions?

Determining what skills to teach

The social skill menu (see Appendix A) can be used to identify areas the student may need to learn about in order to reach individual goals. The menu can be filled out by the student, teachers, counselors, or parents. The menu should not be presented as a list of possible weaknesses, but rather a list of possible areas for instruction to reach the student's own goals. The menu lists skills related to nonverbal behaviors, anger and anxiety management, conversation skills, friendship skills, dating skills, employment skills, dealing with challenging demands, living with roommates, and managing money, transportation and daily needs. Students, teachers, parents and counselors circle the items with which they believe the individual may need help. To prioritize skill lessons, one should:

1. First address skills relevant to problematic behaviors that interfere with the student's goals. For every problem situation, there exists a "replacement" skill to help the student deal with the challenge. If these skills are not taught first, nothing else may be able to be taught.

2. Then consider what other skills might help the student reach their own immediate goals.

3. Plan an initial curriculum recognizing that new skills may have to be added as student's goals and life circumstances change.

Replacement skills for problem behavior. Understanding the situations in which a student has problem behaviors will provide clues as to what skills need to be taught. "Replacement" skills are the skills that will allow the student to deal more effectively with recurring problems. Thus, it is crucial to keep track, not only of problem behaviors, but also the situations in which they occur. For example, if a student engages in angry outbursts when confronted with challenging work, then we know challenging work is a trigger for that student and the skill "Dealing with Frustrating Work" needs to be taught. If the student impulsively makes insensitive remarks that irritate others across most situations, then teaching "Avoiding touchy subjects and insults" should be targeted. If the student argues disrespectfully when others express opposing opinions, then the student may need to learn "How to respectfully disagree with teachers, parents or supervisors."

Target other skills to address the student's goals. Consider the student's wishes in targeting other skills. Some students may want to focus on making friends more than getting a job, while some may want to get along better with their parents or teachers more than develop friendships. Considering their goals to help guide skill selection will maximize the student's motivation to learn.

Create an initial curriculum. After prioritizing replacement skills and identifying additional skills to address the student's immediate goals, I usually select approximately ten skills to teach over the course of ten weeks or more. For many students with average to above average intellectual ability we can cover about one new skill per week for a ten-week program, depending on the student's ability to understand the skill concepts. Although one can teach the knowledge of skills this rapidly, to generalize skills into a student's daily routine, one may need to focus on a smaller set of skills for a much longer period (see Chapter 7). After every ten weeks, one can assess the student's progress (see tracking progress below) and make alterations to their curriculum as their life circumstances and goals change. For example, a younger high school student may initially address handling challenging work and developing friendships. As he ages and his goals change, the student may shift to addressing dating and job-related skills.

Consider how an initial skill curriculum was selected for the following student. CJ was a 17-year-old who wanted very much to keep his job at a local steak house where he prepares silverware and sets up tables. He got the job through his high school vocational program and he has a job coach who gets regular feedback from his employer about his performance. In the past he has continually lost jobs because he would tell others what to do at work and get frustrated when he himself did not know how to handle a situation. Whenever he would lose a job, he became more depressed and angry and it became hard to teach him anything else. To avoid losing his job again, we first prioritized the skills, "Don't impose rules on others," "Dealing with frustrating work," and "Knowing your job responsibilities" in order to help him keep his job. C.J. also tended to perseverate on topics of interest at work and with friends and as a result pushed others away. Since he wanted very much to maintain and build more friendships we also targeted, "Being sensitive to the listener's interests (knowing when to stop talking)," and "Starting and maintaining conversation" to help him in this area. Finally we also targeted some initial dating skill as he had some interest in pursing this area of his life as well. The following is sample curriculum put together for CJ:

1. Don't impose rules on others

2. Dealing with frustrating work

3. Knowing your job responsibilities

4. Knowing when to stop talking

5. Working cooperatively in groups

6. Starting and maintaining a conversation

7. Making phone calls

8. Where to find a date

9. Asking someone out on a date

Targeting skills with a small group of students. For a small group of students (e.g., 4-8 students), the Social Skills Menu can be filled out for each student by the student himself, parent, teacher, or counselor. Again prioritizing for each student the most important skills to teach, we can then put together an initial curriculum for the group, made up of the ten skills that were most frequently identified across all group members. Every ten weeks we will assess students' progress and adjust what skills to teach. Although all students may learn about all skills, each student may only be able to generalize a smaller set of skills (see Chapter 7). Thus as the group progresses, I will begin to target "themes" for each student based upon what I hear about them outside the group and what I see happening in the group. For example, John and Mary may be in the same group learning the same set of skills over many weeks, but it becomes evident that Mary rarely initiates conversation with anyone or asserts her ideas in class or elsewhere. Therefore we target initiating conversations and asserting her ideas as her theme, which will be put on an index card for her to carry around or for others to remind her to remember how to perform these skills on a daily basis (see chapter 7 on generalization). Meanwhile, as we get to know John better in the group we discover that his main issues are quite different. He is not shy like Mary, but tends to say things impulsively that accidentally hurt others feelings and when others annoy him he insults them harshly. The themes to be put on his card become, (a) "Avoid touchy subjects and insults" (things you can think but don't say) to help him avoid making accidentally insensitive remarks, and (b) "Use an 'I' message when others annoy you" to help him find more polite ways to express his upset with others' behavior (see Skill #44, "Conflict resolution/Assertiveness").

Tracking progress. One way to track progress is to create a rating form from the ten or so skills that make up the curriculum you created. See Figure 3 for the rating form used for C.J. based on his skill targets. C.J. himself, his teachers, parents, job coach or counselor rate how well he demonstrates each skill every marking period. This form can be filled out periodically to track progress over the high school marking periods, or before and after treatment. Figure 4 has a blank form that can be reproduced for your use. As described in Chapter 7, some students may use a behavior chart to help them generalize skills, in which case the chart itself can be used to track progress over time.

Where to teach skills: Individual, group therapy or self-instruction

A student's level of self-control and motivation to learn new skills helps guide the choice of individual, group or self-instruction. Those with great difficulties attending and controlling impulses, or who lack motivation to learn, may need to begin with the structure of individual sessions before they are ready for group. Alternatively, those with high levels of motivation and self-control may not only be able to benefit from group, but also be able to set out a course of self-instruction.

Self-control. Often students with AS present with symptoms of Attention Deficit Hyperactivity Disorder (ADHD) showing problems with inattention, impulsivity, and hyperactivity. Some of these students may also show high levels of non-compliance and defiant behaviors that could make it difficult to maintain control in a group setting. In addition to problems with non-compliance, some students present with obsessive interests that distract them from attending in group. Although this may seem like the difficulty sustaining attention associated with ADHD, it may really be a selective focus on a special interest. For example, a student may be obsessively reviewing every step in a video game instead of listening to his teacher. Students may also have obsessive worries or anxieties that prevent them from staying on task. Whether students have ADHD and oppositional behaviors, perseverative interests, or excessive worries, their ability to control themselves in a group setting may be compromised.

Medications may improve some of these self-control difficulties for some students. Stimulant therapy maybe very effective for those who show true ADHD symptoms of difficulty sustaining attention, impulsivity, and hyperactivity. For those whose inattentiveness is primarily related to anxious or worrisome thoughts, antidepressants and anti-anxiety medications maybe more effective. There may be no medications that effectively alter perseverative interests. A variety of medications may also be used to control impulsive behavior or disorganized thought patterns.

All of us, with or without ADHD, anxiety, or perseverative interests, have some difficulties with self-control and attending. The decision about whether they have enough self-control for group is a matter of degree. If a student can be redirected to stay on task using frequent verbal prompts (e.g, "please listen, look at me") or incentives (e.g., "if you follow my instructions then you can have access to the computer") then he or she may be ready to enter a group therapy setting. The student may be "high maintenance" requiring frequent redirection, but nevertheless responsive to that direction. In contrast, if one cannot redirect a student back to task through verbal prompts or incentives or he intentionally defies instructions, then it may be wiser to begin a course of individual therapy prior to considering group. Individual sessions can focus on establishing a positive relationship and working out behavior plans that may then allow the student to build their cooperativeness and self-control to benefit from a group setting.

Motivation to learn and self-instruction. Some students are highly motivated to learn new skills and have the reading comprehension to understand many of the skill lessons on their own. They are fully aware of difficulties that might interfere with reaching personal goals and they ask for help in how to relate better to others. Not only could they benefit from group, but they are also good candidates for self-instruction as they need minimal prompting to learn.

How to group members

There are some distinct advantages to having diverse groups as you can have "typical" peers modeling positive behaviors to those students with more difficulties. However, my experience is that group members have the greatest chance of making genuine reciprocal friendships when they are in groups with students with similar issues and needs. Often students with related disabilities who have felt "alienated" in many other social situations find acceptance and comfort in being in a group with similar students.

A crucial consideration in grouping students together to build friendships and teach skills is to try to keep the level of cognitive ability and receptive language relatively consistent across members. Student's who differ greatly in their ability to comprehend language and abstract concepts may have a difficult time relating to each other. A student with high cognitive ability maybe frustrated by the questions from a student with much lower intellectual ability; and a student with lower ability may be frustrated by the pace of a student with much greater ability. In addition, it is difficult to teach skills to students when their levels of understanding are quite disparate, as some will need much more concrete explanation while others will be insulted by information presented at too low a level. Cognitive ability is ultimately a more important factor for grouping than age or gender. Coed groups and those with students' varying in age can be effective as long as students can relate to each other based on their cognitive/intellectual ability.

One other factor to consider in grouping students is the level of self-control students present. If one student needs constant redirection, it is possible that other group members will tolerate this. However, if there are two or more students with intense needs for redirection, it may be too challenging for the leader to facilitate the group because when direction is focused on one student in need of close monitoring another needy student may begin to act out more. This constant need to redirect may not allow any time to teach skills or help members develop insight about their interactions. In these cases it may be necessary to separate these two students in different groups or to run a much smaller group (e.g., a dyad or trio).

Figure 3

Sample Skill Rating Form for CJ

Student_____ Date: _____

Person filling out this form_____

Directions: Based on your observations in various situations, rate how often the student demonstrates the appropriate use of each skill according to the following scale:

1	2	3	4	5
almost never	rarely	sometimes	frequently	almost always

Skills	Dates			
	9/15	12/15	3/15	6/15
1. Does not impose rules on others	2	3	5	5
2. Dealing with frustrating work	1	3	4	5
3. Knowing your job responsibilities	3	4	5	5
4. Knowing when to stop talking	2	4	4	4
5. Working cooperatively in a group	2	4	4	5
6. Starting and maintaining a conversation	2	3	4	5
7. Making phone calls	1	3	4	4
8. Where to find a date	1	3	3	3
9. Reciprocity and the sequence of intimacy	1	4	4	4

Figure 4

Skill Rating Form

Student_____ Date: _____

Person filling out this form_____

Directions: Based on your observations in various situations, rate how often the student demonstrates the appropriate use of each skill according to the following scale:

1	2	3	4	5
almost never	rarely	sometimes	frequently	almost always

Skills	Dates						
1.							
2.							
3.							
4.							
5.							
6.							
7.							
8.							
9.							
10.							
11.							
12.							

Chapter 6
Skill Instruction:
Teaching skills in a group or individually

The goal of skill instruction is for the student to be able to understand and demonstrate the skill during training. This is different from generalization (see chapter 7), which is about the student using the skill over time in "real life" settings. Teaching a skill is easier to accomplish than generalizing the skill, but both are crucial.

To teach a skill, one must be able to grab students' attention and motivation. Any strategy to learn a skill must be enjoyable in some way or students may tune out. This is particularly pronounced in teens who already resist guidance from adults and resent the interruption in their schedule. I use a number of "devices" to turn a lesson into a more engaging activity, including the use of entertaining role-plays, quiz shows to review information, creative group projects to practice group skills (e.g., creating a commercial, mini-movie, or new game), conversational games, and having students create ways to teach others the skills (e.g., by making a skit, social skill picture book or film to show others). Although the learning process is "spiced" with these fun activities, there is a basic model I follow to teach *most* skills. That model, called "Structured Learning" is described below.

Structured Learning

Structured learning refers to a method of teaching social skills described by Goldstein and colleagues in their book entitled *Skillstreaming* (McGinnis & Goldstein, 1997). Skillstreaming is a valuable tool for social skills training that identifies many key skills for a wide age range of students, yet it is not specific to students with autism or Asperger's Syndrome and does not always provide the level of detail to help such students know specifically what to say and do in different situations. The skills outlined in this manual were selected to address the specific skill deficits demonstrated by students with Asperger's Syndrome, high functioning autism, and social-communication problems. The components for teaching the skills steps are described below:

Structured Learning Steps

1. Didactic instruction (explanation of the skill steps)
2. Modeling of skill steps
3. Role-playing skills with corrective feedback
4. Practice in and outside the group

Most skills in this manual can be taught using all of these components, but some skills would only involve some of these teaching components. For example, "Avoiding touchy subjects and insults" (see Skill #35) involves learning what kinds of things not to say to others. For example, if someone has a huge pimple on his forehead, you can think it but don't say it out loud. Although this skill would be explained, we probably would not model or role-play this skill because students would not know what we were doing if we stood there in silence not saying something (i.e., not saying anything in the face of someone with a large pimple). Instead we would explain the kinds of topics that you should not discuss with others and we might review these situations using a fun quiz show format. For example, we might play *Who Wants to be a Millionaire* and ask questions like, "For $2000, what would you say to someone who was stuttering? (a) Hurry up and get the words out, (b) do you go to speech therapy, (c) don't say anything because that is a 'touchy subject' or (d) do you want to dance?" The answer is "(c) don't say anything because that is a 'touchy subject.'"

1. Didactic instruction

Didactic instruction means providing an explanation of the skill steps. The instructor (teacher, counselor, or parent) might describe the steps of a particular skill, referring to the written steps (e.g., shown on a poster or black board). This portion of a skill lesson should be limited to ten minutes or less as such explanations can be dull, especially for teens. There will be plenty of time to repeat these explanations through modeling, role-playing or other special activities used to practice the skill.

2. Modeling the skill steps.

After the skill has been explained, the instructor models how to do each step of the skill. To model, the instructor needs to consider a situation to act out and may need other teachers or students to help demonstrate the scene. For each skill in Chapter 9, sample situations are provided to use in modeling and role-playing the skill.

Gain the observers' attention. Before modeling the skill, get the observers' attention by giving them an activity that requires them to attend to the demonstration. You can challenge them to try to detect if you model it correctly or not. Then ask what you did right or wrong.

Model all the parts. Modeling it several times in different ways may allow you to demonstrate some subtle but important aspects of the skill. For example, in modeling "Conflict resolution/Assertiveness," one can demonstrate using the right words but the wrong tone of voice, and then ask the students for their reactions. Then one can model the right tone of voice and the wrong words and again get their reactions, stressing why it is important to have both a nice tone and the right kind of words.

Consider whether to model the wrong way. Some skills are hard to understand unless both the right and wrong way are modeled. However, some students might so much enjoy the demonstration of the wrong way that they intentionally reenact the wrong way all the time. If your students enjoy getting attention in negative ways, you may want to think twice about modeling a skill the wrong way.

3. Role-playing the skill with corrective feedback

Acting it out. Students are invited to demonstrate the skill steps while observing students are asked to provide feedback about the performance. The instructor can actively coach the student through the steps. When students are afraid to role-play in front of others, they can be asked to just role-play a portion of the skill or to purposely show the wrong way so they will not fear doing it incorrectly.

Reviewing the skill/providing corrective feedback. Care must be taken to provide feedback in a sensitive way. Both the instructor and other students should first focus on what was done well. Then they can make suggestions for what could be done "better" avoiding statements about what was done poorly or badly. Role-playing and feedback should be repeated until the student can demonstrate the skill steps accurately.

4. Practicing the skills

After students role-play the skill, it is helpful to have them consider when and where they will practice the skills. For each of the skill lessons shown in Chapter 9, there is an accompanying activity page that lists specific engaging activities to practice the particular skill. Helping student visualize when and where they will use the skill will begin the process of generalization, which is discussed in greater detail in Chapter 7.

Getting around resistance to a lesson/ Making lessons fun

To maintain students' motivation for skill lessons and practice, it is crucial to keep the learning activities engaging. In addition to those specific activities listed on the activity pages accompanying the skill lessons in Chapter 9, the following general activities can be used to overcome resistance and/or make the learning process more fun and meaningful:

Ways to encourage participation in skill lessons

1. Prefacing skill lessons with compliments to boost self-esteem
2. Linking skill lessons to real-life goals
3. Using entertaining role-plays
4. Linking skill lessons to fun group activities (see list below)
5. Having students create lessons to teach others

Prefacing skill lessons with compliments. As described in Chapter 3, students may need to be reminded of what they do well before they can tolerate feedback of what they may need help with. Prefacing a skill lesson with reminders to students about what they do exceedingly well typically increases cooperation. This can be done individually or in group sessions. In group I will ask each member what their special talents are and corroborate or add to these positive descriptions. Then I might say "there are some minor issues I want to address with you guys so you can continue to do as well as you are doing." Then comes the lesson on a skill topic

Linking skill lessons to real-life goals. Whatever a student is motivated to do, such as developing a new friend, romantic relationship, or getting a desired internship or paid work experience, skill lessons can be targeted to accomplish those goals. All of us learn better when we know what the ultimate value of a lesson is.

Using entertaining role-plays. Role-plays can be a significant source of entertainment by introducing interesting or famous characters. For example, one adolescent group was fascinated with a past news event in which the boxer, Mike Tyson, had bitten a piece of Evander Holyfield's ear off in a fight. Using their interest, we decided to practice starting and maintaining a conversation by pretending to talk with Mike Tyson after this fight. The activity helped the students learn the concepts of maintaining and starting conversations. Of course to generalize the skill, they later applied the skills to non-pretend situations as well.

Another way to spice up the role-play is to highlight all the wrong ways to demonstrate a skill. For example, one could demonstrate all the wrong things to say and do on a job interview, like dressing inappropriately, refusing to make eye contact, sharing all the self-doubts about one's ability to do the job, and telling the employer all the mistakes that the employer has made in running their company. Satirical role-plays can, by contrast, help students learn the right way while creating some laughs. Caution should be taken with students who show overly silly or oppositional behaviors as they may persist in doing the skill the "wrong" way well after the session.

Linking skill lessons to fun group activities or projects. Here the rationale for learning a skill is so that one can participate in a desired activity or project. Activities might include:

Sample fun group activities

1. **Game shows** that review the skill information. *Jeopardy*, *Wheel of Fortune*, or *Who Wants to Be a Millionaire* are usually well received formats to review or even present skill information. When briefly explaining the skill steps, I might say, "Listen carefully to these skill steps because afterward we will play *Who Wants to Be a Millioniare* to see if you remember them." Group members take turns answering questions for different dollar amounts until the group as a whole reaches the million dollar question. Like in the TV show, they can receive three chances to get help.

2. **Conversational games.** One conversational game borrows a format from the dating industry known as "speed dating" in which participants take turns talking to one person at a time. We have students break up into pairs for 5-minute conversations and then they rotate to converse with a new partner until all participants have spoken with each other. We give them instructions for how to get to know someone new (see Skill #24) or how to start conversations with people they know (see Skill #23). At the end of the activity they play a game to see if they remember anything about with whom they spoke. Students must throw a soft ball to another student and say something they remember about the student and then they get a point. Teachers can try to steal the ball from the students and throw to another teacher, saying something they remember about the other teacher, for which teachers get a point. The game encourages students to not just interrogate those with whom they spoke, but actually listen and remember what the other student has said.

3. **Creative group projects.** We might propose a fun group activity like creating a commercial, short movie, or inventing a new game. In order to do the activity we explain the skills for "Working cooperatively in groups" (see Skill #58).

Creating skill lessons to teach others. Another way to reduce resistance to learning new skills is to have students participate in ways to teach others skills. Through creating picture books, videos or live skits, students can demonstrate the skills to others and learn a skill without having to acknowledge that they themselves needed to learn it. The following lists sample activities to create skill lessons for others.

Activities where students create lessons to teach others

1. **Creating a picture book** of skill lessons to show to others. To get an idea for how these look, see the *Social Skills Picture Book* (Baker, 2001) and the *Social Skills Picture Book for High School and Beyond* (Baker, In press). These books show pictures of actual students demonstrating each step of different skills with dialog boxes indicating what the students are saying. Students can both pose for pictures and help create the picture sequences using an appropriate computer software program or just by pasting pictures on paper and writing in their dialog and thoughts. Participants must decide on: (a) what situation to portray, (b) how to break up the skill into discrete scenes, (c) and what dialog, thoughts or feelings should be portrayed.

2. **Create a video** of skill lessons to show to others. Just like the picture books, students should decide: (a) what situation will be portrayed, (b) how to break up the skill into discrete scenes, (c) and what perceptions, thoughts, or feelings should be portrayed in the video. Characters' thoughts and feelings can be highlighted by a narrator or by taking "breaks in the action" in which the actors themselves discuss their thoughts and feelings

3. **Creating skits** for live performances. The format for creating a live skit is identical to the creation of a video. One important difference, however, is that one needs a live audience. Willing audiences for live skits might include classrooms of younger students, younger siblings, or special needs classes.

Sample format for Group Sessions

Groups may be held in a school setting, community program, or a private therapy office. In schools, groups often meet during lunch, a self-contained special education class, or after school.

vation to learn, skill lessons can be introduced following the same model as in group sessions: Conversation time, skill time, and activity/project time. The therapist can practice conversation skills one on one, coaching the student to start and maintain conversation, talk briefly and take turns, shift topics appropriately, avoid touchy subjects, and listen empathically. Just as in group, the skill lessons can be taught through structured learning: explanation, modeling and role-play.

At the end of each session, plans can be made to help generalize those skills (see Chapter 7). Often parents or teaching staff will be incorporated into these plans when possible by attending the end of a session or by contacting them by phone or email. We might create a cue card, behavior chart or other system to prime the student about the skill steps prior to situations in which the skill is needed. We will also create assignments to practice these skills in natural situations (See Chapter 7). For example, to work on conversation skills, students may plan to participate in lunchtime conversation with peers and review conversational cue cards prior to going to lunch. Those working on how to cooperate with others might plan to participate in several group projects at school to practice those skills. And those working on job readiness skills may have assignments related to getting, maintaining, or appropriately exiting a real job.

Format for self-instruction

As described earlier, self-instruction is only for the most motivated students who actively seek guidance for their social interactions. Although skill acquisition can be conducted through self-instruction, generalizing skills might be easier if the student can also participate in a social skill group to practice skills in a safe, controlled peer environment before trying them out in more natural situations. The following is a list of steps that can be taken by the self-instructing student to begin working independently on skills:

1. Students can begin by considering where in their daily routines do they have most difficulty interacting with others: at home, work, at school, in public places? In each of these locations, details of what situations specifically cause trouble should be noted. These situations can be written on the "Problem Social Situations Log" (see end of this chapter). The student can prioritize which of these situations are most relevant to the student's goals.

2. Then the social skill menu can be reviewed and filled out, identifying social skill lessons that might remedy the difficulties in those specific situations.

3. Of the many skill lessons the student might identify, priority can be given to skill lessons that might remedy those situations that are most relevant to the students' life goals. For example, if the student feels it is more important to get a job than to make friends, priority can be given to employment skills over friendship skills. If the student's most pressing goals are to get through challenging academic situations, skills related to handling school demands might be the priority

4. Students can then begin reading and reviewing skill lessons. It is recommended that students stay with one skill for at least a two-week period before moving on to another skill lesson. It is more important to try to generalize one skill than understand many skills to make real change in one's life. Thus students should read over the suggested ways to practice skill lessons (these suggestions appear in the activity page accompanying each skill lesson in Chapter 9). Also, students can summarize skill steps on a cue card that they can carry with them to remind them of what to do prior to practicing the skill steps in those natural situations (see Chapter 7 for a fuller discussion of generalization).

Problem Social Situations Log

Consider what situations may be problematic for you. Circle those areas that may be challenging.

Home:

- Dealing with parental demands
- Getting along with siblings
- Managing frustrations with yourself (e.g., doing work or playing games)

School:

- Dealing with academic demands
- Dealing with peers
  - Conversations
  - Group work
  - Recreation with friends
  - Teasing
  - Conflicts

Work:

- Dealing with work demands
- Getting along with the boss
- Getting along with colleagues

Public Places:

- Respecting physical space boundaries
- How to meet new people
- Asking for help
- Asserting yourself when needed

Dating:

- How to find a date
- Negotiating interactions on a date

Chapter 7
Generalization of skills

So often a counselor teaches a skill, making sure the student fully understands the steps, only to discover later that the student never demonstrates the skill beyond the lesson time. So the counselor reviews the skill again the next week and yet again the student never uses the skills outside of the sessions. The counselor and the student get frustrated and conclude that "social skills training does not work." Social skills training does work if we plan carefully for generalization. Gresham, Sugai and Horner (2001) in their review of outcomes for social skills training with students with a variety of disabilities point to the persistent weakness in the literature to demonstrate adequate generalization and maintenance of skills taught.

Working with older students and adults often presents even more challenges to generalize skills than with younger students who may have teachers and parents monitoring their behavior during the day and are able to remind their students to use the skills as needed. Older students and adults often do not have people monitoring their behavior and may need to rely more on themselves to remember to use a new skill.

Generalization refers to the ability to perform a skill in situations beyond the training session and to maintain the skill over time. Gresham et al. (2001) describe three aspects of skill deficits that are related to generalization problems: Skill acquisition, performance levels, and fluidity. Acquisition refers to knowledge of skill steps. Students need to know the steps to later demonstrate them when needed. Performance refers to whether the student actually demonstrates the skill steps at acceptable levels of frequency in the situations in which the skills are needed. Fluidity refers to the ability to perform the skill steps accurately and without awkwardness. Fluidity often means that the individual no longer has to "consciously think through the steps" but can actually perform the skill "automatically" without much effort. This is akin to what happens with musicians when they practice a musical piece over and over until they no longer need to read the music and the piece just "flows" from them.

Knowing whether a skill deficit is an acquisition, performance or fluidity problem determines what strategies to use to remedy the deficit. Acquisition problems require more skill lesson instruction. Performance deficits require better use of antecedent control (cuing and prompting of skills) and reinforcement (praising and rewarding skill use, including contrived rewards or natural rewards). Fluidity problems require high levels of practice and repetition with corrective feedback (Gresham et al., 2001).

To realistically practice and repeat skill steps enough to achieve adequate levels of performance and fluidity, it is unlikely that one can generalize many new skills at once. In my experience, true generalization occurs when individuals are reminded about or rehearse no more than one to three new skills every day for several months. Although individuals can learn the concept of many more skills during skill lessons, they may only be able to generalize one to three new skills at a given time. As Gresham et al. (2001) recommend, skills training has to be more intense and frequent than what has been typical in the literature. One 8-12 week course will not do. Focusing on one to three skills, practicing them daily in natural situations for several months at a time is likely to yield much better generalization results.

After students have acquired knowledge of skills, there are three strategies to help achieve adequate performance and fluidity of the skills: **Priming** before the situation in which the skills are needed, frequent **facilitated opportunities to practice** the skills in natural situations (facilitated means someone can coach the student), and **review** of skills use after the situation in which it was needed. Practice in the natural situation is key to being able to later demonstrate those skills in those same natural situations.

Priming

Priming involves some reminder to the individual of what the skill steps are "just prior" to needing the skill. For example, just before going on a job interview, an individual might go over how to answer anticipated questions. Or just prior to starting a frustrating task at school or at work, the individual might review options for dealing with frustrating work. Priming can be verbal and/or supplemeted by a visual aide. Verbal priming involves someone verbally explaining the skill steps prior to the situation in which they will be needed. Cue cards, behavior charts, or copies of the skills in Chapter 9 can serve as visual aides that depict the skill steps.

Cue cards. If students want to change their behavior but can't remember the skill steps, then cue cards or copies of the skill assignments may be ideal. We might write one to three skills on an index card and laminate it. Then we might ask a parent, teacher, job coach, or the student him or herself to review the skill steps prior to the situation in which it will be needed. Although it would be ideal for the student to see the skill steps immediately prior to the situation, this may not always be practical.

Instead the parent, teacher, job caoch, or student might review the skill once in the morning prior to school or work, once at lunch and then again at the end of the day so that the student at least has to think about the skill three times per day. This kind of sustained awareness of the targeted skills on a daily basis over the course of several months often allows students to remember the skill without reminders from others.

Behavior charts. Behavior charts can be used just like cue cards in which no rewards are given, rather the chart itself simply serves as a reminder to use the skill. The student rates him or herself or a teacher, parent, or job coach can rate the student after a specified period of time serving as a reminder for the next period of time. If a student has not fully agreed to try a new skill and thus is lacking in "intrinsic" motivation to perform the skill, then the behavior chart can be used as a *reward* chart in which external rewards are contingent on demonstrating certain targeted skills. In this case self-monitoring may not work and teachers, parents, or employers may need to do the monitoring. There is a sample chart and directions for its use in Figure 5 at the end of this chapter.

Facilitated Practice

In order to practice the new skills, students need opportunities. Sometimes those opportunities are naturally built into the day. For example, a student learning to deal with frustrating work may always have his or her share of challenging work to do during the day. Other times, the practice opportunities need to be carefully planned or created. For example, a student who never initiates conversation with anyone may be asked to call someone on the phone once per day or join others for lunch and initiate conversation once during lunch period. School staff may need to create a "lunch bunch" group in which an adult staff member facilitates conversation among a small group of students at lunch. Without such efforts by adults, some students would not engage in conversation in the larger lunch room.

For students who have difficulty working cooperatively in groups, scheduling group projects in one or more of their classes each semester will serve as a natural opportunity to practice "working cooperatively in groups." The only difference from a typical group project is that these students might be primed ahead of time as to how to work together in groups.

Those working on job skills should have real opportunities to get a job, try to maintain it, and, if necessary, exit the job appropriately. There is no substitute for on-the-job training. The concept of functional vocational assessment requires students to work in an employment setting to assess skill deficits that exist in those setting. Deficits can then be categorized as problems with skill acquisition, performance levels, or fluidity and then remedied through more instruction, better cueing and use of incentives, or more repetition to develop fluidity.

For each skill presented in Chapter 9, I have suggested relevant, natural activities to practice and generalize the skills. Many of these natural activities will bring about their own intrinsic rewards (e.g., making friends, getting a job, dealing effectively with school work). However, sometimes using a contrived reward (e.g., privileges, money, ample praise) can serve as another motivator to help students practice. As discussed earlier, the use of a behavior chart (Figure 5) would be most useful for the student who shows little interest in practicing a skill. Such students would also benefit from all the motivational strategies outlined in Chapter 3, particularly linking the skill to their own personal goals.

Review after Skill Use

After situations have occurred in which skills were needed, the student's performance can be reviewed to increase awareness of the skill. If a student is on a reward chart, the reason the student received the reward (or not) should be reviewed with him or her to enhance learning. For students not on reward charts, the situation can be reviewed verbally or with the help of the cue card of skills described earlier.

In reviewing past situations, care should be taken not to "shame" a student with examples of what they did incorrectly. The following steps can be taken to keep the review constructive and avoid negative judgments:

1. Ask the student what happened in the situation and how he or she dealt with the situation. Avoid judgments about any incorrect ways they handled the situation.

2. Explore how people felt and thought in the situation and discuss what happened as a result of the way the student dealt with the situation.

3. Explore what else he or she could have done in the situation.

4. Finally the student should be asked what he or she might do in the future "to handle the situation even better." Note the positive phrasing here. The adult can add some ideas "to make the future situations even more successful."

Some students may not be able to tolerate any discussion about a past situation as it may make them ashamed. In these instances, it is best not to mention what did happen, but rather what to do if a similar situation comes up again. Wait until sometime after the event when the student is calm and then say, "I wanted to talk to you about something that may happen in the future" (with no mention of the negative event that recently occurred. "Sometime you may . . . ." and the adult can continue to describe a situation that may occur and how the student might want to handle it. Using this method, the student still benefits from a review of a past event, although only the adult helping the student has done the review. From the student's point of view, this is just information to be used for the future.

Figure 5

Sample Daily Behavior Chart

Name: _____ Date: _____

Please rate this student in each target area for each period using the following scale:

       1 = try harder, problem not handled well

       2 = good or no problem

       3 = excellent, problem handled well

Target Behaviors	Period 1	Period 2	Period 3	Period 4	Period 5	Period 6	Period 7	Period 8
Tries When Its Hard Tries it, Asks for help, Asks for 1 min. break, Tries again.								
Accepts Imperfection Does not get mad if corrected or gets something wrong								

If rewards are to be used:

Points needed to earn daily rewards: _____

Accumulated points needed to earn long term rewards: _____

Directions for Using The Behavior Chart

1. This chart should be filled out after each period by the student or a staff person. The number of periods can be adjusted to reflect the student's schedule. The student is rated on how well he or she demonstrated each skill for that period.

2. Decide whether rewards are necessary. Many students do not need rewards to alter their behavior, they just need frequent reminders. If the student does not seem motivated to alter their behavior, the chart can be linked to rewards as described below.

3. **Using the chart as a reminder system without rewards.** The chart can be used as a means to provide frequent feedback to a students. Students can also self-monitor behaviors in an effort to increase their insight into their actions.

4. **Using the chart as an incentive system with rewards.**

   a. **Establish a baseline.** Fill out the chart for a week without providing rewards. Calculate the average daily points.

   b. Use the **average daily points** plus or minus 5 points to set the **points needed for daily privileges.**

   c. Negotiate with the student what kind of privileges will represent daily privileges and what might represent long term rewards. Daily privileges might include free-time in school or home, access to desired equipment like computer games, or getting out of a homework assignment. Long term rewards might include new computer/video games, music, chances to go to a special event, or in school, access to or graduation from a class. For example, some students have worked towards graduating from a class that they no longer wanted to attend.

   d. When students earn the **points needed for daily privileges**, they must cash out and receive their privileges. Any points earned in a day in excess of what was needed to get daily privileges can go into savings for long term rewards.

   e. Only points in excess of **points needed for daily privileges** can be used for savings.

Chapter 8

Training peers to be more accepting of students on the spectrum

Sometimes it is not enough to teach skills just to students on the spectrum. This is particularly the case when special needs students are mistreated, rejected or teased by their peers. To simply address those who are being mistreated does not address the problem. We must intervene with the peer environment that fosters rejection and intolerance.

A growing body of evidence also demonstrates that educating peers about their classmates difficulties and having them participate as peer mentors has positive effects for both the "disabled" students and the "typical" peers (Dunn, 2005; Twemlow et al. 2001; Haring & Breen, 1992; Odom & Strain, 1984). For disabled students, involving peers seems to increase positive social interactions and generalization of those skills. And peers who become peer mentors demonstrate increased achievement test scores and self-esteem (e.g., Twemlow et al., 2001). The research also suggests that without ongoing support, peers may not maintain a high level of interactions with targeted peers (Odom & Watts, 1991). Thus, just as it is important to plan for generalization of skills for "disabled" students, it is equally important to plan for generalization for "typical" peers.

Lessons to increase peer understanding

Lessons can be done in a generic way without using any student's name, or it can involve talking to peers about a specific student, highlighting the students' challenges and assets, and how they as peers can be helpful to that student. The decision to use the student's name or not depends first on the student's and family's wishes, and secondly whether the peers already have a very negative perception of the student. If peers don't know the student and there is little teasing going on, then I might suggest not using the student's name in any presentation. But when they actively dislike the student, then I would suggest using the student's name to try to change the peers' perceptions of the student and his or her behaviors. It is important for peers to know that many of the irritating behaviors the student presents are not intentional and to learn to appreciate some of the student's strengths and talents.

The following maps out the procedures for obtaining the necessary permission and creating the content for presentations to peers. At the end of this chapter are two sample lessons, one for students who want their diagnosis to be discussed, and one for those who prefer that no diagnostic label is used. These lessons can easily be adapted to use without mentioning a specific student.

Guidelines for doing peer presentations

1. Discuss the options for specific versus generic presentations with the student's parents first. If the student's behaviors are very noticeable to peers and cause some negative reactions with peers, then it may be more helpful to do a lesson using the student's name. Have the parents sign a consent form to do this.

2. Have sessions with the target student about his or her assets and challenges (see Chapter 3 on building self-awareness). Together, or with the family, you can map out the challenges and talents you might share with peers if the student gives you permission (see next step).

3. Get permission from the student to talk to his or her peers. I usually say to the student, "Would it be okay to talk with your classmates so they can be more friendly or helpful to you?" If they say no, I say, "Well, I won't if you do not want me to, but can I just show you what I might say?" Then most students will say yes when they see the positive information I could present about them. If they still say no, many will come back months later and ask for me to do it because they realize that their peers continued to tease them. Ideally, the content of what will be said to peers should be created in cooperation with the student. I usually show them an outline of the peer presentations at the end of this chapter and have them add or make changes. The information to present should contain a list of the student's assets and some of their challenges, the reason for any misunderstood behaviors, famous people who have had similar patterns of assets and challenges, and how the student wants peers to help.

4. Select the peers to whom you will speak. Usually we want to select students with whom our targeted student interacts (i.e., those who are in his or her classes). We might select 1-2 students from each of the student's classes. The ideal peers will be those students who are "caring" individuals and would use the information wisely to help the student rather than use the information against the student. Guidance counselors, teachers, and the targeted student are usually the best sources of information for good peer candidates. Peers who do much of the

teasing are not good candidates to help the student, but they need to be spoken to about their behavior by administrators who can let them know the consequences for continued teasing.

5. Send a letter home to the parents of the selected peers informing them that you would like to have them participate in a peer leadership program (See sample letter at end of this chapter).

6. Conduct the peer presentaion, preferably *without* the target student there (see Sample Presentations at end of this chapter).

Peer participation beyond the initial lesson

To help peers continue to show understanding and kindness to targeted students after the initial peer presentation, it is important to create activities that foster peer participation. Wagner (1998) and Dunn (2005) have described several strategies to maintain peer involvement such as those listed below.

Peer leadership programs. In these programs, students are solicited to be helpers to students with social difficulties. They may be involved in promoting interaction during lunch or recess with targeted students or tutoring students with class and homework assignments. In Millburn schools where I regularly consult, we have peer leaders attend **lunch bunch** groups and **after-school groups** with targeted students to help with conversation and cooperative group work skills. Some of our peer leaders come regularly to our "life skills" class to help more severely autistic students. In this class, the peer leaders often engage in highly structured conversation and recreational activities and coach students in academic and work related skills. Peer leaders meet regularly to discuss their experiences and any difficulties they are having with students.

Classroom incentive programs targeting kind behaviors. This kind of program would be useful for "self contained classes" or situations in which students stay in the same class for most of the day. The teacher is encouraged to create an incentive system to reward all students for being helpful and kind towards each other (see Wagner, 1998; Cantor, 1987). I usually target three acts of kindness: (a) invite those who are isolated to join in, (b) stand up for those who are teased (directly or by anonymously getting help for the victim), and (c) offer help to those who are upset. Students are not individually rewarded, but rather the class as a whole gets points every time any student demonstrates one of the kind behaviors. When enough points are accumulated, the class has a celebration.

Sample Peer Presentation (Diagnosis not mentioned)

1. The trainer says, "I am here to ask for your help with a classmate of yours. He is the same as you and different in some ways. How are we all the same? How are we different?"

2. "We are also different in our senses. What are the five senses? Hearing, Seeing, Taste, Smell, and Touch. Some of us differ in how we see, hear, taste, smell things, or are sensitive to touch."

3. "Have you ever heard of the *sixth sense*? The sixth sense is really the social sense." (This notion was adapted from Carol Grey, 1996). "People who have a good friend or social sense:

    a. Can easily talk to others.

    b. Know how to get along with others.

    c. Can easily understand what others are feeling and thinking."

4. "Sometimes people have difficulty with their social sense and they may not know:

    a. How to easily talk with their peers.

    b. How to interact well with others.

    c. How others are feeling or thinking.

    d. And then it is hard to make friends."

5. When the training is about a student who will be named, discuss the student's talents as well as their difficulties with their social sense. Also explain the unintentional nature of any irritating behaviors the student engages in. For example, say:

    a. "John has trouble with his friend sense despite being very intelligent. He has some difficulty knowing what to say to talk with others. Some of you have complained that John sometimes annoys you. What does he do that upsets you?" (As students relay information about what the student does, be ready to explain why he does it, assuring them he does not do it purposely to annoy them. Also explain how they can help the situation rather than create more problems). For example, "Some of you have complained that John talks about topics you do not want to hear even after you ask him to stop. John explained that sometimes the thoughts rush in his head and he is unable to stop talking about it. He does not do it purposely to annoy you. If that happens you can tell him that you do not want to hear about that now and will return to talk with him later when he is done. Don't tell him to 'shut up' or insult him as this will only upset him and *then* he might want to purposely annoy you."

    b. Point out the student's strengths (often associated with particular interests the student has). "John also has some extraordinary talents. He is an avid reader, expert mathematician, and has a wealth of information about transportation systems throughout history. If you ever need to know anything about transportation, he knows more than anyone. He also happens to be an expert on weather systems, so if you ever need to know what or why the weather is doing what it is doing here or in other parts of the country, he is the resident expert."

6. Discuss how talented and valuable individuals can be despite any difficulties with their "social sense." Review famous people who have had trouble with their friend sense despite their terrific talents and successes. These individuals (who have been described as having some symptoms of autism) might include Albert Einstein, Bill Gates, Amadeus Mozart, Thomas Edison, Thomas Jefferson, Marie Currie and Temple Grandin, among others. Review these individuals' special gifts and talents as well as their social difficulties.

7. "I want you guys to understand what it might be like to have trouble with the social sense." Explain that you will conduct an exercise so they can experience what it might be like not to know how to join into a social group. See below:

    a. Tell the students they can be part of a special group if they can figure out how to join in. Those who join in will get something special (e.g., one homework free pass—if you can arrange for them to be excused from one homework assignment that night).

    b. Ask for 3 volunteers who are willing to leave the room while you teach the rest the "secrets" of joining in.

    c. Explain to the remaining students the secret to join into the group. Tell them they must ask, "Can I join?" while showing some "secret" behaviors that you make up (e.g., putting their hands on their hips, tapping their foot, and blinking). Ask for 2 or 3 volunteers to model this for the students who left the room but will shortly return. Have the volunteers practice the secret behaviors before the other students return.

    d. When the 3 students who left the room return, have them try to join in. Tell them to ask if they can join in. After the first student tries to join, ask the entire group, "Did he do it? Can he join?" The students, seeing that he did not put his hands on his hips, tap his foot and blink, will say, "No, he did not do it right." Then have one of the students who knows the secret behaviors model the right way and give them their reward. Then have the students who do not know how to join in try again until one of the students says they do not want to try it anymore.

e. As soon as one of the students gives up, say, "Now you know what it is like not to know how to join in." Ask the student(s) how they felt and why they gave up. Talk about how they were frustrated or embarrassed and how others might have been laughing as they were trying to join in. Explain that is how the targeted student feels when he tries to join in, does not know how, and then people begin to laugh.

f. After the activity, tell everyone what the secret behaviors were and make sure everyone gets the reward (e.g., the homework free pass or whatever else was promised).

8. Ask the students what they can do to help the targeted student or all students with problems with their social sense.

a. Tell the students they can:

- Invite students to join in if they seem isolated or left out.

- Stand up for others who are teased.

- Offer help to others if they are upset.

b. If the sensitivity training is about a particular student then discuss ways to help that student. Ask who among them would like to be a PEER LEADER to help coach the student at lunch and/or during class times. Try to get 5 volunteers for each targeted student so that each peer only helps the targeted student one day per week. Peer leaders can help at lunch or during class time.

(1) At lunch, peers leaders engage and coach the student. They may coach the student to start and maintain conversations and avoid certain topics. They may help protect the student from conflicts with others.

(2) During class, peer leaders might help students with their class and homework and coach them on working cooperatively with others during group projects. They may also continue to protect them from conflicts with others.

9. Schedule follow up meetings with peer volunteers (all meetings are facilitated by a staff member). Peers are asked to participate in several weekly meetings followed by monthly follow ups to help them effectively coach the targeted students.

Sample Peer Presentation (Diagnosis mentioned)

This presentation is identical to the one above, but instead of introducing the concept of "the sixth sense," students are taught about the particular diagnosis the student has, the strengths inherent in that diagnosis as well as the challenges. Then the profile of that particular student is highlighted. The discussion of famous individuals is the same, but students are told that the individuals may have had an autistic spectrum disorder. The joining-in exercise is also the same. See example below:

1. Trainer begins by saying, "I am here to ask for your help with a classmate of yours. He is the same as you and different in some ways. How are we all the same? How are we different?

2. We are also different in our pattern of strengths and challenges. For example, some of us may be great in one area, yet need some help in other areas. For example, some might be great at athletics and socializing, but have a difficult time with schoolwork. Some might be great actors or entertainers, but have difficulty with athletics.

3. One pattern of assets and challenges is when individuals are great with academic work, but have difficulty socializing. This pattern resembles those with something called Asperger's Syndrome. People with Asperger's syndrome may have great intellectual ability and a wealth of knowledge about certain subject areas, but have difficulty socializing. They may have trouble with:

    a. Knowing how to talk to others.

    b. Understanding how other people think and feel.

    c. Managing their feelings when overwhelmed.

    d. Making friends.

    e. Sensitivity to sounds, light or touch.

4. John is someone with Asperger's Syndrome. He is very bright, but has difficulty with socializing.

a. John has trouble making friends despite being very intelligent. He has some difficulty knowing what to say to talk with others. Some of you have complained that John sometimes annoys you. What does he do that upsets you." (As students relay information about what the student does, be ready to explain why he does it, assuring them he does not do it purposely to annoy them. Also explain how they can help the situation rather than create more problems). "For example, some of you have complained that John talks about topics you do not want to hear even after you ask him to stop. John explained that sometimes the thoughts rush in his head and he is unable to stop from talking about them. He does not do it purposely to annoy you. If that happens you can tell him that you do not want to hear about that now and will return to talk with him later when he is done. Don't tell him to 'shut up' or insult him as this will only upset him and *then* he might want to purposely annoy you.

b. John also has a number of great strengths. He is an avid reader, expert mathematician, and a wealth of information about transportation systems throughout history. If you ever need to know anything about this, he knows more than anyone. He also happens to be an expert on weather systems, so if you ever need to know what or why the weather is doing what it is doing here or in other parts of the country, he is the resident expert."

5. Discuss how talented and valuable individuals can be despite having Asperger like features. Review famous people who may have had Aspergers or a related difficulty. These individuals (who have been described as having some symptoms of autism) might include Albert Einstein, Bill Gates, Amadeus Mozart, Thomas Edison, Thomas Jefferson, Marie Currie and Temple Grandin, among others. Review these individual's special gifts and talents as well as their social difficulties.

6. "What is it like to have Aspergers and have difficulty socializing with others?" Explain that you want the students to understand what it is like for students with these difficulties (or for your targeted student). Explain that you will conduct an exercise so they can experience what it might be like not to know how to join into a social group. See below:

a. Tell the students they can be part of a special group if they can figure out how to join in. Those who join in will get something special (e.g., one homework free pass—if you can arrange for them to be excused from one homework assignment that night).

b. Ask for 3 volunteers who are willing to leave the room while you teach the rest the "secrets" of joining in.

c. Explain to the remaining students the secret to joining the group. Tell them they must ask, "Can I join in?" while showing some "secret" behaviors that you make up (e.g., putting their hands on their hips, tapping their foot, and blinking). Ask for 2 or 3 volunteers to model this for the students who left the room but will shortly return. Have the volunteers practice the secret behaviors before the other students return.

d. When the 3 students who left the room return, have them try to join in. Tell them to ask if they can join in. After the first student tries to join, ask the entire group, "Did he do it? Can he join?" The students, seeing that he did not put his hands on his hips, tap his foot and blink, will say, "No, he did not do it right." Then have one of the students who knows the secret behaviors model the right way and give them their reward. Then have the students who do not know how to join in try again until one of the students says they do not want to try it anymore.

e. As soon as one of the students gives up, say, "Now you know what it is like not to know how to join in." Ask the student(s) how they felt and why they gave up. Talk about how they were frustrated or embarrassed and how others might have been laughing as they were trying to join in. Explain that is how the targeted student feels when he tries to join in, does not know how, and then people begin to laugh.

f. After the activity, tell everyone what the secret behaviors were and make sure everyone gets the reward (e.g., the homework-free pass or whatever else was promised).

7. Ask the students what they can do to help the targeted student or all students with Asperger's Syndrome.

a. They can:

- Invite students to join in if they seem isolated or left out.

- Stand up for others who are teased.

- Offer help to others if they are upset.

b. If the sensitivity training is about a particular student then discuss ways to help that student. Ask who among them would like to be a PEER LEADER to help coach the student at lunch and/or during class times. Try to get 5 volunteers for each targeted student so that each peer only helps the targeted student one day per week. Peer leaders can help at lunch or during class time.

(1) At lunch, peers leaders engage and coach the student. They may coach the student to start and maintain conversations and avoid certain topics. They may help protect the student from conflicts with others.

(2) During class, peer leaders might help students with their class and homework and coach them on working cooperatively with others during group projects. They may also continue to protect them from conflicts with others.

8. Schedule follow up meetings with peer volunteers (all meetings are facilitated by a staff member). Peers are asked to participate in several weekly meeting followed by monthly follow ups to help them effectively coach the targeted students.

Content of subsequent meetings with peer leaders

1. In the first follow up meetings, peers are taught how to protect their targeted students from others by: (a) Explaining to others the unintentional nature of any provocative social mistakes the student made without releasing personal information and (b) standing up for them if they are teased, either directly or by getting help from an adult.

2. In the next two or more sessions, peers are taught the skills that their assigned students are working on generalizing. They are also taught how to coach their assigned students on these skills.

3. In subsequent meetings, peers meet to bring up any difficulties they are having with their assigned student(s) or other peers and together the group tries to solve the problems.

NAME OF SCHOOL

Dear Parent(s) or Guardian(s):

Your youngster has been nominated by teachers to be part of a voluntary "peer leadership program" in their school. Peer leaders will be trained to help facilitate social skill development for other students with learning difficulties. Your youngster's participation would involve acting as a coach and buddy to another student one time per week during lunch and recess. Students will still have recess time with their regular class.

The benefit to your youngster may be both enhanced self-esteem and social skill development. We find that most students who take an active role in helping to teach social skills become more socially skilled themselves and more confident.

Participation in the program is voluntary. Space is also limited such that students who want to participate may not be able to do it each month in order to allow other students to have a turn. If you would like your child to be able to participate, please sign the permission form below.

Please feel free to call me at   , ext.   if you have any questions.

Sincerely,

Permission Form

I agree to have my child _____ participate in the peer leader program during the _____ school year.

_____   _____
(Date)   (Please sign here)

Chapter Nine
Skill Lessons

The skill lessons presented in this chapter address the common issues presented by individuals on the autism spectrum and those with other social-communication difficulties. These issues include:

1. Perspective-taking and empathy

2. The use of nonverbal communication

3. Conversation skills

4. Handling frustrations and anxiety

The lessons do not have to be taught in a particular order; however, they are organized such that later skills build on some of the earlier skills. The first section is on nonverbal communication, which is an important component of many of the later complex social skills. The next sections address anger and anxiety management. For those whose anxieties or frustrations interfere significantly with functioning, these skill areas often have to be targeted first. The section on conversation skills is crucial as these skills are prerequisites for the subsequent areas related to building friendships, dating, dealing with school and family demands and employment skills. The last sections deal with employment related skills and the practical skills of managing money, handling emergency situations and negotiating transportation.

Because the skills are partially categorized by situation (e.g., dating situations, friendships, employment) some skills may appear only in one section and yet have relevance for many situations. For example, "Working cooperatively in groups," which appears under the category of "Dealing with school and family demands," has relevance for other situations like friendships, dating, and employment settings. Thus, for those focused on a particular situation (e.g., employment skills) it would be wise to look at the skills in all sections for other relevant skills.

Each skill involves both a lesson and an activity page with ways to teach and generalize the skill. The format for the lessons and activity pages are described below:

Skill lesson format

1. **Rationale**: Each skill begins with a rationale for the skill lessons designed to establish the student's motivation for the lesson, which often involves information about how the student's behavior may affect others' thoughts and feelings.

2. **Skill steps**: The skill is then broken down into component parts that include information about what to do, why, and how to do it.

Activity page format

1. **How to teach**: This includes information about how to **explain**, **model**, and **role-play** the skill steps as well as any other activities to learn the skill. This is appropriate for teachers, counselors, parents, coaches, or self-learners.

2. **How to generalize the skill**: This includes information on how to **prime** students to do the skill, ways to **practice** the skill in natural situations, and how to **review** with students their performance on the skill.

 # Expressing and reading welcoming versus unwelcoming social cues

Rationale

- Being able to *express* a welcoming impression increases the chances that others will like being with us. This is important when meeting new people who might be friends, potential dates, or potential employers. Sometimes when we are nervous or upset, we accidentally give off the impression that we do not welcome others when we might actually wish to connect with those people.

- Being able to *read* the cues that others are welcoming of us helps us to continue to pursue interactions with those who want them, and avoid interactions with those who do not want to interact with you. Pursuing people who are not welcoming of us can be frustrating and lead to trouble (e.g., if people accuse you of harassing them or following them).

Welcoming versus unwelcoming expressions/cues

Behaviors	Welcoming	Unwelcoming
Body language	Turn body towards others Make eye contact Smile	Turn body away Avoid looking at them Frown, make angry or disgusted look
Tone of voice	Pleasant, friendly tone	Overly quiet, muttering to self, or overly loud and harsh
Choice of words	Friendly greetings: "Hi, how are you?" "Hello, nice to meet you."	Unfriendly greeting "Whatever." Grunt
Reciprocity	You or others invite people to get together, respond positively to invitations, or initiate conversations directly or by phone	You or others repeatedly (three times in a row or more) turn down invitations to get together, do not respond to phone calls or gestures to start conversations

Activity Page: Expressing and reading welcoming versus unwelcoming social cues

Teaching

1. **Explain** the rationale for being able to express and read others welcoming and unwelcoming behaviors. Link it to the goals the student has for work, friendship, or dating. Read the chart on the previous page outlining the behaviors showing welcoming versus unwelcoming cues.

2. **Model** the expressions and ask for feedback.

    a. A game-show format can be used here to review the material. Questions can include those in which the teacher models certain behaviors and the students decide whether it is welcoming or unwelcoming. Make sure you model all the categories of body language, tone of voice, and words.

    b. For the reciprocity category, one can ask the student questions about situations in which someone did or did not respond to one or several phone calls or invitations and the students must try to assess the person's desire to get together.

3. **Role-play** with the student's welcoming versus unwelcoming behaviors

    a. Student walks up to group at lunch or recess time: either student or group can practice welcoming or unwelcoming behaviors.

    b. Student approaches another student at a party, dance, or dating situation hoping to make a good first impression.

    c. Student is talking to a friend and asks them to get together or to call or email them.

4. This skill lends itself well to creating picture books where students can pose for pictures demonstrating welcoming versus unwelcoming behaviors (see Chapter 6). Such pictures are available in the *Social Skills Picture Book for High School and Beyond* (Baker, In Press).

Generalization

Priming

Using the chart or a cue card summarizing parts of the chart, remind students before situations in which they should consider how they express or read welcoming social cues. Situations might include:

— Before going to lunch where students pick there own seating arrangements.

— Before picking partners for group projects.

— Prior to going to a party, dance or potential dating situation.

— Prior to attending any new social situation (e.g., club, sports team, music, chorus, etc.).

Facilitated practice

1. Students can practice this regularly if teachers rotate work groups to create opportunities to welcome new students into their group. Lunch groups can also be rotated, yet some students may want to always be paired with each other to foster developing friendships.

2. Students can be challenged to guess who is more welcoming when they attend any group social events at clubs, dances, or parties.

Review

After a new social situation, adults who observed can review with the student how welcoming he or she appeared. Similarly, adults can ask the students who seemed most welcoming.

2 Interest versus boredom social cues

Rationale

- Being able to *express* interest when others are talking increases the chances that others will like being with us. This is important when meeting new people or maintaining ongoing relationships.

- Being able to *read* the cues that others are interested or bored helps us to know whether to continue or stop talking.

Behaviors	Interest	Boredom
Body language	Turn body towards others, lean in a bit. Make eye contact (at least intermittently) Quiet hands and feet (minimal fidgeting)	Turn body away Avoid looking at them Fidget, look at watch or at the clock, or at exit doors. Yawn
Tone of voice	Upward inflection: Oh, Ahh, I see.	Downward inflection that ends in a sigh.
Choice of words	Listener asks questions about what you just said.	The listener does not ask any questions, tries to change the topic, or does not say anything.

Interest versus Boredom expressions/cues

Think about what you could do or say if you are bored (see Skill #29, "Politely ending conversations"). Make an excuse. "I don't mean to be rude, but I have to run and do something right now—I'll talk to you later."

Think about what to do if the other person looks bored while you are talking (see Skill #28, "Being sensitive to the listener's interests"). Say, "Do you want to hear more?" If they say no, ask a question about them like: "So, what is happening with you?"

Activity Page: Interest versus boredom

Teaching

1. **Explain** the rationale for being able to express and read signs of interest or boredom. Link it to the goals the student has for work, friendship, or dating. Read the chart on the previous page outlining the behaviors showing interest versus boredom cues. Explain what to do if you or others are bored.

2. **Model** the expressions and ask for feedback. A game-show format can be used here to review the material. Questions can include those in which the teacher models certain behaviors and the students decide whether they are interested or bored. Make sure you model all the categories of body language, tone of voice, and words.

3. **Role-play** with the students situations in which others are interested or bored.

   a. Student is talking about his or her interests and others become bored.

   b. Student becomes bored when others in a group talk about something he or she has no interest in.

4. This skill lends itself well to creating picture books where students can pose for pictures demonstrating what to do when they see signs of boredom and how to demonstrate that they are interested in others' conversation (see Chapter 6).

Generalization

Priming

Using the chart or a cue card summarizing parts of the chart, remind students before situations in which they should consider whether they are boring others or might have to look interested even if they are bored (e.g., before going to an interview, club meeting, sports team, music lesson, party, dance or potential dating situation). It is important to look interested and not perseverate on one's own interests.

Facilitated practice

1. In a high school setting, students can practice this regularly in a lunch bunch group or after-school club in which an adult facilitates social interaction among a small group of students, coaching them on their interactions.

2. Private social skills groups or hobby clubs might also be places to practice regularly, particularly if there is a facilitator who can coach students in reading the cues of interest and boredom.

3. Students can be challenged to guess who is more bored or interested when they attend any social event, including family get-togethers, clubs, dances, or parties. An adult coach can compare notes with the student about how they are reading the cues.

Review

After a social situation, adults who observed can review with the student how well he or she appeared interested and how he or she read the signs of others' interest.

Sarcasm versus genuine expressions

Rationale

Being able to know whether someone really means what they say is important if you want to know whom you can trust and how to react to others. If you do not read the cues well, you might accidentally insult someone who was complimenting you or you may trust someone who is really making fun of you.

Definition

- Sarcasm is when others' words do not match their body language and thus they really mean the opposite of what they say.

- Sarcastic body language may include rolling one's eyes and looking up or away, making a face of disbelief or confusion, tone of voice that is mocking and draws out the vowel sounds (the opposite of a firm statement where words are spoken in short, staccato tones).

What do people really mean?

Behaviors	Positive statement	Negative Statement
Genuine body language: eye contact, no look of confusion, clear firm tone of voice	Genuine positive communication (probably a compliment)	Genuine negative communication (probably insulting)
Sarcastic body language: looking away or rolling eyes, confused facial expression, mocking long vowel sounds tone of voice	Despite positive words, really a negative communication (probably an insult)	Despite negative words, really a positive communication (probably a compliment)

When you do not know whether someone really meant the words they spoke?

- Ask, "Did you really mean that?"

- If someone says they did mean it, you can be sure they did.

- If someone says they did not mean it, then they may or may not be telling the truth. If you are still unsure, ask others you trust for their opinion about what the person really meant.

 ## Activity Page: Sarcasm versus genuine expression

Teaching

1. Show the students the written skill steps and read through the steps with them, **explaining** the rationale for being able to read sarcasm versus genuine expressions, and defining what sarcasm is.

2. **Model** genuine versus sarcastic expressions and ask students if they can guess your true message. There is no need for students to practice making sarcastic expressions, as it is more crucial for students to learn how to read such expressions. Sample expressions could include:

    a. "You are really good at math," expressed with sincerity. (True meaning: you are really good at math).

    b. "You are a really good writer," stated with sarcastic body language. (True meaning: you are not a good writer).

    c. "You are annoying, get away," spoken with eye contact and a firm clear voice. (True meaning: The person is annoyed and wants you to go away).

    d. "Oh yeah, you are really the worst at computers, totally in the dark ages," spoken with eyes rolling up, a look of disbelief, and a tone that draws out the vowel sounds. (True meaning: Person thinks you are really great with computers).

3. This skill lends itself well to **role-play** activities, like creating picture books where students can pose for pictures demonstrating genuine versus sarcastic comments.

Generalization

Priming

Using the chart or a cue card summarizing parts of the chart, remind students before situations in which others may be sarcastic. Situations may include parties, dances, social mixers where parents and adults are not supervising. It might be helpful to have a buddy to go to such an event with in case the student needs advice about whether someone was being sarcastic or genuine.

Facilitated practice

This skill can be "baitcd" several times per week by having parents, peers or teachers purposely make a sarcastic statement and then asking the student to guess what the true intent was of the statement.

Review

After such baiting situations, one can review with the student whether it was sarcastic and how they know.

 Attending to others

Rationale

- In conversation, in a classroom, on a job, or at a special event (e.g., a religious ceremony), it shows respect to others when you appear attentive to the speaker. Others are insulted when you do not appear to be attending to them.

- It is crucial to position yourself so that you can hear and see the speaker. That way, you won't miss important social cues by not seeing (e.g., if they gesture for others to sit, stand, or point to something important like a homework assignment).

Position your body so you are facing the speaker.

Face the person who is speaking and get close enough to hear them.

Maintain eye gaze.

You do not have to stare, but you need to look at the speaker's eyes or face most of the time. If you find this too difficult, try looking at their forehead instead, or just looking occasionally at their eyes.

Stay relatively still.

Fidgeting distracts others.

Don't interrupt.

Wait for a pause before talking. In class, raise your hand and wait to be called on if you want to talk.

 Activity Page: Attending to others

Teaching

1. Show the students the written skill steps and read through the steps with them. **Explain** the rationale for being able to see others and appear attentive when others speak. Link it to the goals the student has for work, friendship, or dating.

2. Ask another adult or student to read a brief passage from a book (pick an interesting or funny book they would like, to keep their attention) while you **model** good and poor listening. Ask the students to tell you whether you successfully demonstrated each part of the skill.

3. **Role-play** attending to others with the students.

   a. Have the students demonstrate good and poor listening positions while you read from an intriguing book.

   b. Tell students you will test their ability to listen with their eyes rather than their ears. Tell them to pay attention to what you do with your hands and face rather than your words as you direct them in these activities:

      i. Gesture with your hands for them to draw a square while you say, "Draw a circle on piece of paper."

      ii. Ask them to write down homework assignments. Then point to assignments written on the board as you tell them to "do this one, but not that one." See if they understood which ones to write down.

      iii. Ask them to guess what you are looking at in the room.

      iv. Without words, direct them to sit, stand, move to another seat, or attend to something special in the room.

      v. Ask them to guess if you are pleased or annoyed as you ask them to quiet down or to move to another seat. Explain the importance of reading the teacher's level of upset to avoid getting in trouble.

4. This skill also lends itself well to creating picture books where students can pose for pictures demonstrating good versus poor listening positions.

Generalization

Priming

Using the skill sheet or a cue card, remind students to attend to others during important classes, interviews, special events, ceremonies, and when meeting new people.

Facilitated practice

1. Tell the student that you will be "testing" their attention by gesturing for the student to do a variety of things like to follow you, to get something for you, or to look at something. Each day see if they can follow your nonverbal gestures.

2. Classes, religious events, lectures, interviews, and group discussions are all natural activities to practice attending to others.

Review

After a social situation, adults who observed can review with the student how well he or she appeared to be attending.

 Respecting personal space and belongings

Rationale

If you respect others' space and belongings, then they will respect you. Getting physically too close to others or touching their belongings without permission makes others annoyed.

Respect personal space

- **With the general public (those you don't know):** Keep at least an arm's length away (close to two feet). When using public transportation, try to keep one seat between you and others if that is available. Using public restrooms, try to keep one urinal or stall away from others if possible. When sitting in restaurants or during special events (shows, movies, concerts, or sports events), try to keep one seat away from others if available. In crowded public places, you may have to be closer and even come in contact with others because there is no room.

- **With people you know:** Keep about half an arm's length away (close to one foot) from people you know in social situations, like in the classroom, lunch/recess, parties, clubs or sports teams.

- **With close friends and family:** You may get closer and touch people in your family, best friends, or someone you are dating. Always ask permission before you touch.

Respect others' property

- Don't take or borrow others' property without permission.

- Offer to replace or pay for others' property that was damaged while in your care.

 # Activity Page: Respecting personal space and belongings

Teaching

1. Show the students the written skill steps and read through the steps with them. **Explain** the rationale for respecting personal space and belongings and link it to the goals the student has for work, friendship, and dating.

2. **Model** the amount of space given to people in public, social, and intimate settings.

3. **Role-play** can be integrated into a game-show format where students must answer questions about personal space and touching others' belongings (see Chapter 6 for description of using game-show format). Sample questions include:

   a. Show me where you would sit if you were on a bus and people were already sitting like this?

      1. Occupied 2. Empty 3. Empty 4. Empty 5. Occupied

      (draw this or set up seats to simulate). The third seat is the right answer.

   b. Show me how close you should be when sitting with classmates at lunch.

   c. Show me which bathroom stall you would use if they were set up like this:

      1. Empty 2. Occupied 3. Empty 4. Occupied

      (#1 is the right answer because you have a wall on one side, where #3 is surrounded by others).

   d. Show me what you would do if you really liked someone else's laptop that they were not using and was sitting on their desk. (Answer: ask to see it before touching it).

   e. What would you do if you borrowed someone's electronic keyboard and another friend of yours spilled juice on it causing it to malfunction? (Answer: you are responsible to the friend you borrowed it from. You might try to get the student who spilled it to pay for it, but you are responsible to the owner).

Generalization
Priming

Using the skill sheet or a cue card summarizing the skill steps, remind students to respect personal space before situations in which they have previously violated personal space.

Facilitated practice

1. Bait the student with favored items that they might want to see and touch, then remind them to ask before touching.

2. Daily life offers many activities to practice respecting others' space. No need to create a special practice situation.

Review

After social situations, adults who observed can review with the student how well he or she respected space and others' belongings.

 **Personal hygiene**

Rationale

Keeping up your hygiene is important because:

- Good hygiene prevents disease and infection. Lack of cleanliness can serve as a breeding ground for viruses and bacteria.

- It affects your social desirability. Although certain hygiene routines are not health matters but have more to do with conforming to cultural norms, there is still something to be said for some conformity. Minimal conformity may allow you to avoid ridicule and be accepted by peers, schools, and prospective employers. Remember, what you find okay may upset others. For example, you may not be able to "smell" yourself (you are used to it) while others may be repelled.

Hygiene routines

The following is a list of typical hygiene routines. Some are important for genuine health concerns and others are simply about increasing "social acceptability."

- Keeping your **body clean** by regularly showering or bathing. Some shower every day, others shower every other day. The frequency is based on personal choice and on how dirty or sweaty you become during the day.

- Using **deodorant** for underarms should begin with puberty to offset underarm odors.

- **Washing your hair** can be done daily or several times per week depending on how dirty or sweaty your hair gets. Using an anti-dandruff shampoo is often used if you have many visible dry flakes that may make others avoid you.

- **Brushing your teeth** twice a day with toothpaste. Using a mouthwash or mint if your breath is offensive to others (this can happen as a result of certain strong foods, mouth and stomach bacteria, acid reflux, or dehydration).

- **Using tissues** to wipe your nose rather than picking your nose. And by all means do not pick and then put your finger in your mouth.

- Sneezing should be done into a tissue or at least your elbow to prevent sneezing germs onto others.

- Trying to go to a bathroom or **private area if you need to pass gas** rather than near others.

- **Burping or belching** can be done quietly by putting your hand over your mouth.

- Dressing in **clean clothes** that do not smell (undergarments and socks should not be worn for more than one day at a time without being cleaned).

- Many women **shave** their legs and armpits after puberty. Men may shave their faces or grow a beard and keep it trimmed. Like many routines, this is more culturally driven than a health concern.

Motivation and remembering to keep up with hygiene

To help with hygiene maintenance, you may want to keep a schedule with written reminders. If you desire to keep people away and therefore want to be "offensive" consider better ways to do this, for example, by asking others for space rather than making them repelled by you.

6 Activity Page: Personal hygiene

Teaching

1. Show the students the written skill steps and read through the steps with them. **Explain** the rationale for keeping up with hygiene, stressing both the health and social concerns. Emphasize that others do not have to "conform" to social norms entirely (it is okay to be different) but by deviating too sharply from hygiene norms, they may incur rejection from peers, college admissions officers and prospective employers.

2. It may be necessary to **model** and **role-play** some hygiene routines that the student does not know how to do. Also have students design a schedule of how often they should wash their bodies, hair, clothes, brush their teeth, shave, etc.

3. A game-show format can be used to answer questions about other hygiene matters (see Chapter 6 for description of using game-show format). Sample questions include:

   a. If you are at a quiet dinner table with friends and family and you have to pass gas, what should you do?

   b. If you are in class and you have to burp, what should you do?

   c. What would you do if you felt something hard in your nose?

   d. What should you do when you have to sneeze?

   e. What could you do if you were in school and you just had gym and realized your armpits smell bad?

   f. What might you do after eating a pizza with triple garlic before hanging out with your friends?

Generalization
Priming

Use their schedule of hygiene to remind them of what and when to keep clean. Parents may decide to make desired privileges contingent on these hygiene practices when students are very resistant to keeping up with these routines.

Facilitated practice

It may be necessary to coach students through some of these practices if they do not adequately know how to perform them.

Review

During the morning, parents can review the effectiveness of their students' morning hygiene routine. After any period in which the student has been lacking in hygiene, feedback can be presented to the student on how to remedy this. It may be necessary to first get the student's agreement to receive such periodic feedback before there is a problem, as such feedback may be met with shame and subsequent resistance.

 # Dealing with odd motor mannerisms

Rationale

Some of us may make certain motor movements when we are excited, nervous, or bored. These movements may seem odd to others and keep people from wanting to interact with us.

Examples of some odd motor mannerisms

- Hand flapping or clapping hands
- Licking or biting lips repeatedly
- Picking, biting pieces of skin
- Pacing or walking in circles, sometimes walking around the periphery of spaces
- Rocking your body in a chair
- Bouncing legs or clapping knees together in your seat

What to do about odd motor mannerisms

You can stop them, substitute other movements and/or explain them to others, as described below:

1. It may be possible to stop doing these things if you are aware of it. You may need someone to tell you when you are doing it to become more aware of it and try to control it.

2. It may be possible to substitute another movement that others will find less distracting or "odd looking."

    a. Quietly fidgeting with a paper clip or pen may substitute for some hand flapping, clapping, or picking at skin.

    b. You may need to experiment with other sensations that provide similar stimulation but are less noticeable (for example, one student had a piece of cloth he kept in his desk that he would feel rather than fidget on top of his desk with items that made noise.

3. If it is not possible to alter the movements, you may want to explain it to others. When others have an explanation, they are less likely to see a behavior as "odd." For example, one student explained to his peers that he gets restless and likes to run around in circles to relieve excess energy.

 Activity Page: Dealing with odd motor mannerisms

Teaching

1. Show the students the written skill steps and read through the steps with them. **Explain** the rationale for trying to alter or explain these mannerisms. Emphasize that others do not have to "conform" to social norms entirely (it is okay to be different) but by deviating too sharply from norms, they may incur rejection from peers and prospective employers who do not understand the behavior.

2. Only with permission from students, **model** for the students the motor mannerisms they engage in so they can see what it might look like. This is a sensitive area, and thus students must first be willing to consider addressing this before you show them what it looks like. Model possible alternative mannerisms if they are open to altering it. If they are unwilling to alter the behavior, work on explaining the behavior to others.

3. **Role-play** possible alternative mannerisms until students can do them quietly and subtly, or role- play how to explain the behavior to others.

Generalization
Priming

Remind students prior to situations in which they typically get excited, bored or nervous, how they might handle their motor movements.

Facilitated practice

The most important practice opportunity is to give feedback to students when they are engaging in an odd motor mannerism so that they can become aware of it and possibly alter it. You must have the students' permission to offer this feedback because they may not want to be constantly reminded about the issue. They may agree more readily if you explain that you are doing this to increase their awareness of it, but it is up to them whether they want to change it.

Review

Reviewing after the fact is less effective than coaching in the moment. Try to give feedback as soon as you see the student engaged in the behavior (as long as they have given you prior permission to do so).

Overview of dealing with anger

Why Control Yourself?

Being angry in a controlled manner can be productive when it helps you reach your goals. Being angry in an "out of control" way is rarely productive because:

- You may work against your own goals by saying or doing something that insures you will not get what you want and

- You may hurt yourself or others and get in serious trouble.

A Model of Anger

People get angry for a reason. Usually something happens (a trigger) that makes you think something (your perception and thoughts about what happened) that lead to certain feelings (sometimes anger). See diagram below:

Trigger	Something that happens to you. For example, teasing, losing, making a mistake, not getting what you want, waiting too long for things. Other triggers might be related to internal conditions like lack of sleep, physical pain, other physiological conditions that make you more irritable.)
Thoughts	(How you understand what happened. For example, if someone bumps into you, you might think it was on purpose, leading to more angry feelings, or you may think it was accidental, leading to less angry feelings.)
Feelings	(Angry, not angry, sad, scared, happy)

Identifying Your Triggers

The first part of learning to control your anger is to learn about what triggers your anger. When you know the triggers you can make a plan to control your angry outbursts by (a) changing the triggers, (b) changing how you think about and then deal with the triggers, (c) finding ways to keep calm if you get angry, and (d) learning to talk about instead of act out your angry feelings. All of these are described below.

Ways To Control Your Anger

- **Change the trigger** so it is less of a trigger. For example, if certain school work typically leads to many mistakes and subsequent angry outbursts, getting changes to the school assignments or help with the work may make it less of a trigger.

- **Change your thoughts** about the trigger. For example, if mistakes upset you because they make you feel like you are not smart, you can learn to change how you think about making mistakes and see them as opportunities to learn more. Most importantly, you can get ready for situations in which you might make a mistake, so that when it happens it will not take you by surprise.

- Find ways to **keep calm** when you get angry. If you cannot avoid getting angry, then you will need to learn ways to calm down once you are upset. When you are extremely angry it may not be possible to reason with you. Some describe this as the brain being "hijacked" by emotions such that that you lose access to your rational thinking momentarily. During these moments it might be better to try to find a distraction from the angry outbursts through a calming activity, like reading, watching TV, listening to music, taking a walk, playing a game, using humor, or a sports activity.

- **Talking versus acting out your angry feelings** involves learning how to talk calmly to the person you are angry at or to someone else who can help you figure out what to do about the situation.

Activity Page: Overview of dealing with anger

Teaching

1. **Explain** the rationale for controlling anger, and present the cognitive model of how we get angry. Explain that in subsequent skill lessons they will learn to identify the triggers to their anger and then learn ways to prevent or control anger. Explain that this skill is ust an overview of this information.

2. There is nothing yet to **model** or **role-play** as this skill is just about teaching them the information. You can use a game-show format to review the information asking the following questions:

    a. Why is it important to control your anger?

    b. How are your thoughts about an event related to whether or not you get angry? (How we perceive an event determines whether we will be angry or not.)

    c. What can you do to avoid getting angry? (Avoid or change the triggers.)

    d. What is another way to avoid getting angry when something happens that usually triggers you to get angry? (Change the way you think about the trigger.)

    e. What should you do if you do if you are unable to prevent yourself from getting angry? (Find a calming strategy.)

    f. What is the difference between acting out and talking out anger?

Generalization

As this skill involves only information without the expectation for taking action yet, there are no generalization strategies until the students get to the next skills that require them to take action.

 # Identifying the triggers to your anger

Rationale

To begin making plans to prevent and control your anger, it is crucial to know what gets you angry. This skill involves identifying the triggers to your anger or upset.

Using The Daily Anger Record

You can keep track of the moments you lose your temper using the Daily Anger Record (see Skill #14). You can enlist the help of teachers or parents to keep track of these incidents as well, so together you can learn what the triggers are. The record includes information about what the situation was prior to getting angry (clues as to what the trigger was), what you thought, how you reacted and how others reacted.

Common triggers

To help you identify your triggers, consider the following list of common triggers.

- **External triggers**:
  — demanding work — making a mistake
  — being corrected — transitioning from a favored activity to something less
  — getting criticized   interesting (e.g., from a computer game to homework)
  — being teased — losing a game
  — having to wait or not getting to have or do something you want
  — sensory triggers (e.g., loud noise, distracting lights, uncomfortable touches, or repulsive smells)

- **Internal triggers**:
  — physical illness (e.g., viral or bacterial infections)
  — certain foods
  — sleep patterns
  — certain medications can lead to feeling sick, tired, or agitated, which makes it more likely that external triggers will upset you

Make a list of your trigger situations.

On a separate piece of paper, make a list of your triggers. You will use this list in the next two lessons, which focus on helping you avoid or deal better with these triggers.

 **9** Activity Page: Identifying the triggers to your anger

Teaching

1. **Explain** how to use the Daily Anger Record (Part 1: What upset me). Students should be asked to fill this sheet out every time something got them upset or angry, indicating what happened, what they thought about the event (e.g., the other persons' intentions) and how they reacted, and how others reacted.

2. **Model** how to fill out the record using a recent event from you own life that upset you or use the following example: Someone cut in front of you at the supermarket. Show where to write what happened (someone cut in front of you at the market), what you thought (they were inconsiderate and they think my feelings do not matter), what you did (told them that I was on line in front of them and they cut in front) and how the others reacted (they said sorry, but they only had one item and hoped they could go ahead).

3. **Role-play** by asking each student to fill out the Anger Record (just part 1) using a real situation that upset them or give them one of the following:

    a. They got a bad grade from a teacher and they think the teacher mis-graded them.

    b. They were teased by another student.

    c. Their parents did not allow them to go somewhere they wanted to go.

    d. They had to stop watching TV to go do a chore with their parents.

Generalization
Priming

Students should be reminded to fill out Part 1 of The Daily Anger Record when they get upset. This information will be crucial in helping them later make plans to prevent angry outbursts.

Facilitated practice

When students are upset, they can be prompted to fill out the Anger Record and coached through the writing of it.

Review

Students should be reminded to fill out the record after they are upset, or later when they have calmed down . The information will then be reviewed in the next skill lesson.

 # Altering or avoiding the triggers to your anger

Rationale

Once you know your triggers you can create a plan to prevent yourself from getting upset by these situations. Part of this plan involves changing or avoiding the triggering situations.

Review and prioritize your list of triggers

Have your list of triggers ready from Skill #9. Consider tackling one trigger at a time, focusing first on the ones that seem to trigger most of your upsets.

Brainstorm ways to alter your triggers

You will probably want help from teachers, educational consultants (in high school or college), human resources (in employment settings), counselors, parents, and others to help you think of "reasonable" ways to modify your triggers. Keep in mind, that if you want to meet certain requirements for school, you may not want certain modifications. For example, many colleges require that you have a certain number of foreign language credits. If you decided to modify your high school curriculum by getting rid of the foreign language courses, you may not be able to get into certain colleges. Consider the following suggestions to help you alter or avoid some of your triggers:

- **For demanding work**, it may be possible to get modifications to the assignments with the help of teachers, special education specialists in your school or college, or your employer. See the skill "Asking for reasonable modifications" (see Skill #54). Remember, not all modifications are considered "reasonable."

- **For sensory issues**, it may also be possible to get modifications to the environment in which you work (better lighting, quieter rooms, different uniforms that do not cause discomfort). Again, refer to the skill "asking for reasonable modifications" to see how to go about requesting these changes.

- **For teasing and criticism**, you may want to request that someone speak to the students or teachers who may be overly harsh in the teasing or criticism of you. See Chapter 8 on peer sensitivity training.

- **For internal triggers** related to sleep, diet, or medications, try to alter these patterns to avoid being tired, sick, or agitated. You may need to:

  — Avoid certain foods and increase other nutritious foods.

  — Plan to get more sleep or take a sleeping aid if you have insomnia.

  — Avoid certain activities when you are sick (e.g., dealing with a stressful academic or social situation may not be ideal when you have a bad cold).

  — Have your doctor review possible side effect profiles of medications to see if they may be making you tired, irritable, or agitated.

Activity Page: Altering or avoiding the triggers to your anger

Teaching

1. **Explain** the rationale for altering triggers so they no longer cause the same degree of upset. Stress the need to consult with specialists (e.g., education consultants, human resources, or parents and teachers) to consider the types of changes to triggers that can be made.

2. Have students select one or two triggers that are most frequently causing them upset or angry outbursts.

3. For the selected triggers, have students develop a plan for what might done to change the trigger so it would be less upsetting. The plan should include:

   a. Whom should they talk to for help in coming up with ideas for changing the trigger? Consider talking to teachers, educational consultants (in high school or college), human resources (in employment settings), counselors, and parents.

   b. What kinds of changes can be made?

   c. How will those changes be implemented? For many changes in a school setting, the student must first request them of the teacher or special education consultant, and the change may have to be documented in their official school record (e.g., and individualized education plan if they are a special education student) before the change can be made. In many colleges, before any special changes can be made to class demands or the school environment, documentation from a professional indicating the need for the modification must be obtained, and then the student must submit this documentation and request the change in person to the office of support services (see Skill #54, "Asking for reasonable modifications").

4. **Model** and **role-play** asking for the modification from the office of student support services or from a teacher, or employer. The role-play should include providing supporting documentation, explaining the rationale for the modification, and stressing that with such modification the student can accomplish the task.

Generalization

Priming

Students should be reminded to ask for a modification well in advance of a situation in which they might need it rather than waiting until the event. For example, the window to ask for extra time on an exam is days before the exam, not during the exam. Then, if the student does not need the extra time, they do not have to use it.

Facilitated practice

Students can be assigned to carry out their plans to change their triggers with "due dates" for when they will consult with others to get ideas for possible modifications and when they will request those changes.

Review

Students can be given feedback after they have had an angry outburst or upset about the possibility of altering the situation that caused the problem. They can be directed to record the difficulty in the Daily Anger Record and the follow the steps for altering the trigger.

 Better ways to think about and deal with the triggers to your anger

Rationale

Sometimes you can't easily avoid a trigger and will have to learn better ways to deal with it. For example, you would not want to avoid all difficult work because then you would not learn as much. What makes a trigger upsetting or not is how one thinks about or perceives the trigger situation. For every stressful trigger, there is a "better way" to think about it so that you do not get overly angry or frustrated. The following is a list of common triggers and the name of the skills that allow you to deal more effectively with those triggers. Listed next to each skill are particular ways of thinking about the trigger that make it easier to deal with. A full description of each skill is presented elsewhere in this book (see table of contents).

Table of skills to deal with different triggers

Trigger	Name of skill to deal with trigger	Thoughts that help you deal with the trigger
Demanding work	Dealing with frustrating work	It's okay not to know what to do. You can ask to watch others first, get help (the smartest people ask for help), or negotiate doing only part of the work.
Making mistakes	Dealing with mistakes	It's okay to make mistakes-that's how we learn. The smartest people make mistakes.
Getting corrected	Dealing with correction	Correction makes you better. The quicker you correct, the sooner you can do other things.
Losing a game	Dealing with losing	If you lose a game, you may win a friend if you do not get mad.
Getting criticized	Accepting criticism	Constructive criticism is made to help you not hurt you. Accepting criticism helps you grow.

Trigger	Name of skill to deal with trigger	Thoughts that help you deal with the trigger
People complaining about you	Responding to a complaint	Calmly considering the validity of a complaint may help you improve. Calmly disputing false complaints helps others respect you.
Being teased	Dealing with teasing	Don't give others the power to control your feelings. Maybe they were kidding. Their teasing may have more to do with their problems than anything you did.
Not getting what you want, having to wait for what you want, or having to stop doing what you like to do.	Accepting no and waiting for what you want	If you don't get what you want and you don't get mad, you may get something else you want later.

Using the skills to help you deal with your triggers

- Learn the specific skills relevant to your triggers. You may decide to role-play the skills several times a week to remember how to deal with your triggering situations.

- Try to use the skill in real life by putting the skill on a cue card to help you remember the steps before the trigger happens. You may want to enlist the help of teachers or parents to remind you about the skill before entering situations in which you may need to use it. For example, if making mistakes is a trigger, you may use your cue card or ask someone to remind you about how to deal with mistakes just before attempting to do class or homework so you are ready if you happen to make a mistake.

- Consider a reward or loss program. You may want others to create incentives for dealing effectively with triggering situations (i.e., using the new skills) and potential loss of privileges for losing your temper when confronted with a trigger. These conditions may motivate you to use the new skills more than the older angry patterns of behavior.

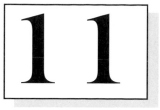

Activity Page: Better ways to think about and deal with your triggers

Teaching

1. **Explain** the rationale for learning to cope with certain triggers that cannot or should not be entirely avoided. Review the model of anger that involves how one thinks about or perceives a situation as determining whether or not one gets angry in response to a trigger.

2. Have students select those triggers that most frequently upset them and then present the skills and thoughts involved that may help them deal better with those triggers. Refer to the skill lesson in the manual that deals specifically with those triggers.

3. **Model** and **role-play** the skills to help students deal effectively with their triggers. For ideas on role-plays refer to the specific skill lessons relevant to the students' triggers listed elsewhere in the manual.

Generalization

(See the generalization suggestions from the specific skill lessons relevant to the students' triggers.)

Priming

This is the most important aspect of preventing angry outbursts. Students must be primed ahead of time to deal with a potential trigger using their new skills.

1. Use a visual cue: Using a cue card, behavior chart, or other reminder is crucial here. Ideally we want the student to review the information just prior to the situation in which they may need it. For example, if a student is about to do challenging work that will likely result in some mistakes, we might want to remind the student how to handle frustrating work and deal with mistakes just prior to doing that work. Similarly, if students have a hard time dealing with losing, then reviewing this skill is crucial just before playing a competitive game.

2. Such an immediate reminder may not always be possible, so we might schedule regular times within the day to review a skill in preparation for upcoming triggers. For example, a student might be reminded before school or work in the morning, once again at lunch time and again after work or school. Such regular daily reminders over several months may help the student

generalize the skill more permanently so that reminders can then be faded. Having the skill steps written on a cue card makes it easier to schedule these daily reminders.

3. The Daily Anger Record is another means to help prime and plan for upcoming triggers. Students can fill out the journal after an event occurs in an effort to help them plan for the next time that trigger occurs.

Facilitated practice

Students must receive enough coaching from others on a particular skill so that when the trigger occurs, they can use the skill.

Review

After an angry outburst, students can get feedback on the skill they can use next time to deal more effectively with the triggering situation. If the student is reluctant to talk about the past outburst (i.e., because it embarrasses them) then do not review what happened. Instead focus only on preparing before the next possible trigger. The Daily Anger Record is an ideal way to review how a student handled a trigger. The journal can be used for both individual and group counseling. For counseling situations, students can fill out the first half about what happened to upset them, and then the second half related to how to handle the trigger can be saved for the counseling session.

Daily Anger Record (Page 1: What upset me)

Date: _____

Name: _____

Trigger: _____
What happened prior to getting angry. Was it demanding work, making a mistake, being teased, not getting what you want, sensory issues, physical illness certain foods, interrupted sleep, or medication side effects?

Thoughts (the way you perceive the situation): _____

How you reacted (what you felt and what you did): _____

How others reacted (what others said or did after you got mad): _____

Calming yourself when angry

Rationale

The previous lesson was aimed at helping you find ways to avoid getting angry by preparing ahead of time for possible triggers. This will not always be possible as unexpected things may happen that make you upset. Thus it is important to learn ways to calm yourself once you are already angry so you don't hurt yourself or others or get in trouble.

Calming Strategies

The following are useful calming strategies:

- **Self-talk**. Something you say to yourself to help remind you to keep calm. Some examples from real students are:

  — "I do not want to break something I will want later."

  — "It's not worth it."

  — "Will this really matter one week from now?"

  — "Staying calm will help me get what I want eventually."

- **Distractions** to get your mind off what is upsetting you.

  — Remove yourself from the situation.

  — Count to ten.

  — Take deep breaths.

  — Think of pleasant images.

  — Listen to music.

  — Watch TV.

  — Play a game. (video, sports, or thinking game).

  — Draw.

  — Read.

  — Talk to a friend.

Choosing a Strategy

Pick procedures that work for you in a variety of settings. You may decide to have one calming strategy for home, another for work or school, and another for public settings. Write down your strategy for each setting using a combination of self-talk and distractions.

The importance of practice

When you are angry is not the time to try to learn how to calm because it is hard to think when you are upset. You must practice when you are calm until the strategy is almost automatic (you can do it without thinking). You may need to practice the strategy once per day for several months until you can do it without thinking. Then you may be able to do it when you really are upset.

 Activity Page: Calming yourself when angry

Teaching

1. **Explain** the rationale and review the calming strategies. Give the students a list of the strategies so they can pick and choose those that may work for them.

2. Have students select or invent a strategy that they can use at home, school or work, and in public settings. Have them write down the strategies on a cue card for reminders later.

3. **Model** and **role-play** the particular strategies they choose.

Generalization

Priming

Students must be reminded to use the calming strategy before they get angry, as it is quite difficult to remember to do it once they are angry. Thus if one can predict what triggering situations are coming up, then the students can be ready to use their calming strategy if necessary along with any other coping skills they have learned from skill lesson #11. As a rule, it is helpful to review each morning before school or work what to do if they get angry.

Facilitated practice

This is the most important aspect of this skill. Students must practice their calming strategy every day, when they are not angry, perhaps for months before the strategy can be done automatically without any thought from the student. This level of repetition is crucial because students can rarely think logically when they are very angry and thus the routine must be able to be carried out without conscious thought. Students might be given points towards rewards to motivate rehearsing their calming strategy. In the moment of anger, students can be reminded to use their calming strategy, and then adults should give the student some space to avoid provoking him or her further and to allow the student to use the calming strategy on their own volition.

Review

After an angry outburst, students can be reminded of how they might have dealt with the particular trigger and what calming strategy might have worked. If the student is reluctant to talk about the past outburst (i.e., because it embarrasses them) then do not review. Instead focus only on preparing before the next possible trigger.

 ## Talking versus acting out your feelings

Rationale

- **Acting out your feelings** means raising your voice, threatening or causing physical harm to yourself or others. Such displays of anger frighten people and thus others may fear being with you. You may also get in trouble and not get what you want.

- **Talking out your problems** means telling someone how you feel in a calm way. You have a much better chance of getting what you want when you talk out your problems with others.

Get calm first

To talk to someone calmly, you may first have to use one of the calming strategies from the previous skill (Skill #12). Often we have to take time to calm down before we can approach someone to talk about it. Don't take your anger out on others with whom you are not angry. If you do not want to talk to anyone, say, "It's not you, I am just upset about something and need some time before I talk."

Talking to others

You can talk directly with the person you are angry with or talk to someone you trust about the problem. Here are the steps to take:

1. **Schedule a time to talk.** Sometimes people are not ready to listen if they are busy or very angry. Thus it is important to schedule a time to speak rather than just insist on talking when you want to. Say, "Can I speak to you privately for a moment?" If they say no, ask when you can schedule a time to talk. If they still say no, ask to talk with someone else you trust.

2. **How to talk to others.** In a calm voice, let the person know how you feel. Tell the person how you feel in a positive way. Use an "I" message (see below).

I feel _____ _____

(Feeling word)

when you _____

(Describe their actions. Don't insult them.)

because _____.

(Describe why you feel that way)

What I want you to do is _____.

3. **Take turns talking and listening.** To effectively talk out a problem, you must listen as well as talk. Use these steps to guide the process:

   a. When you are done telling them how you feel, let them respond.

   b. Before you talk again, ask "Is there more?" If there is, then listen.

   c. When they say they are done, then you can talk again using the "I" message.

   d. Continue until both of you have said what you wanted to say.

Activity Page: Talking versus acting out your feelings

Teaching

1. **Explain** the difference between acting out and talking out feelings, and explain the steps for talking calmly to others.

2. **Model** and **role-play** how to talk calmly to others. Use situations that really happened to the students to model and role-play or the following situations:

   a. You get together with your friends and you are angry about an interaction you just had with your family. You are snickering and turning away from your friends as if you are angry with them. What could you say to talk instead of act out your feelings? (Answer: You could say, "It's not you guys, I am just mad about an argument I had with my parents.")

   b. You heard that a friend of yours said you were a mean person. How could you talk to the person rather than act out your feelings? (Answer: remember to schedule a time, and calmly use an "I" message.)

   c. Your teacher or boss told you to do a task one way and when you did what they asked, they told you that you were wrong and should not have done it that way. How can you talk to them about this? (Answer: remember to schedule a time, and calmly use an "I" message.)

Generalization
Priming

When students are angry with a particular person, they can be reminded to schedule a time to talk out their feelings with that person or to talk with a trusted friend. Those helping the student may want to role-play the scenario just prior to the student approaching a person with whom he or she is angry.

Facilitated practice

Conflicts with parents and peers are inevitable. These are times that students can be coached to talk through the problem rather than "act out." Sometimes it is helpful for students to receive incentives (or points towards an incentive) for talking versus acting out feelings.

Review

After a student "acts out" he or she can be redirected to the steps for talking out feelings instead.

 # Putting it all together: Using the Daily Anger Record

Rationale

Keeping track of instances in which you were angry can help you identify your triggers so you can prepare for them. The Record can also serve as a visual reminder of how to respond to these situations.

Filling out the record

Each time you get angry, fill out a record following these steps.

1. On Page 1, indicate what happened that made you angry, what you thought, how you felt and reacted, and how others reacted.

2. Then on Page 2 think about how you can deal with the situation. It is often helpful to fill out this page with the help of others, such as a counselor, parent, or trusted friend or advisor. Fill out each section on:

   a. Changing or avoiding the triggering situation.

   b. Learning a skill to change how you think about and deal with the trigger.

   c. Finding ways to calm down.

   d. Talking out the problem with someone you trust or the person who upset you.

Daily Anger Record (Page 1: What upset me)

Name: _____ Date: _____

Trigger:

What happened prior to getting angry. Was it demanding work, making a mistake, being teased, not getting what you want, sensory issues, physical illness, certain foods, interrupted sleep, or medication side effects?

_____

_____

_____

Thoughts (the way you perceived the situation):

_____

_____

_____

_____

How you reacted (what you felt and what you did):

_____

_____

_____

_____

How others reacted (what others said or did after you got mad):

_____

_____

_____

_____

Daily Anger Record: (Page 2: Plan of Action)

Ways to change or avoid the trigger:

(change work demands; alter sensory issues like noise, smells, lights; avoid those who tease; get more sleep, eat better or explore possible medication changes)

_____

_____

Change my thoughts: (Use the thoughts below as a guide or create your own.)

_____

_____

Dealing with frustrating work	It's okay not to know what to do. You can ask to watch others first, get help (the smartest people ask for help), or negotiate doing part of the work.
Dealing with losing	If you lose a game, you may win a friend if you do not get mad.
Accepting criticism	Constructive criticism is made to help you not hurt you. Accepting criticism helps you grow.
Dealing with teasing	Don't give others the power to control your feelings. Were they kidding? Their teasing may have more to do with their problems than anything you did.
Accepting no or waiting for things	If you don't get what you want and you don't get mad, you may get something else you want later.

Ways to calm myself:

(Use self-talk, count to ten, take deep breaths, think of pleasant images, listen to music, watch TV, play a game, read, talk to a friend, write or draw ways to get your mind off what is bothering you.)

_____

_____

Plans to talk out problems:

(Schedule a time to talk, and then use an "I" message).

I feel _____ when you _____

because _____ . I want _____ .

Activity Page: Using the Daily Anger Record

Teaching

1. Remind students how to fill out the Daily Anger Record (Part 1: What upset me). Students should be asked to fill out this sheet every time something got them upset or angry, indicating what happened, what they thought about the event (e.g., the other persons' intentions), how they reacted, and how others reacted. Then **explain** how to fill out Part 2 of the anger record where they consider how to deal with the trigger situation. Stress the usefulness of talking with someone else about the upsetting situation to help brainstorm ways to solve the problem.

2. **Model** how to fill out the record using a recent event from their life or your own. If students are meeting in a group, have the group collectively brainstorm about possible ways to handle the upsetting situation.

3. **Role-play** by asking each student to fill out the Anger Record (just part 1) using a real situation that upset them or give them one of the following:

    a. They got a bad grade from a teacher and they think the teacher mis-graded them.

    b. They were teased by another student.

    c. Their parents did not allow them to go somewhere they wanted to go.

    d. They had to stop watching TV to go do a chore with their parents.

4. Have a discussion about ways to handle the upsetting situation so that each student can fill out Part 2 of their Daily Anger Record.

Generalization

Priming

The Daily Anger Record is a means to help prime and plan for upcoming triggers. Students can fill out the journal after an upsetting event occurs in an effort to help them plan for the next time that trigger occurs.

1. The record can serve as a visual cue or the information can be transferred to a cue card. Ideally we want the student to review the information just prior to the situation in which they may need

it. For example, if a student is about to do challenging work that will likely result in some mistakes, we might want to remind the student how to handle frustrating work and deal with mistakes just prior to doing that work. Similarly, if students have a hard time dealing with losing, then reviewing this skill is crucial just before playing a competitive game.

2. Such an immediate reminder may not always be possible, so we might schedule regular times within the day to review a skill in preparation for upcoming triggers. For example, a student might be reminded before school or work in the morning, once again at lunch time and again after work or school. Such regular daily reminders over several months may help the student generalize the skill more permanently so that reminders can then be faded. Having the skill steps written on a cue card makes it easier to schedule these daily reminders.

Facilitated practice

It is important to practice the strategies they list on Part 2 of the Daily Anger Record.

1. Calming strategies should be practiced every day (perhaps for several months) if they are to become "automatic" so that a student can use the procedure when they are actually angry.

2. It is equally important to practice the skills related to the students' particular triggers. For example, if teasing is a trigger, they need to role-play handling teasing several times a week. Or if not getting what they want is a trigger, then they need to role-play "accepting no" several times a week. Practicing dealing with their particular triggers in combination with priming them before the triggers can make meaningful reductions in the number of angry outbursts.

Review

The Daily Anger Record is an ideal way to review how a student handled a trigger. The journal can be used for both individual and group counseling. For counseling situations, students can fill out the first half about what happened to upset them, and then the second half related to how to handle the trigger can be saved for the counseling session.

 # Dealing with anxiety and fear—understanding the alarm reaction

Rationale

Anxiety and fear can be constructive (helpful) or destructive (damaging).

Good and bad anxiety

- **Constructive anxiety and fear.** Fear can be crucial to keeping us healthy and alive when it helps move us from those situations that might pose real danger or harm. Fear creates what is known as an "alarm" reaction which moves us to fight or flee in response to a perceived danger. Physiologically, this alarm reaction speeds our heart and breathing rate and sends blood to our arms and legs so we can run or fight. All of this is helpful when it organizes our bodies to avoid dangerous situations. Examples of constructive fears are:

  — Fear and avoidance of walking into a busy highway.

  — Fear and avoidance of an angry person carrying a loaded gun.

  — Fear of a wild predator-type animal, such as a lion out of its cage.

- **Destructive anxiety and fear** occurs when we have "false alarms." These are situations in which we perceive a danger, have the alarm reaction, fight or flee from a situation, yet the situation is not really dangerous at all. If such false alarms interfere with desired functioning in school or work, then it becomes a "problem." Examples of these "false alarms" might include:

  — Fear of socializing with people who might in fact be nice to us.

  — Fear of trying to get a job (for which you are really qualified).

  — Fear of trying any new work (even when help is available).

  — Fear of asking someone out on a date (even when they seem interested in you).

Don't let the anxiety control you

Although you may not always be able to stop the feeling of anxiety that comes with false alarms, you do not have let that feeling stop you from functioning. You do not have to listen to the part of your brain that tells you to be afraid of something that is not a "real" danger.

Treating your anxiety with Cognitive Behavior Therapy

Cognitive Behavior Therapy (CBT) has been shown to be very effective alone or in conjunction with medications to help you overcome your anxiety and fears in a lasting way. CBT has several parts:

- **Challenging your anxious thoughts with more positive thoughts.** CBT involves examining the evidence for your fearful thought versus the evidence that the situation is not something to fear. The Daily Record of Anxious Thoughts (at end of the anxiety section) is based on the work of Burns (1990) and Beck (1979). The first column asks you to track situations that lead to anxious thoughts, the next column asks you to indicate your anxious thoughts, and the last column asks that you consider rational alternative thoughts that challenge your belief in the anxious thoughts. The form also asks you to rate how much you really believe the anxious thought (from 0-100%) versus the rational alternative thought (from 0-100%). The goal is to reduce your belief in the anxious thoughts and increase your belief in the rational thoughts. NOTE: Part of challenging your anxious thoughts may come from understanding the source of your anxiety as coming from something other than a real threat. For example, your anxieties may have been inherited from past generations. Have others in your family had such false alarms? Alternatively, you may have once had some "real" danger (a traumatic event), which led your brain to be on the "lookout" for other dangers when in fact the danger is now over.

- **Personal experiments to test out your beliefs:** Gradually facing the feared situations. It is crucial to slowly face your fears so you can discover that nothing bad actually happens and your anxiety can lessen. If instead you avoid the feared situation, the relief from not facing the situation may cause you to avoid further situations until there is very little you are willing to do. To set goals for testing one's beliefs, one usually sets up a list of situations from least to most feared and attempts to gradually face each step on the list.

- **To help you reduce your anxiety enough to face your fears, you may also want to use any of the following strategies:**

  — Try using **relaxation strategies** prior to facing a feared situation. These might include listening to music, meditation, deep breathing techniques, and progressive muscle relaxation strategies (see handout on relaxation techniques at the end of the anxiety section).

  — **Vigorous exercise** (for about thirty minutes or more each day) is a powerful anxiety and depression reducer. Try exercising the morning of the day you will face a feared situation.

Some studies demonstrate that such vigorous exercise can be as effective or better in relieving depression and anxiety than antidepressant medications.

— **Various medications** can greatly reduce anxiety and fear responses. Check with your doctor or a psychiatrist about these possibilities, as some of these can be habit-forming while others are not. Medications may be especially helpful when the anxious beliefs are "overvalued" (i.e., the person is certain that the beliefs are true) and delusional (i.e., the beliefs are about things that are not really possible). This is different from the situation in which the individual believes that their beliefs are probably not true but continues to be bothered by them.

 Activity Page: Dealing with anxiety and fear—understanding the alarm reaction

Teaching

1. **Explain** what an "alarm reaction" is and the difference between constructive and destructive anxiety, showing students examples of both. Explain that the series of skills on anxiety are aimed at helping them reduce "false alarms" or at least not to be controlled by them. Describe the components of Cognitive Behavior Therapy and how this has been proven to help reduce false alarms and allow students to face their fears.

2. Give examples of fears or anxieties you might have had over the years or anxieties the students are willing to share with you (e.g., fear of starting a new class, meeting someone new, trying a sport, public speaking, doing a daring stunt, approaching certain animals, etc.). Then use these examples to illustrate:

   a. **What are constructive versus destructive anxieties?** For example, fearing a daring stunt might be constructive anxiety, whereas fearing meeting someone new might be normal, but destructive if it stopped you from meeting new people.

   b. **How could one challenge anxious thoughts with positive alternatives?** For example, discuss what the evidence is for fearing meeting someone new. Historically, what has happened when you met someone new? Did they insult, reject or hurt you or were they usually nice?

   c. **What personal experiments could one do to test out one's beliefs?** For example, one could gradually meet new people, by first just saying hello when introduced or meeting only one new person before meeting others. Then one can examine what happened. Did the person insult them or reject them or were they nice?

   d. **What relaxation strategies or other anxiety reducers could one use to reduce their fear long enough to try to face their fear?** Consider the relaxation strategies listed, exercise, or medications.

Generalization

As this skill involves only information without the expectation for taking action yet, there are no generalization strategies until the students get to the next skills that require them to take action.

 # Dealing with unpleasant, intrusive thoughts and compulsive behaviors

Rationale

Though they are not always negative, anxious obsessions can be unpleasant and lead to compulsions.

What are anxious obsessions?

Sometimes we have pleasurable obsessions associated with a particular interest. For example, a student might enjoy talking about his favorite movies over and over again. Although this may bother others, it does not bother him because it is a pleasurable thought. (We would refer him to a skill lesson called: Being Sensitive to the Listener's Interests: Knowing When to Stop Talking). When we have obsessive thoughts that frequently intrude into our awareness and are unpleasant we often see this as part of an anxiety disorder called Obsessive–Compulsive Disorder (OCD). Examples of unpleasant, intrusive obsessions associated with OCD might include:

- Thoughts of being contaminated by germs leading to possible illness.

- Worries that one has forgotten to do something (e.g., lock a door, turn off an oven) and that could lead to something terrible happening.

- Thoughts that we have caused harm to someone (e.g., one student feared that she might have accidentally hurt someone whenever she heard an ambulance go by even though she could not have possibly hurt anyone).

- Disturbing thoughts of harming people they like despite having no desire to do so. Unlike someone who is angry and wants to harm someone, here the person is horrified to be having such thoughts.

- Some students have had obsessive thoughts that they are defective, ugly, or perceived as bad or dangerous. When the focus is on a particular feature of one's face or body, this is often referred to as Body Dismorphic Disorder.

What are compulsions?

Compulsions are repetitive, purposeful behaviors that are performed in response to an obsessive thought, often in an attempt to neutralize or prevent a dreaded event associated with the obsession.

The compulsions become problematic when they take up a great deal of time or cause the student harm. Examples might include:

- For those obsessed with fears of germs, compulsions might include frequent washing of hands and body. When washing becomes excessive it can lead to health risks (e.g., dry, cracking, bleeding hands from being over-washed).

- For those whose obsessions focus on fears of forgetting something (like locking a door, turning off the oven), compulsions might include frequent checking behavior. Checking behavior can become so time-consuming that the individual cannot get to school or work or socialize.

- For students who fear accidentally harming someone, sometimes the compulsion involves excessive praying and avoiding situations where they falsely believe they might be at risk of hurting someone.

- For those who obsess over an imagined defect or fear of being perceived as bad or dangerous, the compulsion may involve constant efforts to alter their appearance or behavior. For example, one student mistakenly thought others would perceive him to be a terrorist just because he had a Middle Eastern background. He went to great length to cut his hair and hide any features associated with his Middle Eastern background. The rituals to keep this appearance took many hours and he avoided going out until his hair was just right.

Treating Obsessive-Compulsive Behaviors with CBT

Cognitive behavior therapy (CBT) has been proven helpful in the treatment of Obsessive-Compulsive Disorder (OCD). The treatment has several components outlined below. For clear symptoms of OCD that interfere with your functioning, it is best to work with a professional therapist familiar with CBT to guide the treatment. You might want to ask your school, parents or other advisors for referrals to qualified therapists who have successfully treated individuals with OCD. For mildly intrusive thoughts and compulsive behaviors that do not interfere significantly with social and work functioning, you can follow the guidelines below:

- **Challenging your anxious thoughts with positive alternative thoughts.** Using the "Daily Record of Anxious Thoughts" begin tracking when you have an anxious thought. Fill in the column for what situation occurred and what anxious thoughts you had. Then follow these steps:

1. Ask yourself, "What evidence is there really for this anxious thought?"

2. Ask yourself, "Could it just be the anxious part of my brain lying to me again?"

3. Ask yourself, "What evidence is there against this anxious thought?" Your answers to these questions will help you come up with rational alternatives to the anxious thoughts.

4. If you are having trouble coming up with rational alternatives, don't be afraid to ask others for their answers to the questions above. Since they may not be as anxious, they may be able to share with you rational alternatives.

5. Write in the rational alternative responses and rate the percentage that you believe your anxious thoughts and your rational alternative thoughts. See sample form for a student named Jay. Jay has a mix of obsessive-compulsive behaviors, body dysmorphic disorder (i.e., beliefs that certain features of his face and body are defective), and subsequent avoidance of social situations. He believes that his Middle Eastern features (particularly his hair) will make others think he looks like a terrorist and so he compulsively dyes his hair and covers it up or avoids going out. Notice that each day Jay fills this out, which he did with the help of his father, his belief in the anxious thoughts declined and the belief in the rational thoughts increased.

6. Practice using this form each day if possible, and after a month you may find it much easier to generate the rational alternatives yourself.

- **Personal experiments to test your beliefs:** Gradually facing the feared situations. It is crucial to slowly face your fears so you can discover that nothing bad actually happens and your anxiety can lessen. Set up a list of situations from least to most feared and attempt to gradually face each step on the list (see Anxious Situations Hierarchy Form at the end of the anxiety section). Although initially you may believe some harm will befall you if you face one of the situations, if you begin facing the fears you will soon discover that there was really nothing to fear. See sample Anxious Situation Hierarchy for the student named Jay. Jay has a combination of obsessive thoughts about how he looks to others and subsequent social fears that prevent him from going places. Jay was afraid to go out with his hair uncovered for fear others would think he was a terrorist (see his Daily Anxious Thoughts Record). He spent hours a day making sure his hair was dyed just right and covered by hats. If the dye or the hat were not perfect, he would avoid going out. After learning to challenge his anxious thoughts, he was ready to try to venture out, at first with his hair dyed and covered, and then eventually with no dye or hat.

- **Try using some of these alternative strategies to decrease your anxiety further so you can begin facing the fears on the hierarchy.**

  — Try using **relaxation strategies** prior to facing a feared situation. These might include listening to music, meditation, deep breathing techniques, and progressive muscle relaxation strategies (see handout on relaxation techniques at the end of the anxiety section).

  — **Vigorous exercise** (for about 30 minutes or more each day) is a powerful anxiety and depression reducer. Try exercising the morning of the day you will face a feared situation. Some studies demonstrate that such vigorous exercise can be as effective or better in relieving depression and anxiety than antidepressant medications.

  — **Various medications** can greatly reduce anxiety and fear responses. Check with your doctor or a psychiatrist about these possibilities, as some of these can be habit-forming while others are not. Medications may be especially helpful when the anxious beliefs are "overvalued" (i.e., the person is certain that the beliefs are true) and delusional (i.e., the beliefs are about things that are not really possible). This is different from the situation in which the individual believes that their beliefs are probably not true but continues to be bothered by them.

Activity Page: Dealing with unpleasant, intrusive thoughts and compulsive behaviors

Teaching

1. **Explain** what unpleasant obsessions and compulsive behaviors are and illustrate with the examples shown on the skill sheet. Stress the importance of working with a professional therapist when symptoms significantly interfere with social and school/work functioning. Describe the components of Cognitive Behavior Therapy and how this has been proven to help reduce OCD symptoms. When going over the skills involved with Cognitive Behavior Therapy, **explain**, **model** and **role-play** one skill at a time. Start with how to challenge their anxious thoughts (examine the evidence for their anxious thoughts).

2. Challenging anxious thoughts with positive alternatives:

    a. **Explain** how to challenge their anxious thoughts using the Daily Anxious Thoughts Record using Jay as an example.

    b. Then **model** this procedure using anxious thoughts that the student(s) experience. Model how to come up with alternative rational thoughts to challenge the anxious thoughts. Write this down on a large dry erase board so the student(s) can see how it is done.

    c. Have students **role-play** the procedure using their own anxious thoughts. Be sure to help them come up with viable rational thoughts to challenge their anxious beliefs.

3. Then go over personal experiments: gradually facing the feared situations.

    a. **Explain** the rationale for testing out your beliefs rather than avoiding and how to set up a fear hierarchy.

    b. **Model** the creation of a fear hierarchy using Jay as an example,

    c. **Role-play** creating a fear hierarchy using the situations they fear. Have each student develop their own list of situations they may gradually confront.

4. Then go over the other strategies they might want to use to help them lower their anxiety enough to confront their feared situations:

a. **Explain** the use of relaxation, exercise, and medications to help lower anxiety. Give them the relaxation techniques sheet.

b. **Model** and **role-play** the relaxation exercises.

c. Have them write out an action plan of what strategies they will practice or pursue. For example, if they want to explore the medication possibility, help them create a plan for how they will contact a professional who can discuss with them such options.

Generalization
Priming

Anxiety is about anticipating events. It is typical that the waiting for the event is actually more stressful than the event. For this reason, priming well in advance of a feared event can sometimes backfire and cause more anxiety since the student has nothing concrete yet to deal with. It is better to prime soon before the event so the student can begin challenging their anxious thoughts and gradually confront the situation without having too much time to develop more anxious thoughts. In OCD, the feared events are intrusive thoughts, but those thoughts are usually connected to some environmental event (e.g., touching someone or something, leaving the house, seeing oneself in the mirror, facing the public). To prime for any of these anxious situations:

1. Use the anxious thoughts record as a visual cue of positive coping thoughts to combat the fear. Using a cue card, behavior chart, or other reminder is crucial here.

2. Use some of the relaxation methods or exercise to alter the student's mood.

3. Although you can use medication, it is not wise to use medication just before an anxious situation in preparation as this often leads to dependency and addiction. If medication is to be used, it is preferable to use it on a fixed schedule (e.g., once a morning) rather than as an immediate aid to anxiety.

Facilitated practice

1. It is crucial to practice challenging anxious thoughts with the aid of the Daily Anxious Thoughts Record. Consider using it once to twice a day until the student can challenge their thoughts more automatically.

a. First help the student come up with the alternative rational thoughts as they express their anxious thoughts. Write these alternatives down on the Daily Anxious Thoughts Record.

b. Then parents, counselors, or other helpers can reverse roles and pretend to be the student expressing the anxious thoughts and have the student come up with the rational alternative with the help of the written record. This role reversal is crucial in helping the students begin to do the work of challenging their thoughts rather than depending on others to make them feel better.

2. The most crucial practice is that of gradually confronting feared situations. Students may need a lot of encouragement and coaching to face situations, and prompts to use their alternative rational thoughts and relaxation strategies. Getting them to just face part of the situation is crucial as each exposure may lessen their anxiety over time. It is crucial to continue to explain this to the student, stressing that each time they face their fear it will get easier.

3. It is equally important to practice their relaxation strategies or to keep up with daily exercise. If they are taking medication, it is important to take it consistently, as many medications do not work unless they have a chance to build up in your system through consistent use.

Review

The Daily Anxiety Record can be used to review how a student handled a feared situation and to discuss the evidence for their anxious versus rational alternative beliefs. After a student confronts a feared situation, ask the student to tell you whether anything terrible happened or if they discovered that nothing bad really happened. Use the event to demonstrate how the alternative rational thoughts were supported and the anxious beliefs were unsupported. Write this information down on the record as proof that there is really nothing to fear so that you can show it to the student next time the student is asked to confront a situation.

Dealing with social fears

Rationale

Social fears involve excessive anxiety about being judged or evaluated poorly by others or fear that one might do something that would be humiliating or embarrassing in front of others. These anxieties cause one to avoid the social situations and thus limit being able to work or interact with others. Fears might include: Not being able to talk in front of others, being afraid to eat in front of others, not being able to use a public restroom, or not being able to look at others.

Treating social fears

We would treat social fears just as we treat other fears, with examining the evidence for the anxious thoughts, personal experiments (gradual exposure) to test out the beliefs, and strategies to reduce the intensity of the anxious feelings. The one additional approach would be to find ways to modify the social situations to make them less anxiety provoking so that individuals are more willing to enter those situations (see below).

- **Modify the social situations.** Often social situations are very unstructured with no obvious rules and thus students do not know what to do or say in those situations. Feeling that they do not know what to do adds to students' anxieties. One way to structure social situations is to add rules for how to interact. The following lists some ways to add that structure to a social situation:

  — Use the skills throughout this book to help students prepare for a social situation. For example, the conversation skills give students a map of what to say in social situations with people they do or do not know. Similarly, the work skills map out how to work cooperatively with others.

  — Have students enter a more structured social setting. At lunch time in a school, the cafeteria can be a very unstructured time. Having an adult facilitate a lunch bunch group and help students find topics to talk about can help structure the social experience so that students will feel successful. Similarly, in the dating industry, there are less structured events where individuals must independently meet and start conversations, or more structured events where individuals are given a schedule of partners to talk with for brief conversations. One model called "speed dating" has individuals scheduled to have brief conversations with a series of partners that they have been matched with and various topics are suggested to help each pair find something to talk about. At the end, the individuals indicate to an administrator with whom they may want to talk again and where there is a match, the administrator brings them back together.

— Social situations centered around a particular activity (sports, movies, shopping, sightseeing) offer a focus for the interaction rather than relying on the individuals to independently structure the conversation.

• **Challenging your anxious thoughts with positive alternative thoughts.** Using the "Daily Record of Anxious Thoughts," begin tracking when you have an anxious thought. Fill in the column for what situation occurred and what anxious thoughts you had. Then follow these steps:

— Ask yourself "What evidence is there really for this anxious thought?"

— Ask yourself "Could it just be the anxious part of my brain lying to me again?"

— Ask yourself, "What evidence is there against this anxious thought?" Your answers to these questions will help you come up with rational alternatives to the anxious thoughts.

— If you are having trouble coming up with rational alternatives, don't be afraid to ask others for their answers to the questions above. Since they may not be as anxious, they may be able to share with you rational alternatives.

— Write in the rational alternative responses and rate the percentage that you believe your anxious thoughts and your rational alternative thoughts are true. See sample form for the student named Jay who has fears about his looks, which cause him to avoid public social situations. He believes others think he looks like a terrorist and he dyes his hair and covers it up to avoid the fear that others will think he is a "bad" person. He then avoids going out where people can see his hair. Notice that each day Jay fills this out, which he did with the help of his father, his belief in the anxious thoughts declined and the belief in the rational thoughts increased.

— Practice using this form each day if possible, and after a month you may find it much easier to generate the rational alternatives yourself.

• **Personal experiments to test your beliefs: Gradually facing the feared situations.** It is crucial to slowly face your fears so you can discover that nothing bad actually happens and your anxiety can lessen. (see Anxious Situations Hierarchy Form). Although initially you may believe some harm will befall you if you face one of the situations, if you begin facing the fears you will soon discover that there was really nothing to fear. See sample Anxious Situation Hierarchy for the student named Jay. Jay has a combination of obsessive thoughts about how he looks to others and subsequent social fears that prevent him from going places. Jay is afraid to go out with his hair uncovered for fear others will think he is a terrorist (see his Daily Anxious Thoughts Record). After learning to challenge his anxious thoughts, he was ready to try to venture out, at first with his hair dyed and covered, and then eventually with no dye or hat.

- **Try using some of these alternative strategies to decrease your anxiety further so you can begin facing the fears on the hierarchy.**

  — Try using **relaxation strategies** prior to facing a feared situation. These might include listening to music, meditation, deep breathing techniques, and progressive muscle relaxation strategies (see handout on relaxation techniques at the end of the anxiety section).

  — **Vigorous exercise** (for about 30 minutes or more each day) is a powerful anxiety and depression reducer. Try exercising the morning of the day you will face a feared situation. Some studies demonstrate that such vigorous exercise can be as effective or better in relieving depression and anxiety than antidepressant medications.

  — **Various medications** can greatly reduce anxiety and fear responses. Check with your doctor or a psychiatrist about these possibilities, as some of these can be habit-forming while others are not. Medications may be especially helpful when the anxious beliefs are "overvalued" (i.e., the person is certain that the beliefs are true) and delusional (i.e., the beliefs are about things that are not really possible). This is different from the situation in which the individual believes that their beliefs are probably not true but continues to be bothered by them.

Activity Page: Dealing with social fears

Teaching

1. **Explain** what social fears are. Describe the components of Cognitive Behavior Therapy and how this has been proven to help reduce social fears. When going over the skills involved with Cognitive Behavior Therapy, **explain, model and role-play one skill at a time**. Start with how to challenge their anxious thoughts (examine the evidence for their anxious thoughts).

2. Challenging anxious thoughts with positive alternatives:

   a. **Explain** how to challenge their anxious thoughts using the Daily Anxious Thoughts Record using Jay as an example.

   b. Then **model** this procedure using anxious thoughts that the student(s) experience. Model how to come up with alternative rational thoughts to challenge the anxious thoughts. Write this down on a large dry erase board so the student(s) can see how it is done.

   c. Have students **role-play** the procedure using their own anxious thoughts. Be sure to help them come up with viable rational thoughts to challenge their anxious beliefs.

3. Then go over personal experiments: gradually facing the feared situations.

   a. **Explain** the rationale for testing out your beliefs rather than avoiding and how to set up a fear hierarchy.

   b. **Model** the creation of a fear hierarchy using Jay as an example,

   c. **Role-play** creating a fear hierarchy using the situations they fear. Have each student develop their own list of situations they may gradually confront.

4. Then go over the other strategies they might want to use to help them lower their anxiety enough to confront their feared situations:

   a. **Explain** the use of relaxation, exercise, and medications to help lower anxiety. Give them the relaxation techniques sheet.

   b. **Model** and **role-play** the relaxation exercises.

c. Have them write out an action plan of what strategies they will practice or pursue. For example, if they want to explore the medication possibility, help them create a plan for how they will contact a professional who can discuss such options with them.

Generalization

Priming

Social anxiety is often worse when anticipating events. It is typical that the waiting for the event is actually more stressful than the social event. For this reason, priming well in advance of a feared social event can sometimes backfire and cause more anxiety since the student has nothing concrete yet to deal with. It is better to prime soon before the event so the student can begin challenging their anxious thoughts and gradually confront the situation without having too much time to develop more anxious thoughts. To prime for these anxious social situations:

1. Use the Daily Anxious Thoughts Record as a visual cue of positive coping thoughts to combat the fear. Using a cue card, behavior chart, or other reminder is crucial here.

2. Use some of the relaxation methods or exercise to alter the student's mood.

3. Although you can use medication, it is not wise to use medication just before an anxious situation in preparation, as this often leads to dependency and addiction. If medication is to be used, it is preferable to use it on a fixed schedule (e.g., once a morning) rather than as an immediate aid to anxiety.

Facilitated practice

1. It is crucial to practice challenging anxious thoughts with the aid of the Daily Anxious Thoughts Record. Consider using it once to twice a day until the student can challenge their thoughts more automatically.

   a. First help the student come up with the alternative rational thoughts as they express their anxious thoughts. Write these alternatives down on the Daily Anxious Thoughts Record.

   b. Then parents, counselors, or other helpers can reverse roles and pretend to be the student expressing the anxious thoughts and have the student come up with the rational alternative with the help of the written record. This role reversal is crucial in helping the students begin do the work of challenging their thoughts rather than depending on others to make them feel better.

2. The most crucial practice is that of gradually confronting feared situations. Students may need a lot of encouragement and coaching to face situations and prompts to use their alternative rational thoughts and relaxation strategies. Getting them to just face part of the situation is crucial as each exposure may lessen their anxiety over time. It is crucial to continue to explain this to the student, stressing that each time they face their fear it will get easier.

3. It is equally important to practice their relaxation strategies or to keep up with daily exercise. If they are taking medication, it is important to take it consistently as many medications do not work unless they have a chance to build up in your system through consistent use.

Review

The Daily Anxiety Record can be used to review how a student handled a feared situation and to discuss the evidence for their anxious versus rational alternative beliefs. After a student confronts a feared situation, ask the student to tell you whether anything terrible happened or if they discovered that nothing bad really happened. Use the event to demonstrate how the alternative rational thoughts were supported and the anxious beliefs were unsupported. Write this information down on the record as proof that there is really nothing to fear so that you can show it to the student next time the student is asked to confront a situation.

 Dealing with new feared situations

Rationale

It is quite normal to have some fear of new situations since we may not know precisely how to handle those situations. We may fear making a mistake, getting hurt, or getting embarrassed for not knowing how to deal with the new situation. However, if such fears prevent us from ever entering a new situation, the ability to learn and function will be quite limited. All aspects of life involve confronting new situations. For example, in school, work and social settings we are often presented with new work or tasks or new people to meet.

Let others know

As a first step in dealing with a new feared situation, let others know how you feel. Sometimes we make the mistake of running away or getting mad without telling people the real underlying feeling of fear. Running away or getting mad can get you in trouble, whereas telling people you are fearful may actually elicit their help. For example, if you are confronted with new work in school and you are afraid to try it, let the teacher know your concerns, then he or she may be more willing to help and more understanding of your delay in doing it. If instead you start goofing off to avoid the work, refusing to do it in an angry way or asking to leave to go to the bathroom for most of the period, the teacher will likely be annoyed and might want to punish you.

Ask to watch others first

Sometimes watching others in a new situation can alleviate some of our own fears. We can become more familiar with the situations before having to dive into the situation ourselves. As an example, if your peers asked you to participate in some dorm room game with them at college and you were afraid it might be dangerous or that you might not do it right, ask them if you can watch others do it first so you can get familiar with it.

Ask for help

Asking for assistance in the new situation can also alleviate our fears of making a mistake or getting embarrassed because we are unsure of what to do. For example, if you are at work and your boss asks you to perform a new task and you fear making a mistake, ask for help the first time until you understand how to do it. Don't fear asking for help, as the smartest people will inquire about how to do something so they do it right. On the other hand, don't keep asking for help with the tasks that you can already do. Save asking for help for things you really cannot do yourself yet.

Then try it

After you have watched others deal with the situation and/or asked for help, it is time for you to try dealing with the situation.

What if you are too afraid to try it?

If you continue to be too fearful to approach the new situation after watching others, then it may make sense to use the Cognitive Behavior Therapy approaches described in the previous skills:

- **Challenge your anxious thoughts with positive alternative thoughts.** Using the "Daily Record of Anxious Thoughts" begin tracking when you have an anxious thought. Fill in the column for what situation occurred and what anxious thoughts you had. Then follow these steps:

  — Ask yourself "What evidence is there really for this anxious thought?"

  — Ask yourself "Could it just be the anxious part of my brain lying to me again?"

  — Ask yourself, "What evidence is there against this anxious thought?" Your answers to these questions will help you come up with rational alternatives to the anxious thoughts.

  — If you are having trouble coming up with rational alternatives, don't be afraid to ask others for their answers to the questions above. Since they may not be as anxious, they may be able to share with you rational alternatives.

  — Write in the rational alternative responses and rate the percentage that you believe your anxious thoughts and your rational alternative thoughts. See sample form for the student named Jay who has fears about his looks, which cause him to avoid public social situations. He believes others think he looks like a terrorist and dyes his hair and covers it up to avoid the fear that others think he is a "bad" person. He then avoids going out where people can see his hair. Notice that each day Jay fills this out, which he did with the help of his father, his belief in the anxious thoughts declined and the belief in the rational thoughts increased.

  — Practice using this form each day if possible, and after a month you may find it much easier to generate the rational alternatives yourself.

- **Personal experiments to test your beliefs:** Gradually face the feared situations. It is crucial to slowly face your fears so you can discover that nothing bad actually happens and your anxiety can lessen. Set up a list of situations from least to most feared and attempt to gradually face each step on the list. (see Anxious Situations Hierarchy Form). Although initially you may believe some harm will befall you if you face one of the situations, if you begin facing the fears you will soon discover that there was really nothing to fear. See sample Anxious Situation Hierarchy for the student named Jay. Jay has a combination of obsessive thoughts about how he looks to others and subsequent social fears that prevent him from going places. Jay is afraid to go out with his hair uncovered for fear others will think he is a terrorist (see his Daily Anxious Thoughts Record). After learning to challenge his anxious thoughts, he was ready to try to venture out, at first with his hair dyed and covered, and then eventually with no dye or hat.

- **Try using some of these alternative strategies to decrease your anxiety further so you can begin facing the fears on the hierarchy.**

  — Try using **relaxation strategies** prior to facing a feared situation. These might include listening to music, meditation, deep breathing techniques, and progressive muscle relaxation strategies (see handout on relaxation techniques).

  — **Vigorous exercise** (for about 30 minutes or more each day) is a powerful anxiety and depression reducer. Try exercising the morning of the day you will face a feared situation. Some studies demonstrate that such vigorous exercise can be as effective as or better than antidepressant medications in relieving depression and anxiety.

  — **Various medications** can greatly reduce anxiety and fear responses. Check with your doctor or a psychiatrist about these possibilities, as some of these can be habit forming while others are not. Medications may be especially helpful when the anxious beliefs are "overvalued" (i.e., the person is certain that the beliefs are true) and delusional (i.e., the beliefs are about things that are not really possible). This is different from the situation in which the individual believes that their beliefs are probably not true but continues to be bothered by them.

Activity Page: Dealing with new feared situations

Teaching

1. **Explain** the rationale and skills steps for dealing with a new feared situation.

2. **Model** and **role-play** telling others you are nervous or fearful, asking for help and asking to watch others do it first. Examples might include:

   a. Doing a new task in school or at work.

   b. Playing a new game.

   c. Being asked to do a new chore at home.

3. If students need more help to confront the situation, review the use of Cognitive Behavior Therapy. When going over the skills involved with Cognitive Behavior Therapy, **explain, model and role-play** one skill at a time. Start with how to challenge their anxious thoughts (examine the evidence for their anxious thoughts).

   a. **Explain** how to challenge their anxious thoughts using the Daily Anxious Thoughts Record using Jay as an example.

   b. Then **model** this procedure using anxious thoughts that the student(s) experience. Model how to come up with alternative rational thoughts to challenge the anxious thoughts. Write this down on a large dry erase board so the student(s) can see how it is done.

   c. Have students **role-play** the procedure using their own anxious thoughts. Be sure to help them come up with viable rational thoughts to challenge their anxious beliefs.

4. Then go over personal experiments: gradually facing the feared situations.

   a. **Explain** the rationale for testing out your beliefs rather than avoiding them and how to set up a fear hierarchy.

   b. **Model** the creation of a fear hierarchy using Jay as an example,

   c. **Role-play** creating a fear hierarchy using the situations they fear. Have each student develop their own list of situations they may gradually confront.

5. Then go over the other strategies they might want to use to help them lower their anxiety enough to confront their feared situations:

   a. **Explain** the use of relaxation, exercise, and medications to help lower anxiety.

   b. **Model** and **role-play** the relaxation exercises.

   c. Have them write out an action plan of what strategies they will practice or pursue. For example, if they want to explore the medication possibility, help them create a plan for how they will contact a professional who can discus with them such options.

Generalization
Priming

Anxiety is about anticipating events. It is typical that the waiting for the event is actually more stressful than the event. For this reason, priming well in advance of a feared event can sometimes backfire and cause more anxiety since the student has nothing concrete yet to deal with. It is better to prime soon before the event so the student can begin challenging their anxious thoughts and gradually confront the situation without having too much time to develop more anxious thoughts. To prime for an anxious situation:

1. Remind students that they can tell others they are fearful rather than run away or act out their fear. They can ask for help or to watch others first.

2. Use the Daily Anxious Thoughts Record as a visual cue of rational-coping thoughts to combat the fear. Using a cue card, behavior chart, or other reminder is crucial here.

3. Use some of the relaxation methods or exercise to alter the student's mood.

4. Although you can use medication, it is not wise to use medication just before an anxious situation in preparation, as this often leads to dependency and addiction. If medication is to be used, it is preferable to use it on a fixed schedule (e.g., once a morning) rather than as an immediate aid to anxiety.

Facilitated practice

1. Practice challenging anxious thoughts with the aid of the Daily Anxious Thoughts Record. Consider using it once to twice a day until the student can challenge their thoughts more automatically. First help the student come up with the alternative rational thoughts as they express their anxious thoughts. Write these alternatives down on the Daily Anxious Thoughts Record. Then parents, counselors, or other helpers can reverse roles and pretend to be the

student expressing the anxious thoughts and have the student come up with the rational alternative with the help of the written record. This role reversal is crucial in helping the students begin do the work of challenging their thoughts rather than depending on others to make them feel better.

2. The most crucial practice is that of gradually confronting feared situations. Students may need a lot of encouragement and coaching to face situations and prompts to use their alternative rational thoughts and relaxation strategies. Getting them to just face part of the situation is crucial as each exposure may lessen their anxiety over time. It is crucial to continue to explain this to the student, stressing that each time they face their fear it will get easier.

3. It is equally important to practice their relaxation strategies or to keep up with daily exercise. If they are taking medication, it is important to take it consistently, as many medications do not work unless they have a chance to build up in your system through consistent use.

Review

The Daily Anxiety Record can be used to review how a student handled a feared situation and to discuss the evidence for their anxious versus positive alternative thoughts. After a student confronts a feared situation, ask the student to tell you whether anything terrible happened or if they discovered that nothing bad really happened. Use the event to demonstrate how the alternative positive thoughts were supported and the anxious beliefs were unsupported. Write this information down on the record as proof that there is really nothing to fear so that you can show it to the student next time the student is asked to confront a situation. Also remind them to tell others how they feel rather than simply acting out their fears.

Relaxation techniques

Exercise #1: The Relaxation Response (Benson, 1976)

Developed to: Help you cope better with stress and anxieties, sleep better and relieve fatigue, conserve the body's store of energy, and make you alert and focused

Steps to follow:

1. Find a quiet calm environment with few distractions.

2. Sit quietly in a comfortable position.

3. Close your eyes.

4. Deeply relax all of your muscles beginning with your feet and progressing up to your face (you can do this by squeezing each muscle tightly and then relaxing it).

5. Breathe through your nose. Become aware of your breathing. As you breathe out, say the word "one" silently to yourself.

6. Breathe in......out...... "one."   In........out...... "one."   Breathe easily and naturally.

7. Continue this for 10-15 minutes or as long as is comfortable.

8. Don't worry if you are not successful in achieving a deep level of relaxation. Let relaxation occur at it's own pace. If you get distracted by your thoughts, try to ignore them by not dwelling on them and return to breathing and repeating "one."

9. The more you practice this, the easier it will become.

Exercise #2: The Relaxing Breath

Dr. Andrew Weil's yoga-derived "Relaxing Breath" (aka "4-7-8 Breath") is a simple technique people can use to address various health problems, from stopping panic attacks to improving digestion.

1. Sit comfortably and place the tip of your tongue against the bony ridge near your upper front teeth. You will keep your tongue in this position throughout the exercise.

2. Exhale with a *whoosh* sound through your mouth.

3. Now close your mouth and breathe in quietly through your nose to the count of four.

4. Hold your breath easily to the count of seven. Then exhale through your mouth with a *whoosh* to the count of eight.

5. You have now completed one breath. Repeat the cycle three more times for a total of four breaths.

You can try to practice this twice a day. Do not do more than four breaths at one time for the first month of practice. Over time, you can work up to eight breaths. While you may notice only a subtle effect at first, breath work gains power throughout repetition and practice.

Daily Record of Anxious Thoughts

Situation/Date	Anxious thoughts (% Believe) Is there any real evidence for this thought or is it just the anxious part of my brain lying to me again?	Positive Alternative(% Believe) What evidence is there against the anxious thoughts?

Jay's Anxious Situations Hierarchy

(Jay has obsessive-compulsive behaviors, body dismorphic disorder, and subsequent social fears)

For each situation, indicate how anxious it makes you using the scale below:

1	2	3	4	5	6	7	8	9	10

Calm   Slightly Nervous   Anxious   Very Anxious   Extreme Anxiety

Situations	Anxiety Rating (1-10)
1. Going to a store without a hat, with hair not dyed and no sunglasses and looking people in the eyes while checking out.	10
2. Going to the gym, without a hat, hair not dyed and saying hello to others.	10
3. Walking in the neighborhood without a hat on and hair is not dyed.	9
4. Going to the grocery store without a hat and hair is dyed, and no sunglasses.	8
5. Going to the gym without a hat, but hair is dyed and no sunglasses.	8
6. Going to a store with a hat, hair is not dyed, and sunglasses.	7
7. Going to the gym with a hat, hair is not dyed, and sunglasses.	7
8. Going to the gym or a store with a hat, hair is dyed, and wearing sunglasses.	5
9. Walking in my neighborhood with my hat, sunglasses, and dyed hair.	4
10. Calling people on the phone to order something.	3

 Saying hello's and goodbye's

Rationale

If you do not greet people or say goodbye, people may think you do not like them, even if the real reason is that you feel too shy to talk. Remember to make eye contact, stand at least an arm's length away, and use a nice tone of voice.

Situations to greet people

- Each day, when you see someone you know, you should say, "Hello, how are you?" You do not need to keep saying hello to the same person later that same day.

- When you or someone else is leaving, you should say, "Goodbye."

Formal versus informal language

- **With authority figures** (e.g., teachers, bosses, supervisors), use more formal language like "Hello," "Good morning," "Goodbye," and "Have a good night."

- **With peers and family**, you an use more informal language like "What's up" or "Catch you later."

 **Activity Page: Saying hello's and goodbye's**

Teaching

1. **Explain** the skills steps, highlighting the idea of greeting each person you know once during the day.

2. **Model** and **role-play** appropriate greetings and goodbyes making sure to demonstrate appropriate physical space, eye contact, and tone of voice. You can use the following situations as examples:

   a. Saying hello and goodbye to authority figures (e.g., teachers, bosses, administrators). Stress the use of a more formal language with these authority figures (e.g., "Good morning. How are you?" or "Goodbye, have a good evening").

   b. Saying hello or goodbye to peers (other students or coworkers). Here you can show that the use of informal language may be tolerated (e.g., "What's up?" and "Later").

Generalization

Priming

Verbal and written reminders (e.g., notes to self, cue cards) to greet hello and goodbye can be used prior to going to work or school as a way to maintain polite behavior in these settings.

Facilitated practice

Regular school and work activities contain enough practice opportunities. There is no need to create contrived practice situations unless the student needs more work on the form of the greeting.

Review

It is crucial to give feedback to student after an opportunity in which the student should have greeted or did greet others. Feedback about eye contact and tone of voice is as important as information about the words chosen.

Introductions

Rationale

Sometimes you will be in situations where you need to talk with people you don't know. You will need to introduce yourself. Sometimes you will be with people who do not know one another, yet you know them both. It is expected that you will introduce them to each other.

Introducing yourself

- When you need to talk with people you don't know (e.g., you are going to work with them or they are visitors in your home), you need to introduce yourself.

- Tell them your name and ask for their name. Then say, "Nice to meet you."

Introducing others to one another

- When both people are not busy, say, "Do you know one another?"

- If they don't, tell them each others' names:

  — Say to the first person, "This is _____" (referring to the second person).

  — Then tell the second person, "This is _____" (referring to the first person).

- If you forgot their names, say, "I'm sorry, I forgot your names. Would you mind introducing yourselves?"

- Then try to explain how you know each person so the two people will know something about one another.

 Activity Page: Introductions

Teaching

1. **Explain** the skills steps for introducing yourself. Highlight the kinds of situations you might want to introduce yourself. For example:

   a. You have to interact with someone at work or in school that you do not know (e.g., you are both assigned to do a project together).

   b. Someone new comes to your home.

2. **Explain** the skill steps for introducing others to each other. Describe situations in which you would be called upon to do this. These are situations in which you are with two people you know who do not yet know each other.

3. **Model** and **role–play** appropriate introductions making sure to demonstrate appropriate physical space, eye contact, and tone of voice. You can use the following situations as examples:

   a. You are asked to work with someone that you do not know.

   b. You are walking with a friend, classmate or co-worker you know and come across another friend, classmate or co-worker that does not know the person you are walking with.

   c. You have a new friend visit your home and they have not yet met your family.

   d. A friend or family member picks you up from a class you are taking. Introduce them to your friends in the class.

Generalization
Priming

Verbal and written reminders (e.g., notes to self, cue cards) to introduce yourself or others can be used prior to situations in which you will meet new people or others will meet for the first time.

Facilitated practice

You can set up practice opportunities by inviting new people to come to a class or work site or by inviting friends to your home to meet your family.

Review

Privately (not in front of the new people) give feedback to students about how they introduced themselves or others focusing on the timing, words used, eye contact and tone of voice.

Politely interrupting

Rationale

Sometimes we want to say something while others are talking or busy. If we interrupt at the wrong time or too often, others will be upset.

Wait for the right time to interrupt

Scan the environment before saying anything (look to see if people are busy working or talking).

- **In classroom situations**:

  Raise your hand and wait to be called on.

  Do not shout out.

- **When others are talking or busy**: Walk up in the line of vision of the persons you want to speak with. WAIT for a pause in their conversation or WAIT for them to ask what you want. You may have to get closer and put your index finger up to get their attention.

- **In dangerous situations:** Don't wait to report a dangerous situation like a fire or if someone is about to get hurt.

If you are waiting for a long time

Say, "Excuse me," or "Sorry to interrupt," then ask your question.

Know when to be quiet

Stop interrupting if someone asks you to wait a moment or to stop talking.

Activity Page: Politely interrupting

Teaching

1. Explain the skills steps for interrupting in class and in other situations such as group conversations, or when someone is working or on the telephone. Stress how even if you interrupt politely (i.e., wait for a pause and say excuse me) it can upset others if you interrupt more than they want. When people say "Stop!" or "Wait!" that is a signal that they may be annoyed if you keep interrupting. It may be helpful to give some students a rule for how many interruptions they can make in a given time period (e.g., three interruptions per class) rather than rely on their ability to pick up on others' reactions as a guide for interrupting.

2. **Model** and **role-play** appropriate interrupting. You can use the following situations as examples:

   a. You want something from a parent, teacher, or supervisor who is on the phone.

   b. Delivering a note or package to someone who is busy working in a school or job setting..

   c. You need to report a dangerous situation to a teacher or parent who is on the phone.

   d. Asking a teacher for help or permission to leave during class.

   e. People are talking about a project you have a question about.

Generalization
Priming

Verbal and written reminders (e.g., notes to self, cue cards) to scan the environment and wait for a pause should be given prior to sending a student to give a message to someone or to talk with a teacher, boss, or supervisor who may be busy. Some students who are very impulsive may benefit from using a behavior chart with waiting for a pause as a target that leads to rewards.

Facilitated practice

Daily life offers numerous opportunities to practice this skill. In all likelihood, impulsive students will continue to interrupt a little and each inappropriate interruption is an opportunity to practice the right way. When the student interrupts, he or she should be asked to correct him or herself by waiting for a pause and then talking. Without this correction, the interrupting may inadvertently be reinforced if others respond to the interruption instead of correcting the student. You can also bait the skill by temporarily ignoring a student who needs something to see if the student can wait or get attention politely.

Maintaining and joining a conversation

Rationale

The basis of keeping a conversation going is to "tune in" to what your partner is saying and ask and tell about what they said. Even if you are not really interested in the topic, showing an interest helps you build or maintain friendship with that person. You can always find ways to shift the topic later after you have first shown an interest in what they are saying. Remember to show a good listening position and not to interrupt them. Then use the table below as a guideline to think about what to say to keep the conversation going.

Ask and tell about what the others say

Keep the conversation going by asking on-topic questions and making on-topic comments related to what the other person(s) says. One hint is that you can ask the same question someone asks you or comment about what the other comments about. For example, if they ask how your weekend was, you can ask them how their weekend was. If they comment that they loved a particular movie, you can share your opinion about that movie.

Asking and Telling table

ASK (about what the other said)	TELL (comment about what the other said)
Who _____ ? What _____ ? Where _____ ? When _____ ? Why _____ ? How _____ ? What else _____ ?	Ah huh. I see. I also _____ . I _____ . My _____ .

Joining into a group conversation

Listen to what the people are saying and try to identify the topic. Then when there is a brief pause, **ask or tell about the topic to join in**.

Activity Page: Maintaining and joining a conversation

Teaching

1. **Explain** the skills steps for maintaining a conversation. Show how asking and telling about a topic is also the basis for joining others' conversations. Put the Asking and Telling Table up on a board or make it into a poster to use as a visual aid to maintaining conversations.

2. **Model** asking and telling on the topic of what others said. You may want to pick a topic and demonstrate on and off-topic comments and questions to more clearly demonstrate what it means to be on-topic. While making reference to the Asking and Telling Table you can use the following situation as an example: Ask someone about his or her weekend plans. Show how you would ask and tell to follow up on what they say. For example, if they say they are going to a movie, ask about what movie. After they say what movie, comment about whether you have seen it or are also going to see the movie. Ask what else they are going to do. If they say they will go to a restaurant, model an incorrect off-topic follow-up question like, "do you like video games?" Explain how this may be perceived by the other person as rude.

3. **Role-play** asking and telling. This can be done as a class activity with each student taking turns asking and telling, or more natural conversations in which two people talk or students talk in a small group. Remember to have the Asking and Telling Table available as a visual aid to help students think of what to ask or tell. It is wise to have students develop comfort and ease in talking with one other person (a dyad) than practicing in a group situation. Group situations often require that students track several conversation strands at once and thus are much more challenging.

   a. Classroom activities:

   - **Class asks and tells about one student.** One person starts a topic such as what he or she did over the weekend and everyone else takes turns asking or telling about what the student said.

   - **Guess-who game.** One person pretends to be a famous character (but does not tell the others who he is). The others begin by asking what the person has been doing lately. Then they take turns asking and telling in response to the character's answers. After a minimum of five questions, the students can then begin guessing who the student was pretending to be.

b. Dyads:

- **Practice with an adult.** Students can start by asking how the adult's day is going and then trying to keep it going by asking and telling in response to the adult's answers. Adults should not be the ones to carry the conversation, but rather allow for silent moments without asking the student questions so that the student can think of questions and comments to make.

- **Mock interviews.** Students can take turns interviewing each other as if they were famous people. They have to ask and tell to keep the conversation going, but they answer as if they are a famous character. Sometimes this is a fun way to begin practicing asking and telling before moving on to asking and telling in a more naturalistic way.

- **Freeze game:** Ask students to walk around until you say freeze, then turn to the nearest person and have a conversation. We give them a topic such as "What they did last weekend" or "what they will do after school or work." Have them keep the conversation going by asking and telling. Students with more difficulty doing this may need some prompting from an adult to keep the conversation going. At the end, have each pair tell what they learned from their partner. This can also be done without the "freeze" by just pairing students up for brief conversations.

- **Rotating conversation game.** We have students break up into pairs for six-minute conversations and then they rotate to converse with a new partner until all participants have spoken with each other. We give them instructions for what to talk about (e.g., find out about the person's past week or upcoming plans, or about their interests. They are instructed to ask and tell to keep the conversation going for six minutes. They are also told at the end of the activity that they will play a game to see if they remember anything about with whom they spoke. We usually play a game of "keep away," teachers against students, using a soft ball. Students must throw the ball to another student and say something they remember about the student and they get a point. Teachers can try to steal the ball from the students. If the teachers get the ball, then they can throw to another teacher saying something they remember about the other teacher for which they get a point. The game encourages students to not just interrogate those with whom they spoke, but actually think about and remember what the other student has said.

c. Facilitated Group Conversations

• **Through a lunch bunch, group therapy, or other group gathering**, an adult can help facilitate conversations by prompting students to start and maintain conversations by asking and telling. Quiet students need to be encouraged to ask or tell about what another student may have just said. It may be necessary to quiet the other members to give that shy student a chance to ask or tell. Similarly, the student who goes on and on about their own interest can be encouraged to ask about what another group member just said rather than continue to tell about him or herself.

Generalization
Priming

The Asking and Telling Table (or all of Skill #25, "POSTER: Summary of Starting and Maintaining Conversations") can be converted into poster form and used as a visual aid for groups of students when practicing conversations. Students are encouraged to copy Skill #25 and carry it with them as a personal guide to conversing. They can review it prior to entering social situations in which they are unsure of what to say (e.g., mealtimes at school or work, parties, dating situations, and new social situations).

Facilitated practice

All of the activities described above under "role-playing" the skill can be used to practice conversation skills. To improve, it is imperative that students practice several times per week in a naturalistic way. That means they must eventually move beyond the games in which they pretend to be others and begin to talk with each other in dyads and small groups about common interests and their experiences.

Review

Correct off-topic questions and comments by having them say something on the topic before shifting the topic (see Skill #27 "Politely changing topics" for information on how and when to shift topics).

Starting conversations with people you know

Rationale

In order to make and maintain friends, it is important to show that you care about others. One way to show you care is to ask people questions.

Use the guidelines below to think of questions to ask them to start a conversation.

Present: Ask questions about what they are doing in the moment. — "What are you doing?" — "What's that [referring to something the person is holding]?" — "What do you think about this class?"
Past: Ask questions about the recent past. — "How was your class?" — "What did you do this week?" — "What did you do last weekend?"
Future: Ask questions about the immediate future. — "What are you doing after school?" — "What are you doing after work?" — "What are you doing this weekend?"
Person's interests or routine: Ask about one of their interests or about something they do, like sports, hobbies, work, or clubs they may be in. — "How is your job going?" — "Did you watch your favorite show the other night?" — "Have you gotten any new video games lately?"

Ask and tell to keep the conversation going

Use the Ask and Tell Chart from Skill #22 to help you think of ways to continue the conversation.

Activity Page: Starting conversations with people you know

Teaching

1. **Explain** and **model** the various conversation starters as you show them Skill #23 or the poster of Starting and Maintaining Conversations which contains this information.

2. **Role-playing in real conversations.** Rather than just build knowledge of conversation starters, these activities allow students to practice starting and maintaining conversations while actually talking with others.

   a. Classroom activities:

      • **Class asks and tells about one student:** Classmates ask one student a conversation starter and subsequent follow-up questions and comments. Then another student gets to be the center of attention while the rest ask him/her a conversation starter and subsequent follow-up questions and comments.

      • **Guess who game.** One person pretends to be a famous character (but does not tell the others who he is). The others begin by asking conversation starters. Then they take turns asking and telling in response to the character's answers. After a minimum of 5 questions, the students can then begin guessing who the student was pretending to be.

   b. Dyads:

      • **Practice with an adult.** Students can start by asking how the adult's day is going and then trying to keep it going by asking and telling in response to the adult's answers. Adults should not be the ones to carry the conversation, but rather allow for silent moments without asking the student questions so that the student can think of questions and comments to make.

      • **Mock interviews.** Students can take turns interviewing each other as if they were famous people. They have to ask and tell to keep the conversation going, but they answer as if they are a famous character. Sometimes this is a fun way to begin practicing asking and telling before moving on to asking and telling in a more naturalistic way.

- **Conversation stations.** Various posters are placed around the room with a conversation starter printed on it. Pairs of students are directed to the stations to begin a conversation using the particular conversation starter. Then students are asked to say what they learned from the other student.

- **Freeze game:** Ask students to walk around until you say, "freeze" then turn to the nearest person and start a conversation. Students can be given the conversation starter or come up with it themselves. Have them keep the conversation going by asking and telling. Students with more difficulty doing this may need some prompting from an adult to keep the conversation going. At the end, have each pair tell what they learned from their partner. This can also be done without the "freeze" by just pairing students up for brief conversations.

- **Rotating conversation game.** We have students break up into pairs for six-minute conversations and then they rotate to converse with a new partner until all participants have spoken with each other. We give them instructions for what to talk about (e.g., find out about the person's past week or upcoming plans, or about their interests. They are instructed to ask and tell to keep the conversation going for six minutes. They are also told at the end of the activity that they will play a game to see if they remember anything about with whom they spoke. We usually play a game of "keep away," teachers against students, using a soft ball. Students must throw the ball to another student and say something they remember about the student and they get a point. Teachers can try to steal the ball from the students. If the teachers get the ball, then they can throw to another teacher saying something they remember about the other teacher for which they get a point. The game encourages students to not just interrogate those with whom they spoke, but actually think about and remember what the other student has said.

c. Facilitated Group Conversations

- **Through a lunch bunch, group therapy, or other group gathering**, an adult can help facilitate conversations by prompting students to start and maintain conversations by asking and telling. Quiet students need to be encouraged to ask or tell about what another student may have just said. It may be necessary to quiet the other members to give that shy student a chance to ask or tell. Similarly, the student who goes on and on about their own interest can be encouraged to ask about what another group member just said rather than continue to tell about him or herself.

Generalization

Priming

The list of conversation starters (or poster of Starting and Maintaining Conversations) can be converted into poster form and used as a visual aid for groups of students when practicing conversations. Students are encouraged to copy the poster and carry it with them as a personal guide to conversing. They can review it prior to entering social situations in which they are unsure of what to say (e.g., mealtimes at school or work, parties, dating situations, and new social situations).

Facilitated practice

All of the activities described above under "role-playing" the skill can be used to practice conversation skills. To improve, it is imperative that students practice several times per week in a naturalistic way. That means they must eventually move beyond games of knowledge (i.e., being able to tell about different conversation starters) and begin to talk with each other in dyads and small groups about common interests and their experiences.

Review

Correct idiosyncratic conversation starters (e.g., ones that center only around the student's own interest or offensive topics) and have the student replace it with a more relevant conversation starter (e.g., about common interests or about the other person's recent past). Also correct off-topic questions and comments by having them say something on the topic before shifting the topic (see Skill #27, "Politely changing topics," for information on how and when to shift topics).

Getting to know someone new

Rationale

In order to develop new friendships, it is important to find out about others' lives to see what you might have in common.

How to talk with someone you don't know

- **Begin by asking a question** about something the person is doing or about something you both are interested in:

  — "What are you doing?" or "What are you working on?"

  — "What do you think about this class?"

- **Introduce yourself.** Tell them your name and ask for their name.

- **Categories to ask about:** The goal is to look for what you both have in common. Common interests are the basis for possible friendships.

Safe questions

School: What school did you transfer from? What year are you? What is your major?

Work: What do you do for work? Where is your workplace?

Town: Where are you from?

Fun: What do you like to do on the weekend? What kind of music do you listen to?

Family: Do you have any brothers or sisters? What are their names?

Getting to know them better

If you have something in common, one way to get to know them better is to ask them to get together to do the activity you have in common. For example:

- Listen to music you both like.

- Go to a movie you both like.

- Do a game or sport you both like.

- Go to a restaurant for food you both like .

Activity Page: Getting to know someone new

Teaching

1. **Explain** the steps of getting to know someone new. This involves two previous skills. Step 1, the ice-breaker, is really like one of the conversation starters from Skill #23 (present conversation starters) which focuses on what you see or know about the person in the moment. Step 2 is introducing yourself (Skill #20).

2. **Model** the skill steps for breaking the ice, introducing yourself and then getting to know the other person using any of the following situations. Each situation lends itself to a particular ice-breaker (see hints):

   - You are eating lunch with your classmates. (Hint: You can ask what they are eating or how it tastes as a way to begin.)

   - You see someone playing with a handheld game or communication device. (Hint: "What are you playing?" could be a way to begin.)

   - You see someone wearing a T-shirt that has the name of a school on it. (Hint: You could ask them if they go to that school and comment that you heard it was a good school as a way to begin.)

   - You are in line at a movie theater and you see someone you recognize but do not know from school or work who is also in line. (Hint: You can say hi and ask what they are going to see as a way to begin.)

   - You are sitting next to someone new in class or work. (Hint: You can ask if they are new to the school or work as a way to begin.)

3. **Role-play** using any of the following activities (make sure the getting to know you skill steps are posted as a visual aid (use poster of Starting and Maintaining Conversations as visual aid for several skills):

   a. Classroom activities:

- **Class asks and tells about one student:** have a new person come to the class and have the students break the ice, introduce themselves, and then take turns asking questions to get to know him or her.

- **Guess-who game.** One person pretends to be a famous character (but does not tell the others who he is). The others begin by asking questions to get to know the person. After a minimum of 5 questions, the students can then begin guessing who the student was pretending to be.

b. Dyads:

- **Mock interviews.** Students can take turns interviewing each other as if they were famous people. They have to use the question categories listed to get to know the other person.

- **Rotating conversation game.** We have students break up into pairs for six-minute conversations and then they rotate to converse with a new partner until all participants have spoken with each other. Have them use the getting-to-know-you categories to find out about each other. They are instructed to ask and tell to keep the conversation going for six minutes. They are also told at the end of the activity that they will play a game to see if they remember anything about with whom they spoke. We usually play a game of "keep away," teachers against students, using a soft ball. Students must throw the ball to another student and say something they remember about the student and they get a point. Teachers can try to steal the ball from the students. If the teachers get the ball, then they can throw to another teacher saying something they remember about the other teacher for which they get a point. The game encourages students to not just interrogate those with whom they spoke, but actually think about and remember what the other student has said.

Generalization

Priming

The list of questions to get to know others (or poster of Starting and Maintaining Conversations) can be copied so that students can carry it with them as a personal guide to conversing. They can review it prior to entering social situations in which they may talk to new people (e.g., mealtimes at school or work, parties, dating situations, and new social situations).

Facilitated practice

All of the activities described above under "role-playing" the skill can be used to practice conversation skills. Students are encouraged to enter new social situations (parties, dances, dating situations) to practice this skill. Parents and friends can continue to role-play this skill in preparation for such events.

Review

Correct students if they ask questions that only center around their interests, redirecting them to the questions listed in the skill. Also correct off-topic questions and comments by having them say something on the topic before shifting the topic (see Skill #27, "Politely changing topics," for information on how and when to shift topics).

 **POSTER: Summary of Starting and Maintaining Conversations**

Getting to know new people

Name: What's your name? Mine is _____.

School: Where do you go to school? What are you studying?

Work: What kind of work do you do or want to do?

Town: Where are you from? Where are you living now?

Fun: What do you like to do for fun?

         Hobbies, TV, movies, books, places they like to go, games, sports, food.

Family: Do you have a big family? Parents, siblings, spouse, kids, or pets?

Talking with people you know

Tell: Guess what (something you did)

         Did you hear (some news you heard about)

Past: How was your_____? (week, weekend, day, vacation)

Present: What are you _____? (doing, reading, working on, eating)

Future: What are you going to do __? (after group, this weekend, over vacation)

Interests: How is _____? (something they are interested in or they do like work,

         hobbies, sports, or a common interest)

Keep Conversations Going

Ask	Tell
Who	Ah huh.
What	I see
When	I like_____
Where	I also _____
Why	I never _____
How	My _____
What Else	

Conversation repair strategies

Rationale

Sometimes there is a breakdown of communication where the person expressing an idea needs to try to restate what they have said or the person receiving the information needs to ask for clarification. How we make these repairs is crucial to maintaining a positive interaction. In general **it is best to take responsibility for the communication problem rather than blame the other** for not listening or expressing themselves well. Taking responsibility means doing something positive to fix the problem. The following lists several repair strategies.

When you don't know the answer to a question

Do not just keep silent. Let the other person know that you need more time or do not know the answer. Say, "I don't know" or "Let me think" if you need more time to think about the answer.

When you don't understand a question

Tell the person that you do not understand. Request that they ask you again.

Giving enough background information

Since other people do not know all that you know, you may have to give background information about what you are saying so it is clear to them. The background information you give depends on how much information the other person may have. For example, your grandmother may not know about a new online game you play, but a peer who has played the game will know what it is if you begin discussing the game by its name. As a general guideline:

- When talking about people, tell whether they are friends, family members, co-workers, students, celebrities, etc.

- When talking about a thing, explain whether it is a TV show, game, electronic device, animal, food, location, or something else.

When your partner does not understand

If you express an idea and the other person does not seem to understand, then take some responsibility for the miscommunication by saying, "I may not have expressed that well, let me say it differently." Don't blame the listener for not understanding as this will make the listener less interested in continuing to talk with you.

Activity Page: Conversation repair strategies

Teaching

These are really four skills that all share a common theme: repairing communication breakdowns. The most important part to teach is that each of us must take responsibility to fix the problem, which means using these repair strategies rather than waiting for the other person to fix the problem.

1. **Explain** the skill steps for each of the four skills pointing to a visual of the steps.

2. **Model** and then **role-play** the steps of each skill using the following sample situations:

   - **Saying I don't know.** These are questions that you understand but do not know the answer to:

     — What is the name of the elementary school that your grandmother went to?

     — Who won the World Series in 1971?

     — Who was the first person to fly across the Atlantic Ocean?

   - **Saying "I don't understand."** These are questions that you may not understand what is being asked, such as:

     — Someone asking you to do something in a foreign language.

     — A confusing question like, "Can you grab that," in which the person gives no indication of what to grab.

     — A question in a field that you do not know much about so the question is hard to understand, like "If the Heisenberg Principle is correct, then can we really know the activity of sub-atomic particles?"

   - **Giving background information:** Students can play a game where they talk about something without saying what it is and others have to figure out what they are talking about. These are sample situations in which one should provide more background information:

     — Relating that Phil and Eileen are coming over to the house (without explaining who they are to those who do not know them).

— Telling someone who does not know about camera technology that you bought a 7.2 megapixel digital one with a docking station.

— Indicating you are going to get a hybrid to save gas (without indicating you are talking about a car).

- **When your partner does not understand.** These are situations in which the student must say, "I may not have expressed that well, let me say it differently."

  — Any of the situations from the "giving background information" can be used to practice.

  — Explaining something using an overly complicated vocabulary such as "I believe my epidermis is blemished with crimson blotches due to the beta ray exposure." (Translation: I think my skin is freckled from the sun).

Generalization

Priming

Consider the following situations as those in which the students may need to anticipate using these skills:

- Attending challenging classes where they may not understand or know the answer to many questions

- When they are going to be expressing complicated concepts to others (e.g., if teaching, presenting in front of a class, participating in a group project, or when with other individuals who do not share the same knowledge base as the student).

Facilitated practice

Daily life certainly offers many opportunities for communication breakdowns, however, to create more opportunities, parents or teachers can bait the students to use these skills by:

- Asking questions that the student does not know the answer to

- Asking questions or giving directions that are overly complicated so that the student will need to ask for clarification

- Pretending not to know about someone or something the student is talking about so they have to fill in the background information

- Pretending not to understand what the student is saying so they have to explain it again

Review

Whenever students fail to respond to a question, they can be redirected to say that they do not know or to ask for an explanation. Similarly, if students do not express themselves clearly, the student can be redirected to give the appropriate background information or say, "I may not have expressed that well, let me say it differently."

Politely changing topics

Rationale

Interrupting others' conversation with comments that are not related to what the other people are saying can make them annoyed. The following outlines the steps for changing topics without upsetting others.

How to change the topic

- First, listen to what people are saying. Ask or tell at least once to show you are listening, or wait until the other person stops talking.

- Then change the topic by:

  — Asking to change the topic. Say, "Do you mind if I change the topic?"

  — Using a linking statement. Say, "Speaking of _____ (original topic), did you know that _____ (related topic)."

Activity Page: Politely changing topics

Teaching

1. **Explain** the skill steps for when and how to shift topics pointing to a visual poster or blackboard with the written steps.

2. **Model** and **role-play** the skill steps using the following sample situations:

   a. You were not listening to your friends so you have no idea what they were saying, but you desperately wanted to tell them about a new computer you got. (Hint: try to listen and ask a question about what they said first or at least wait for a pause, then ask to switch the topic).

   b. People are talking about something they did last weekend and you want to talk about what you are going to do this weekend. (Hint: remember to ask or comment about their weekend before transitioning to your plans; you can say, "Speaking of weekends . . .")

   c. Someone is talking about a movie you are not really interested in and you would rather talk about a movie you liked. (Hint: remember to ask or comment positively about their movie before transitioning to yours).

   d. Transition from others talking about a museum trip to discussing a sports outing. (Hint: you can use "speaking of trips . . .").

Generalization

Priming

Consider the following situations as those in which the students may need to anticipate using this skill:

- Entering a room where people have already been talking. They need to listen first before changing the topic.

- When they are talking to others who they know talk about things they are not usually interested in.

Facilitated practice

Daily life offers many opportunities for changing topics. However, to create more opportunities, parents or teachers can bait the students to use this skill by talking about an uninteresting topic until the student tries to change the topic.

Review

Whenever students shift topics abruptly without transitioning, redirect them to ask or tell first, wait for a pause, or ask to change the topic. For those who always ask to change the topic but do not listen to others, require them to ask or tell about what others said before they change the topic.

28 Being sensitive to the listener's interests

Rationale

When you talk about topics that are not of interest to others or take a long time to talk, listeners may become bored.

Talk about topics that are of interest to your listener

If you know the listener, you may already know what kinds of topics he or she likes to discuss or those topics that are interests common to you both.

Look at the listener while you are talking to check for signs of interest or boredom

Ask the listener

If they look bored say, "Do you want to hear more?"

If the listener is bored

- Ask the listener if they want to talk about something else.

- Cut to the main point. In one sentence, finish what you are saying (e.g., say, "To make a long story short . . .").

 Activity Page: Being sensitive to the listener's interests

Teaching

1. **Explain** the skill steps for being sensitive to the listener's interests, pointing to a visual poster or blackboard with the written steps. In addition to the verbal explanation, it may be helpful to review pictures and demonstrations of bored versus interested nonverbal expressions. The social skills picture book (Baker, 2003; Baker, In press) are both good resources for looking at pictures of these expressions).

2. **Model** the skill steps. You can talk to someone about your weekend plans as you have someone else model interested versus bored expressions. Then show how you identify bored expressions and check to see if they are interested. Model how you can:

   a. Ask the listener if they want to talk about something.

   b. Cut to the main point of what you were saying.

3. **Role-play** the skill steps using the following sample situations:

   a. Have them think and talk about common interests with another student they know (i.e., to avoid boring their partner).

   b. Have them talk about an interest that only they like looking for signs of interest or boredom in their partner.

   c. Have them tell a long story (e.g., all that they did on a summer vacation) and then cut to the main point.

   d. Have them start a conversation just as others have to leave (e.g., at the end of a class, or as others are walking out the door).

Generalization
Priming

Alert the student to the fact that they may need to use this skill most when:

- They are talking about their own interests, especially if the interests tend to be obsessions or strong interests.

- When class is over or people need to leave and they are still talking.

- When they are talking to people they just met who may be too polite to share their disinterest in what the student is discussing.

Facilitated practice

Although daily life offers many opportunities for trying to be sensitive to listeners' interests, parents and teachers can create more opportunities by baiting the students to use this skill. They can purposely look bored as the student talks to see if the student remembers to check on the listener interest. Be sure to remind the student not to go around looking bored when others speak, as this is rude and was done here only to help the student practice.

Review

Whenever students perseverate (talk on an on) about a topic, redirect them to check for signs of interest, check if the listener wants to hear more, and to change the topic, give a brief summary, or stop talking.

Politely ending conversations

Rationale

Ending a conversation too quickly can appear as though you do not like or care about the other person. To maintain a good relationship with others, it is important to end a conversation without hurting the others' feelings.

Steps for ending the conversation:

- Think about why you want to end the conversation.

  — You may need to do some work or get to class, or go to an appointment.

  — You might just be tired of talking to the person.

- Explain why you must stop the conversation.

  — If you need to go somewhere or do something, say, "I do not mean to be rude, but I have to go." Then describe where you must go or what you must go and do.

  — If you're just tired of talking to the person, don't tell them that because it might hurt the person's feelings. Instead say that you have other things to do at that moment.

- Then say, "All right, see you later."

Activity Page: Politely ending conversations

Teaching

1. **Explain** how and why to end a conversation pointing to a visual poster or blackboard with the written steps. Stress that if you are bored, it would be rude to express that. Some students might need a lesson on when it is okay not to tell the whole truth (i.e., when it protects others' feelings and does not hurt anyone else).

2. **Model** and **role-play** the skill steps. Here you can show the right way and perhaps the wrong way (where one abruptly ends the conversation without a word or a curt "goodbye"). The following are situations that can be used.

   a. You are talking to another student about a class or job and you realize you have to get to another class or appointment.

   b. You are talking to a teacher who goes on and on and you get tired. Show how to give a polite reason to end the conversation.

Generalization

Priming

Alert the student to the fact that they may need to use this skill most when:

- They are talking to someone who tends to talk too long.

- When they are in a rush to do something and have no time to talk.

Facilitated practice

Although daily life offers many opportunities for ending conversations, parents and teachers can create more opportunities by baiting the students to use this skill. They can talk too long so that students will want to end the conversation or at least change the topic.

Review

Whenever students abruptly end a conversation, redirect them to ask or tell about what the other is saying and then politely explain why they are ending the conversation.

Answering the telephone and taking messages

Rationale

An important part of keeping friends is talking to your friends when they call you on the phone. If you never receive their calls, they may think you are not interested. It is also important to be able to take a phone message for a family member or coworkers. If you are not able to accurately take and give phone messages, then family members or coworkers might be upset with you.

How to begin the call

- When someone says hello, say, "Hello, who is calling please?"
- Ask, "Who do you want to speak to?"

If it is a friend calling for you

- **Say, "Hello, how are you?"**
- **If they do not say anything, then ask why they called:** To ask something, to get together, or just to talk.
- **Answer their questions. If they just want to talk, then ask them questions, too.**

  Past: "How have you been doing?"

  Present: "What are you up to?"

  Future: "Do you have any interesting plans?"

  Interests: "How is school, your job, a team or club going?"

- **Ask or tell to keep the conversation going.**

Ask:	Tell:
Who, What, Where	I _____.
When, Why, How	I also _____.
What else	My _____.

- **To end the conversation**, explain why the conversation must end.

  Say, "I have to go do some work right now so I better be going. See you later."

  Then wait for them to say goodbye before hanging up.

If the other person was calling for someone else

Offer to get the other person if they are available or take a message if they are not available.

Getting the other person:

- Say, "Hold on please," and quietly go tell the person they have a call.

- Give the person the phone if they want to talk.

- If they do not want to talk, tell the person on the phone they are not available and ask to take a message.

Taking a message:

- Ask for the caller's name, phone number, and any message they want to leave with you.

- Write the information down.

- Ask them to repeat it if you did not understand.

- Tell the person you are going to repeat the information back to see if you got it right.

- If you got the message right say, "Okay, thank you, goodbye now."

- Don't forget to tell the person they have a message.

Calling friends on the telephone

Rationale

An important part of keeping friends is contacting them between visits. If you never call your friends, they may think you are not interested.

How to begin the call

- When someone says hello, say hello and give your name.
- Ask if your friend is there.

If your friend is there

- **Say, "Hello, how are you?"**
- **Explain why you called** (e.g., to ask something, to get together, or just to talk).
- **Start the conversation with a question:**

  Past: "How have you been doing?"

  Present: "What are you up to?"

  Future: "Do you have any interesting plans?"

  Interests: "How is school, your job, a team or club going?"

- **Ask or tell to keep the conversation going.**

Ask:	Tell:
Who, What, Where	I _____.
When, Why, How	I also _____.
What else	My _____.

- **To end the conversation**, explain why the conversation must end.

  Say, "I have to go do some work right now so I better be going. See you later."

  Then wait for them to say goodbye before hanging up.

If your friend is not home, ask to leave a message

- Tell them your name and phone number.
- Ask if they got it.
- Then say thank you and goodbye.

If you get an answering machine

- Wait for the tone

- In a slow, clear voice say, "This is _____ (your name) calling for _____ (your friend's name). My phone number is _____ (your phone number)."

- Say, "Thank you. Bye now." Then hang up.

30-31 Activity Page: Phone calls

Teaching

1. **Explain** the importance of talking on the phone to reaching career and personal goals. Making phone calls is typically an important part of maintaining friendships and conducting business in the job world. Validate for students that most people are somewhat anxious calling people they do not know, but the more they practice using the phone, the more comfortable they will get (see Skill #18, "Dealing with new feared situations").

2. **Model** and **role-play** the skill steps. Have conversation pairs practice in the same room but with their backs to each other so they cannot see each other (as is the case with typical phone calls). Remember to demonstrate appropriate beginnings and endings to conversations. The following are situations that can be used:

   a. You call up a friend to ask about a work assignment and your friend is not home (practice leaving a message).

   b. You call up a friend to ask about a work assignment and your friend is home (practice getting the requested information and having a brief conversation).

   c. You call a friend just to talk.

   d. You are calling an employer to find out about the availability of a job position. The manager is not there and no one else knows (practice leaving a message).

   e. You are calling an employer to find out about the availability of a job. The manager is there and has the information (find out about how to apply and thank the manager).

   f. You answer the phone at home and take a message from someone trying to reach your parent. You do the same at work with someone trying to reach your boss who is out right now.

   g. You answer the phone and it is your friend calling to ask to get together.

Generalization

Priming

When students set out to practice making or receiving a phone call, they can certainly have with them a copy of these skills at hand since the other person on the phone will not notice. They should use this visual before making or when expecting a phone call.

Facilitated practice

Students are encouraged to practice calls between skill sessions. Often at the end of a group social skills session, students will identify what other group member they will call before the next session. Sometimes a therapist or parent can make the call to help the student practice. On occasion, rewards have been offered for practicing this skill the first couple of times until a student develops more comfort on the phone.

Review

When adults have participated in the conversation, they can review with the student what went well and what else the student can say next time. Encouragement more than criticism will overcome anxiety.

 # Where to find friends

Rationale

Although it would be nice, friends do not always just come to you. You may need to do some minimal work to find and develop friendships. The following describes the kind of settings in which you may find suitable friends.

What is a friend?

A friend is someone whom you like and who likes you. Friendship cannot be forced, as both individuals must freely want to be with the other. There is a difference between being "friendly" and "being friends." Friendly means being nice and polite to others. "Being friends" means you want to seek each other out to talk, get together, and share life's experiences. Usually common interests, similar ways of thinking, and common experiences are some of the things that bring friends together. Although friends need not be exactly alike, some commonalities help people relate to each other and seek each other out. Their commonalities give them something to talk about and a means for selecting activities to do together.

Where to find potential friends

If friends are people with whom you share some commonalities, it makes sense to look for friends among people who might share your interests or experiences. The following lists some of the possible locations for meeting people with similar experiences or interests.

- High schools, colleges, and community centers often have **clubs based on interests** (e.g., radio, music, television/video, photography, journalism, history, science, science fiction, sports, politics, video games, card games, chess, theatre, etc.).

- High schools, colleges, and community centers often have **teams** to join like athletic teams, debate teams, chess teams, trivia teams, and chorus or musical bands. Joining a theatrical group to put on a play is also an excellent way to connect with others.

- High schools, colleges, and community centers may also have **clubs based on common ethnic experiences** (e.g., Latin-American club, Caribbean students club, Pan-Asian club, etc.).

- If a club is not there that matches your interests or experience, you may want to consider starting **your own club** in your school or community to draw people with similar interests.

- **Support groups** that help students with a variety of emotional issues (e.g., divorce in the family, grief, social isolation, substance abuse, coping with medical problems, etc.) may be excellent places to meet friends with common experiences.

- **Specialized classes or electives** may draw people together with special interests. Thus people who are taking certain college prep courses, vocational classes, or who share your major in college may be potential friends.

- **The virtual world** can be an easy way to find people with common interests and experiences through websites that allow you to converse about particular interests and online gaming that allows you to play games with others over the internet. Caution is advised for dealing with people you meet on the web as you never know who they really are and many predators use the internet to find people to steal from or potentially abuse. If you plan to meet someone in person that you met online, it would be wise to do that with a parent or another adult in a public place to insure your safety. In addition, do not divulge any financial information (e.g., credit card or bank account numbers) to individuals you meet online as they may be trying to steal from you.

After you meet, then what?

Use the format presented in Skill #24, "Getting to know someone new," to help you learn about your common interests and possibly plan an activity together.

Activity Page: Where to find friends

Teaching

1. **Explain** the importance of making an effort to find friends. Then discuss the importance of some commonality in interests or experience that form the basis for people coming together to be friends. Outline the different places that students may find suitable friends.

2. This skill cannot be easily modeled or role-played. Instead, students can **create an action plan** that details their interests and where they might search for potential friends as described in the following steps:

   a. Have students list their interests among possible school, community, or online resources using the clubs and activities described in the skill sheet.

   b. Ask students to indicate which activities they already participate in, and those that they might be willing to explore.

   c. Ask them to identify any particular peers that they might have seen in those settings who might share their interests or experiences.

   d. Ask them to write what they might say to begin a conversation with those individuals to "break the ice" and try to get to know them (see Skill #24, "Getting to know someone new").

   e. Students with a great deal of anxiety about initiating conversation with someone new may need to review some of the anxiety management skills prior to committing to a plan to meet someone (see Skills #15-18).

Generalization

Priming

Creating the action plan described above is key to priming this skill. In addition, students may want to review Skill #24 and role-play several times before talking to new students.

Facilitated practice

Students are encouraged to carry through with their action plans. On occasion, rewards have been offered for practicing this skill the first couple of times until a student develops some comfort with the new friends.

Review

It may be helpful to review the students' efforts after participating in a setting in which they could have met someone new. Any obstacles to initiating with that new person should be explored. If anxiety is getting in the way, one should consider ways to break down the task (e.g., just saying "hi" to someone rather than beginning a whole conversation) or get help from an adult who can facilitate introductions between students so that the student does not have to initiate on their own. The anxiety management skills (#15-18) may also help here.

Don't try too hard too soon

Rationale

Friendship is based on mutual interest where both people freely choose to be with the other person. Although you have to make some effort to make friends with someone, pursuing the person too strongly can make the person feel threatened or smothered and not want to be your friend. A real friend is someone who likes you and wants to be with you, not someone who is coerced to be with you.

When you meet someone the first time

If you get to know someone from a club or class or other setting and discover you have common interests, you may want to follow these steps in pursuing the friendship:

1. You can suggest **getting together with them "sometime" (do not specify a time or date yet)** around a common interest (see Skill #24, "Getting to know someone new"). This loose suggestion of getting together can help you "test out" if the other person is interested in you.

2. If they say they definitely want to get together with you (and their facial expression and tone of voice indicates excitement too), then you may want to make a firmer plan with a specific date and time during this first encounter with them.

3. If they say yes or maybe (and their tone of voice and facial expression seem more neutral) then you may not want to ask them again during this first encounter with them. You may have to wait until you speak with them again during the next class, club meeting or chance encounter.

4. If they say no or make an excuse that they would not be able to get together, then they are probably not interested and you may not want to ask them again.

After a second meeting with someone

During a second meeting with someone in which you are in the same class, club, or activity together, you can try to get to know them further using the following steps:

1. Using the questions from Skill #25, Summary of Starting and Maintaining Conversations, try to get to know the person better. You can ask how they have been since you last saw

them. You can ask about any special interests of theirs you learned from the last time you met them. And you can continue to get to know them using the categories from Skill #24, "Getting to know someone new."

2. You can suggest again, "Maybe we should get together sometime?" If they respond positively in the words, tone and facial expression, then set up a time and date.

3. If they make an excuse or say no, then do not pursue them again. Let them make the next move. If they are interested in you then it is their turn to ask you.

General Rule #1: Three strikes and you're out

Since friendship is based on mutual interest, there should be a balance between the number of times you initiate get-togethers or make phone calls to them and the number of times they initiate get-togethers with you or call you. If you are doing all the initiating or phone calls, then it may be that you like them but they are less interested in you.

- If you have asked to get together three times and all three times they said no, then they are probably not interested and you should not pursue them unless they later ask you to get together. The exception to this rule is if they have another compelling reason for saying no (e.g., they were out of town, sick, or they are very anxious about getting together).

- If you have made three phone calls over the last three weeks trying to reach them and they have not returned your calls, then do not pursue them further unless they call you. The exception to this rule is if they have another compelling reason for not calling (e.g., they were out of town, sick, or they have trouble using the phone).

General Rule #2: If someone says no

If someone says to you directly that they are not interested in pursuing the friendship with you, then do not pursue them. To do otherwise at this point would be considered harassment. Look to other possible friendship opportunities.

General Rule #3: How often is too often?

There is no absolute rule about how often you can get together with someone or call them on the phone as long as both seem to enjoy the frequency of talking with each other. However, if one does not know how often to get together or how often to call, the following can serve as a general guideline:

- Do not call more than once per week.

- Do not ask to get together more than every other week.

Activity Page: Don't try too hard too soon

Teaching

1. **Explain** the importance of balancing making an effort to find friends and giving friends enough space to discover for themselves that they like you. Post the steps on a poster or blackboard and review what to do on the first meeting, second meeting and the rules for subsequent meetings.

2. **Model** and **role-play** the skill highlighting the nonverbal as well as verbal signals that others may give to indicate interest or disinterest in pursing a friendship. Try using the following situations to model and role-play:

   a. You meet someone in a school activity (e.g., band, chorus, after-school club, school play, sports team). Use the "Getting to know someone new" skill to get to know them (see Skill #24). Suggest getting together and have the person respond in the following ways: with an emphatic yes, with an ambivalent sounding yes, with an uninterested maybe, or with a no.

   b. Pretend you just had a get-together at the mall with a friend that lasted most of the day and you want to extend it to dinner that night as well. Role-play with the other student showing varying levels of interest in this plan.

3. Use a game-show format to help students think about whether they should pursue or not pursue another student. Use the following questions to provoke discussion:

   a. You met someone from a school club and had two conversations at two different times with them. You asked them to get together and they said yes, call me. You called them twice during the week and they did not return your call. What would you do?

   b. You just had your first get-together with a new friend and it seems to have gone well. Should you suggest getting together again tomorrow? Should you suggest getting together again next week? Should you not suggest another get-together but just say you will call them soon?

   c. You overhear a new friend of yours saying that they are going to go somewhere you really want to go (e.g., a movie you want to see, or a store you wanted to go to). Should you ask to come along? Should you say you wanted to go to that place sometime? Should you say nothing and see if they invite you?

Generalization

Priming

Students who tend to try too hard too soon should be prompted to use this skill prior to meeting anyone new and prior to the end of a get-together (so they do not try to set up another get-together too soon).

Facilitated practice

All new social situations and ongoing friendships are opportunities to work on this skill.

Review

It is crucial to provide feedback to students if they push others too hard to be friends. Ideally this feedback should come from friends, but friends may be too hesitant to say how they feel. Instead, the feedback may come from a caring adult who sees how others are reacting to the student. The feedback should focus on asking the student to let others make the next move rather than giving up hope on that person entirely (unless the person said directly they are not interested).

Review

It is crucial to provide feedback to students if they are smothering another student and not allowing them to see other people. Ideally this feedback should come from friends, but friends may be too hesitant to say how they feel. Instead, the feedback may come from a caring adult who sees how others are reacting to the student. The feedback should focus on asking the student to give the other student space by not calling or trying to get together and letting the friend decide when they will get together again.

 Avoiding touchy subjects and insults

Rationale

We should avoid accidentally saying things about others that upset them. Doing this too often may make others dislike us. In addition, we may want to be careful about sharing private information about ourselves. Revealing too much to the wrong person can make us victims of teasing.

Definitions

Touchy subjects are words and ideas that others may regard as personal and talking about them may make people feel uncomfortable, upset, hurt, sad, or mad. **Insulting comments should never be made to others**, while some personal topics can be discussed after you know someone long enough.

- **Insults are negative comments** about:

  — how others look

  — their personality

  — where they live (e.g., their home)

  — something they made (e.g., food, artwork, writing)

  — something they performed (e.g., sports, speech, singing, dancing)

- **Touchy subjects** are not necessarily insulting but may make others uncomfortable. The following may be considered touchy subjects:

  — Race, religion, and sexual orientation are usually touchy subjects when you first meet someone. After you become friends, it may be okay to ask about these topics.

  — Asking adults about their age

  — a physical disability (e.g., a speech problem, paralysis, awkward physical movements)

  — a life-threatening illness in the person's family or network of friends

  — the loss of a job or death of a family member or friend

What to do with touchy subjects and insults

- If it is an insult, do not say it at all.

- If it is a touchy subject, let them bring it up first before you discuss it.

- If their behavior is hurting or bothering you, you can tell them with an "I message". For example, "I feel _____ when you _____ because _____. I want you to _____. "

What to do with touchy subjects about yourself

- Do not tell all your private information to just anyone, as some people may tease you.

- Decide whether the person you are talking to is a close friend and someone you can trust not to tell others.

- Ask them to keep the information confidential (i.e., do not tell others).

 Activity Page: Avoiding touchy subjects

Teaching

1. **Explain** the rationale and the definition of touchy subjects with the help of the skill written up on the blackboard or a poster. This skill is difficult to role-play because the right response is usually to do nothing. As such, it is helpful to discuss numerous situations rather than act them out. You may decide to adopt a game-show format to review these situations.

2. **Using the game-show format.** For each situation, students can indicate whether they think it is a touchy subject, an insult or okay, and if they would say anything. In some situations students should say nothing, while in others, the student should wait for the other person to bring it up, and in other situations the student can say how they feel. Example situations:

   a. Telling someone they have a good singing voice (not touchy).

   b. Telling someone that they "walk funny" (touchy).

   c. Telling someone that you are annoyed because they keep interrupting you (touchy, but you can use an "I message" here).

   d. Asking your teachers about their sex lives (touchy).

   e. Telling the teacher that they look good for an older person (touchy, even though it sounds like a compliment).

   f. Telling your teachers that your parents tried drugs once (touchy—personal information).

   g. Asking a peer how he got so good at playing the piano (not touchy).

   h. Asking a classmate why they got a low grade on a test (touchy).

   i. Suggesting that your friend see your dermatologist to clean up her skin (touchy).

   j. Saying you like your boss' new haircut (not touchy).

   k. Telling someone that you often wish you were a member of the opposite sex (touchy—only tell those friends who will not tease you or spread rumors about you).

   l. Asking someone you just met if they are a virgin (touchy).

   m. Asking someone you jut met what race they are (touchy).

n. Your friend says that her parents are from different religious backgrounds so you ask which religious backgrounds they are from (not touchy—because she brought up the subject first).

o. You meet two college students who are dating one another and you ask if they are going to get married (touchy).

Generalization

Priming

Those students who do not regularly edit themselves will need to be prompted before entering situations in which they will see individuals who are different from them.

Facilitated practice

You can bait this skill by purposely doing something odd (e.g., walking differently, putting a large band aid on your forehead) and then prompt the student to think, rather than say out load, any touchy comments.

Review

When students make an insensitive remark, tell them that is a touchy subject or insult and explain how the comment might make others feel.

 Complimenting

Rationale

Complimenting others is a good way to make or maintain friendships, help you relate better to someone who is potentially upset with you, and a safe way of showing an interest in others (e.g., flirting).

What to say

- Say something nice about their appearance (e.g., "You look great," or "Nice haircut!").

- Say something nice about something they accomplished (e.g., "That was a great story that you wrote!" or "You aced that test!"

- Say something nice about a talent of theirs (e.g., "You're a great artist," or "You're a great writer."

How to compliment

- Tell them in a sincere tone of voice.

- Don't overdo it. Compliment someone no more than once or twice per day; more may be perceived as fake. They may think you are just trying to get them to be nice to you if you compliment all the time.

Activity Page: Complimenting

Teaching

1. **Explain** the importance of complimenting others and describe the categories of things to compliment. Remind them that sincerity in your tone of voice and facial expressions is crucial so that the compliment is not seen as sarcastic.

2. **Model** and **role-play** the skill highlighting nonverbal aspects as well the words used. Compliment several of the students. Indicate how it would sound if the compliment were insincere (e.g., overly complimentary or sarcastic). To practice, have each person compliment the person to their left until everyone has been complimented.

Generalization

Priming

Students should consider complimenting prior to meeting someone new, going for a job interview, going on a date, or meeting anyone else they are trying to impress.

Facilitated practice

As an assignment, students can practice complimenting one person each day regarding their appearance, talents or recent accomplishments.

Review

It is important to provide feedback to students if their compliments do not sound sincere, directing them to how to make them more genuine sounding (e.g., by altering tone of voice or reducing the overall frequency).

Respecting others' views

Rationale

Respecting others' rights to share their ideas, even when you disagree, is crucial to maintaining relationships with friends, teachers, or employers.

Respecting others' views

There will be times that you believe you are right and others are wrong. You may even think that others are silly or unintelligent to believe what they believe. If you want to get along with them, then here is how you might handle this situation:

- Don't insult them by referring to their idea as silly, unintelligent or just wrong. Respect others' right to have their own opinion. Say, **"Well that's your opinion. I have a different opinion."**

- State your ideas as strong opinions, not facts. Use words like, **"From my point of view . .."** or "I believe…"

If you have to work together

When you disagree about what to do and you have to work together, be willing to compromise. That means do a little of what you want and what they want (see Skill #58, "Working cooperatively in groups").

If they change the rules

Often teachers and parents will change the rules about how a game or task is to be completed. You may not like these new rules, but you must respect others if you decide to tell them that you do not like those rules. You can:

- Accept the new rules. You may have to accept the rules ultimately if the person is an authority like a teacher or parent.

- Respectfully express your disagreement: "In my opinion, the older rules were better." Do not use insulting remarks like "these rules are stupid, silly, or wrong."

Activity Page: Respecting others' views

Teaching

1. **Explain** the importance of talking to others in a respectful way even when you disagree with them. With the phrases written up on a poster or blackboard, explain how to talk with someone when you disagree.

2. **Model** and **role-play** the skill steps. Suggested role-plays:

   a. Initially, explore students' preferences for things they do not have strong opinions about (topics like favorite restaurants, movies, or books).

   b. Instructors can also change the rules for how some task should be completed and coach the student to respect the new rules even if they prefer the old rules. One can do this with classic games or any routine that the adult decides will be done differently today.

   c. The next activity requires the permission of the students, as you will be asking if it is okay to really challenge them to remain calm and respectful. Then challenge them about something more important to them, like their choice of sports teams, religion, or political values. For example, an instructor might say to a member of one political party that only members of other political parties are sensible. Then prompt the student to show respect as they voice their disagreement.

Generalization

Priming

Certain situations can be anticipated in which the student will be confronted with others with markedly different opinions. The following are some of the situations before which to prime students:

- When they will be working on group projects and have to select ideas together.

- When they will be talking to someone who has very different opinions about valued topics (e.g., sports teams, politics, or religion).

- When a task is going to be done differently.

Facilitated practice

It is most helpful to coach students when working in diverse groups so they do not say something that insults others. One can also bait the skill by challenging the students' values and then reminding them to express their different views respectfully. Also, parents and teachers can purposely alter the rules of a game or routine and prompt the student to either accept the new rules or respectfully share a dissenting opinion. Students may initially need incentives to be willing to accept new rules, compromise and stay respectful.

Review

Students need feedback immediately if they begin to get angry or disrespectful in the way they handle their disagreements with others. Redirect them to how to respectfully handle their disagreement.

Don't impose rules on others (minding your own business)

Rationale

Generally, people do not like it when you tell them what to do or tell on them for violating a rule. In fact, if you act like the boss or tell on them, some students will begin to tease or harass you.

Mind your own business

When you see others break a rule or do something wrong, it is not your business to tell them what to do. It's only your business when their actions might affect you or cause harm (see below).

When it might be your business

It might be okay for you to tell others what to do or tell on them if:

- Someone is causing you harm (i.e., directly bothering you with words or actions). Here you can use an "I message" or tell on them. For example, "I feel _____ when you _____ because _____. I want you to _____.

- Someone is going to do something dangerous.

- You are the legitimate person-in-charge (e.g., a supervisor or the leader of a group/team).

Activity Page: Don't impose rules on others (minding your own business)

Teaching

1. **Explain** the rationale for not telling others what to do and then outline the exceptions when it might be okay to tell others what to do. After teaching the skill through explanation, you can use a game-show approach to review the situations described in the skill.

2. Use a game-show format like *Who Wants to Be a Millionaire* to review when it is or is not okay to impose rules on others. The following are sample questions:

   a. Explain why you should mind your own business.

   b. If a classmate is not listening to the teacher, should you tell them to pay attention? (No)

   c. If a student is not listening to the teacher and is also making distracting noises, what should you do? (You can ask them to be quiet if the noise is bothering you.)

   d. If you see classmates outside smoking cigarettes, what should you do? (Probably nothing. Although smoking is dangerous, it is not immediately dangerous.)

   e. You see someone in the supermarket going through the express checkout aisle with more than the allowed ten items. What should you do? (Nothing, unless you are behind them and in a hurry, in which case you might politely mention it to them.)

   f. Your boss at a local food store says that he is not going to take the trash out tonight before locking up the store, even though that's the rule of the store. What should you do? (Probably nothing, unless leaving the trash in the store causes some kind of danger.)

Generalization

Priming

Students will need priming prior to situations in which the rules of a game or routine are changing, or instances in which they are around students who do not generally follow rules.

Facilitated practice

Bait the skill by doing something wrong (e.g., leaving lights on in unoccupied rooms or sneaking your own food into a movie theater) and then coach them not to impose rules on others.

Review

Review situations in which the student unnecessarily imposed rules on others. Remind students to mind their own business unless someone bothering them or doing something dangerous.

Avoid bragging

Rationale

Sometimes students think they need to tell everyone what they're good at so people will like them. But bragging may actually make others dislike you.

Definitions

"Bragging" is when you show off or exaggerate your talents or accomplishments in front of others. It is okay to be aware that you may be better at something than someone else , but it is not wise to say that out loud. It is also unwise to insult someone else's abilities (see Skill #35, "Avoiding touchy subjects and insults").

How to avoid bragging

Modesty looks and sounds like . . .

- **Think but don't talk about** all the things you are good at, unless someone directly asks you.

- **Refrain from comments about being better** at something than the person you are talking with.

- Present your strengths as **good but not "the best"** or better than all those around you. For example, "I am pretty good at . . ." rather than "I am better than all of you at . . . ."

- If someone has difficulty with something, **don't talk about how easy it was for you**.

Activity Page: Avoid bragging

Teaching

1. **Explain** the rationale and steps for avoiding bragging. Make sure students don't go to the other extreme and begin putting themselves down.

2. **Model** how to describe a talent in a modest fashion without acting better than others by saying, "I am good but not the best at _____."

3. **Role-play** the skill using real situations the student experienced or the following sample situations:

    a. Have two students talk about their grades using **bragging versus modest comments**.

    b. Have two students talk about a favorite video game they play using **bragging versus modest comments**.

    c. Have students tell what they would say if a student was having trouble with their work. Show bragging comments ("Oh, that's easy!") versus helpful comments ("Do you want some help?").

Generalization

Priming

Students who are particularly good at a subject should be reminded not to brag or flaunt their abilities. Students who tend to brag may also need to be primed before any competitive situation.

Facilitated practice

You can bait the skill by talking about your ability with something that they are actually better than you at and coaching them to refrain from commenting about how much better they are than you.

Review

Review bragging behaviors, highlighting how they may make others feel about the bragger.

 # Dealing with peer pressure and avoiding setups

Rationale

Sometimes following the suggestions of your peers can be very helpful while other times it can lead you to serious trouble, including problems with the police. It is therefore crucial to know when pressure from peers is helpful and when it is not.

Definitions

Peers are your classmates or friends. Peer pressure refers to their influence on you. Peers can have a positive or negative influence.

- **Positive peer pressure** involves peers helping you to reach your goals and be productive (e.g., helping you with work, making friends, or getting a job).

- **Negative peer pressure** involves peers influencing you to do things that may get in the way of your goals or get you in trouble (e.g., convincing you to drop out of school, get involved in criminal activity, do drugs, or engage in other risky behavior).

Handling negative peer pressure:

1. Don't be afraid to disappoint someone who is trying to get you in trouble.

2. Make eye contact and speak firmly.

3. Refuse to do what they say (e.g., say, "No, I won't").

4. Explain why you are refusing if you want to try to continue the friendship.

5. Walk away.

What if you are desperate for friends?

Sometimes we may wish to make friends so much that we do things that peers suggest even when we know it may not be a good thing. People who try to make you do bad things are not really your friends, they are just using you. Instead seek out those people who will really care about you (see Skill #32, "Where to find friends").

Avoiding setups—when you do not know if it is positive or negative

"Setups" are when people act like they are being nice, yet the advice they give is really meant to hurt or embarass you (e.g., telling you to come to a party at a particular house when really, there is no party and it is just a stranger's house). When you can't tell if someone is really being nice or not, ask someone you do trust, like a parent or teacher.

Activity Page: Dealing with peer pressure and avoiding setups

Teaching

1. **Explain** the rationale for handling peer pressure and the definitions of good and bad peer pressure. Discuss the pull to conform to such pressure when one is desperate to make friends.

2. Help them see their other options for finding friendships with people who do not ask them to do dangerous or hurtful things just to feel accepted. Have students make a list of people who care about them and who have a positive influence. Use the skill "Where to make friends" to help them see their options to find other friendships.

3. Have students also make a list of individuals who can be trusted to guide them when they're not sure whether peers are asking to do something positive or negative.

4. One can use a game-show format to **model** and **role-play** how to react to different peer pressure situations. For each situation below, students can be asked to decide if it is positive, negative, or unclear peer pressure, and how they would respond.

   a. A classmate pressures you to do some volunteer work related to your interests (positive).

   b. Friends encourage you to come with them to a frat party at a local college (unclear, ask someone you trust).

   c. Coworkers try to convince you to tell your boss that he's a terrible supervisor (negative, ask someone you trust).

   d. Cool students offer to be your friends if you lend or give them money (negative).

   e. Classmates call you a wimp for doing all of your homework (negative).

   f. Your friends confront you about why you are always late to class (positive).

   g. A bunch of students tell you that it is "pajama day" at your high school tomorrow and even show you a flyer (unclear, ask someone you trust).

   h. A student tells you that another student insulted you behind your back (unclear, check it out before you get mad at the other student).

Generalization

Priming

Students should be primed before interacting with teenagers known to engage in risky behaviors.

Facilitated practice

To practice the skill in the safety of home, parents, other adults, or siblings can tell the student to do something that would have a negative effect. If the student does not refuse, then coach him or her on how to refuse or seek help..

Review

Provide feedback to students if they have succumbed to negative peer pressure, exploring with them why it may have happened. Did they know it was negative peer pressure? Did they want to do it anyway just to belong? Remind them of other friendship opportunities and the need to ask for advice if they are unsure of the consequences of certain behaviors.

Empathic listening

Rationale

One of the most important parts of being a good friend is the ability to listen to your friend in a way that shows you understand them. Often listening makes the other person feel better than telling them how they can solve their problem. People sometimes do not want you to "fix" their problem, but just listen and show that you understand their problem. Good listening is really a gift you give to your friends that make them like being with you. It is most difficult to listen empathically when others are mad at you. When this happens refer to the skill on "conflict resolution."

Steps to empathic listening

Empathy refers to understanding others feelings. Sometimes empathy means to even feel what the other person feels. Empathic listening means listening in a way that shows you understand the other person and might even feel what they feel. Follow steps 1-4 to demonstrate your understanding of the other person's feelings. Step 5 is optional, in which you communicate that you also feel what the other person is feeling.

1. **Show a good listening position:** face them with some eye contact that indicates you are listening.

2. **Reflect back what you heard:** After the person has spoken, check to see if you heard what they said. Say, "Let me see if I got that, you said that . . . ." (Repeat back in your own words what you heard them say. Then say, "Is that right?")

3. **Ask, "Is there more?"** You want to let them have the time to say what is really on their mind and not rush to interrupt or try to tell them what to do.

4. **Validate their feelings:** This means, indicate that you understand how they might feel given what they described, even if you yourself might not feel the same way. You can say, "It makes sense that you feel that way given what happened." This may be particularly hard if the other person is upset with you. But remember, you do not have to agree. You just have to show you understand (see also Skill #44, "Conflict resolution/Assertiveness").

5. **Empathize.** This last step involves communicating to the other person that you feel what they feel. First, your face and tone must communicate a similar feeling that they feel (e.g., looking sad if they are sad, or excited and happy if that is how they feel). You can say, "I feel _____ too given what happened to you."

Avoid invalidating their feelings

- Try not to offer a solution to the problem before you show that you understand the other's feelings.

- Don't say things that will make the other person feel like it is not okay to feel the way they do, like saying, "That's no big deal, get over it."

- "If the other person is upset with you, do not say they are wrong to feel that way. Validate their feelings (i.e., say you understand how they feel) and then ask if you can tell how you feel. When you tell how you feel, you can explain how you think and feel differently even though you understand how they feel. You can use an "I message" here: "I feel _____ when you _____ because _____. I want _____.""

Activity Page: Empathic listening

Teaching

1. **Explain** the rationale and steps for empathic listening using the sample phrases provided.

2. **Model** each skill step the right way and perhaps the wrong way to show how one can accidentally be unsupportive or invalidating. Have someone else pretend that they had minor car accident and you listen to their story demonstrating the right and wrong way for each step.

   a. Show the right and wrong listening position.

   b. Show accurate versus inaccurate reflective listening.

   c. Show how to ask if there is more to the story versus interrupting the person with ideas about what to do, where to take the car, etc.

   d. Show how to validate someone's feelings, demonstrating an understanding of how upset they may be versus invalidating their feelings by saying it is not big deal.

   e. Show how to communicate that you feel upset along with them versus saying that you would never feel upset over something so minor.

3. **Role-play** the steps by having peers talk with each other. Each peer can come up with one thing that made them very happy or very upset, or they can use the following situations to practice.

   a. A student describes winning a scholarship and is very happy.

   b. A student describes how their older brother won a scholarship and they feel they never win anything so they are feeling upset.

   c. A student tells his friend that he is upset because the friend never sits with him at lunch. Show how the friend could validate the student's feelings and then say how he thinks and feels (e.g., he may feel that he does sit with the student sometimes, but other times wants to be able to sit with others).

   d. Have a student talk about something another student may not care much about so that the listener has to work hard to show their understanding. For example, have a student say he is very upset because someone walked in front of him on his way to an elevator and slowed him down slightly. See if the student can validate the other's feelings even if he does not understand why this is so upsetting.

Generalization

Priming

Students need to be reminded to be empathic listeners whenever their friends are upset or very happy. Sometimes this can be anticipated when one has heard news that a friend has experienced an event that probably caused strong emotions.

Facilitated practice

Although life offers many chances to listen empathically, adults can bait this skill to give students a chance to practice. One can tell the student about a situation that made them very upset or happy and coach them to listen, and validate the others feelings. To really challenge the student, one can create situations that the student really would not care about but must work hard to show understanding (e.g., having a male student listen to a girl talk about breaking a fingernail and how upset she is since she works hard to get her nails done).

Review

Provide immediate feedback to students if they say something invalidating to others. Try to stop it before the student says too much to upset the other person. Redirect them to the skill steps, particularly how to show their understanding even if they would not themselves feel that way.

Showing caring for others' feelings through supportive statements

Rationale

Showing you care for others may be the most important skill for maintaining close friendships and intimate relationships. It is equally important for getting and maintaining employment, as showing you care for others makes people want to be around you. In addition to listening empathically (see previous skill), there are a variety of responses you can make to show you care for the other person.

Steps for showing you care for others

1. **Pay attention to signs of positive or negative feelings.** It is important to know whether others are basically happy or upset in order to know how to approach them. Many of us can do this if we are paying attention. Some of us may first need help in identifying the cues for negative versus positive feelings. (See the activity page for ideas on how to learn the cues for positive versus negative feelings.)

2. If someone looks very happy, say, "You look happy, did something good happen?" Tell them you are very happy for them.

3. If someone looks upset, keep some distance so you don't bother them, and calmly ask **"Are you okay?"** Then depending on what they say, you can make a supportive comment. For example, you could:

   - **Share a related experience**. Say, "Something like that happened to me . . ."

   - **Validate and empathize** with the other person's feelings. Say, "I understand how you feel. I feel that way, too, sometimes."

   - **Challenge any negative self statements**. For example, if the other person says everyone hates me, say, "I like you and I know others who do, too."

   - **Offer a distraction.** See if the person wants to do something else to avoid thinking about the issue for a while.

   - **Just listen**. They may not need or want any help to solve the problem. Often, people want to be understood more than to have someone offer advice. So ask if they want advice before offering it.

4. Be careful about trying to get the person to laugh. If you make jokes, the person may feel you don't care about their problem, or that you think what they're saying is unimportant.

Activity Page: Showing caring for others through supportive statements

Teaching

1. **Explain** why it is important to show caring for others' feelings. Describe the steps for identifying others feelings and how to follow up with a variety of supportive statements. Many students can accurately identify others' feelings when their attention is drawn to others. However, some students will need help with this. What is most important is for students to be able to identify positive versus negative feelings, as this will tell them how to approach others. The following activities may help those students to identify others feelings:

   a. **Model** the facial expressions and tone that accompany positive versus negative feelings, like happy versus sad or mad.

   b. Review the various facial expressions in magazines, TV shows, and movies.

   c. One software program called Mind Reading (Baron-Cohen, 2002) might be particularly helpful in learning to identify basic emotions.

2. **Model** and **role-play** the steps for showing care for others. It may be useful to make a poster of the supportive statements when modeling, role-playing, or practicing this skill.

3. One way to model and role-play is through a game I call "Make Me Happy." Encourage a student to tell about something that upset them. Then the other students must take turns making supportive statements using the list of supportive statements as a guide. If no student can think of a real situation that upset them, they can use the following scenarios:

   a. A student shares how his older sister seems to be better than him at everything.

   b. A student says she cannot handle the workload at school.

   c. A student complains that no one seems to like him or call him.

   d. A student says that his parents are divorcing and worries that he won't see one of them as much as he used to.

Generalization

Priming

Students can be primed to use this skill when information is known that a particular friend had an experience that may make them upset or very happy.

Facilitated practice

Although most every day there is a natural opportunity to practice this skill, adults can also bait the skill by sharing an upsetting event. If the student does not respond, then prompt the student to make supportive statements.

Review

Correct inappropriate ways to show understanding, such as when the student does not see that someone is obviously upset, or tries too hard to help when the other person does not want help.

Deepening relationships— sharing personal information

Rationale

The basis for friendship often changes as students age. At very young ages, children pick friends based on proximity, and sharing of common activities and toys. During older elementary ages, students often select friends based on common interests. Beginning in middle school and beyond, friends begin to select each other based on sharing deeper feelings, thoughts, and private experiences. When friends decide to share personal information with each other, it is a sign of mutual trust and responsibility. Each trusts that the other will be responsible and keep their personal information confidential. They honor each other with the sharing of information that they would not share with just anyone. This sharing of private information is the basis of emotional intimacy.

What kinds of information might be considered "personal"

Personal information is any information that you would not want just anyone to know. It is information that you save for those you trust will be supportive and empathic when they hear the information and who will keep it confidential (i.e., they will not tell others without your permission). The following might be considered personal information:

- **Past experiences** you have had that left you with strong positive or negative feelings

- **Worries and wishes** you have about the future

- Thoughts, concerns and **feelings about yourself** or those close to you

- **Strong religious or political beliefs**

To whom should you reveal personal information

The decision to reveal personal information is based on your level of comfort with someone and your desire to develop a closer relationship. You need to be able to trust that the person will not tcase or insult you for your thoughts and feelings and will keep the information confidential if that's what you want.

- People you just met and have not had any conversations with yet may not be those to whom you want to reveal personal information.

3. Students may want to consider making a list of those people they would trust with their private thoughts and feelings and with whom they would like to further develop their friendship. They can make a plan to share information over the next weeks with those people.

Generalization

Priming

Students will need to be prompted before entering situations in which they will be around individuals who cannot be trusted to hear about the students' private matters.

Facilitated Practice

Students can be coached to share similar experiences, thoughts, and feelings and be supportive of each other with those that they trust. Small group therapy situations are ideal for this, yet if this opportunity is not available, students may want to plan to share personal information with closer friends or those they trust.

Review

Anytime the student shares personal information too soon or with those who cannot be trusted, discreetly provide feedback about with whom they might want and not want to share this information. Similarly, if the student does not respond supportively to hearing about their friend's personal information, then direct them to be more empathic and supportive.

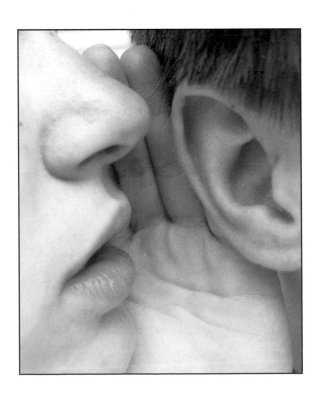

Conflict resolution/Assertiveness

Rationale

Everyone has conflicts with other people sometimes, even when you try hard to avoid problems. Conflicts may involve situations in which others did or said something that bothered you or they were bothered by something you did or said. How you handle these conflicts determines whether you will continue to have a positive relationship with the other person. It is important to be assertive with others rather than passive or aggressive.

Definitions

- **Aggressive** means to communicate or try to get what you want in a way that hurts others. Insulting others or yelling quickly ends communication and the possibility of resolving a conflict.

- **Passive** means to do nothing such as letting others say and do things that bother you without saying how you feel or asking them to stop. Sometimes being passive can actually seem aggressive. For example, if someone asks you to help them and you do not respond, that may be perceived as hostile. The "silent treatment" in which you do not respond to anything someone says is often considered a "passive-aggressive" action and perceived by others as a hostile response, even if the silent person is really just trying to avoid conflicts.

- **Assertive** means to communicate or try to get what you want in a respectful way without hurting others. This is a positive method for trying to resolve conflicts.

Steps for trying to resolve conflicts

The key to resolving conflicts is to take turns talking respectfully without interrupting and to try to understand the other's feelings. One must understand the other person's feelings in order to resolve the conflict because any possible solution will have to address both your and the other person's feelings. If you only understand your point of view, you may not be able to offer a solution that is agreeable to the other person.

1. Ask the person if you can **schedule a time to talk**; say, "When would be a good time to talk with you about something?" Sometimes people need time to prepare for a difficult discussion, so it is best schedule a time rather than just start telling them how you feel.

2. **Prepare yourself** for the discussion; think about what you want to say. What did they do or say that upset you? What do you want them to do? Do you want them to stop doing something, apologize, or help you in some way?

3. **Tell the other person what you want in an assertive way.**

   a. Use a firm but friendly voice and make eye contact.

   b. With family and friends you can use an **"I statement"**:

   "I feel _____ (feeling word)

   when you _____ (what they did or said)

   because _____ (the reason it upset you).

   What I want or need is _____ (what you want from them, offering a possible solution)."

   c. With Authority figures (teachers, employers) you can use a phrase like **"With all due respect..."** followed by something like an "I statement" in which you explain what you think, feel, and/or want.

4. Give them a turn to talk while you listen. You may want to interrupt to defend your position, but don't, because that will only lead to arguing. Try to summarize what they said, showing you understand even if you disagree.

5. Take turns talking. When you understand their view, you can begin offering solutions that work for both of you.

Activity Page: Conflict resolution/ Assertiveness

Teaching

1. **Explain** the rationale, stressing the importance of understanding the other person's perspective in order to be able to resolve a conflict and reach an agreement with others. Then explain the steps for effective communication, including scheduling to talk, and taking turns asserting yourself and listening empathically.

2. **Model** these steps with another person. Pretend you are mad at this person because he did not stand up for you when others said they did not know why he was friends with you. Pretend the other person wanted to stand up for you but was afraid to say anything because he thought the others would make fun of him. Allow this information to come out as you take turns asserting yourselves and listening empathically.

3. **Role-play** the steps. Suggested role-plays:

   a. A friend keeps criticizing the way you dress.

   b. Someone borrows some money and does not pay you back when they said they would.

   c. A friend demands to go somewhere with you, but you want to go somewhere else.

   d. No one is listening to your ideas during a group project.

   e. Your boss accuses you of slacking off and you disagree.

   f. A teacher accuses you of cheating when you did not.

   g. A parent gives everyone in the family a gift except for you.

Generalization

Priming

Cue students to use the skill when they complain of a conflict with peers, colleagues, or authority figures. Have them role-play what they might say to that person.

Facilitated practice

Tell the student you are going to do things to bait the skill. For example, take something of theirs (e.g., a pen or pencil) just as they need it, or prevent them from leaving when you know they have to go somewhere, or accuse them of something they really did not do and then coach them to assert themselves positively.

Review

Correct inappropriate ways to express frustration like aggressive or passive responses. Redirect to schedule a time to talk and to be assertive.

Dealing with teasing

Rationale

This skill is about finding ways to calmly stand up for yourself and gain respect. It is crucial to *stay calm* because some people who tease do it to upset others. If you get upset or act aggressively, then they might do it more and you may get in trouble. If you act passively others may think they can continue to insult you.

How to deal with teasing

1. **Stay calm.** If they want to hurt you or just get your attention, getting upset will only make them want to do it more.

2. **Check it out before getting upset.** Find out if they are just kidding. If you were teased and hurt by others in the past, you may automatically believe others are trying to hurt you now even if they are not. Ask, "Did you mean that?" Sometimes they really do not mean it. They may have been teasing you to be playful and get your attention. What they really want is to interact with you. Hopefully this will make you less annoyed to know they really did not intend to hurt you. If you still cannot tolerate it, then treat it as teasing and use the steps below.

3. **Don't take it personally.** The other person's teasing may have more to do with them than you. They may have problems that make them angry and mean to many people, not just you. Think to yourself, "It does not matter what the other person says. What is important is what I think and what my friends think." You may not be able to stop others from teasing, but you can learn not to let it hurt your feelings.

4. **Use the following four-step strategy** to try to get them to stop. If they stop with an early step, then you do not have to go to the next step.

    a. Tell the person to stop.

    b. Tell them you do not really care what they say.

    c. Walk away if possible. "I can't hear you."

d. If they continue despite your walking away, or if they threaten to harm you, tell an authority (school personnel, supervisor, or your parent). Research is clear that certain bullies will not stop until authorities are informed. If one authority does not take this seriously enough, tell another authority until someone responds by removing the bully or providing you with protection .

Activity Page: Dealing with teasing

Improving the peer environment

Even when students do all the right things so as not to get teased, peers may continue to tease them. Our job as adult authorities, teachers, or supervisors is to try to improve the peer environment so that our students do not get teased. We may need to:

a. Provide sensitivity training to peers who witness the teasing or occasionally tease (see Chapter 8). This involves explaining that the things our student does that may annoy them are not intentional and they can help rather than hurt the student (see Chapter 8 for full details)

b. Report students who do the teasing to an authority (e.g., vice-principal in a school or supervisor in an employment setting.). We may need to report this frequently until the students are warned of the consequences of their actions. I often talk to students doing the bullying in the following way: "I do not know if it is true, but there have been reports that you are teasing *other students*. I want others to respect you and I need you to respect others. If anyone bothers you, you can tell me and I will take care of it, but if we get reports that you are continuing to tease others, you will have to talk with the administration who will discuss with you the consequences." **I do not use the "victim's" name here** because I do not want the teaser to retaliate against the teased. If students continue to tease after this warning, there needs to be a consequence. At this time they may discover who reported them. That person must then be protected and the teaser warned about consequences that would ensue if they retaliated.

Teaching

1. **Explain** that dealing with teasing is a two-way street. It involves training both the person getting teased and the peers who do the teasing or witness it. Go through the skill steps for handling teasing. Remind them that even if the student learns all the right ways to deal with teasing, peers may still tease. Thus it is their job to not let the teasing get to them and to follow the steps to try to get others to stop, but that it is ultimately our job as teachers, supervisors, or

other authorities to make others stop teasing them (see "Improving the peer environment" above).

2. **Model** and **role-play** the skill steps. It is preferable to model and role-play how to respond to the actual words the student hears when teased. However, the instructor must get permission from the student to use these words so as not to upset the student. The goal is not to upset anyone, just to practice handling these situations. Never tease or let others tease the student without first getting the student's permission. When students do not want to share what they actually get teased about, practice with words that don't really bother them. For example, say, "I really like your shirt, but can I pretend that I don't?" and then say, "That's a sorry-looking shirt," or something similar.

Generalization

Priming

Students should be prepared for situations in which they will be around peers that might tease and where there is less adult supervision. These situations usually involve times when students are not occupied with an activity and may use teasing to entertain themselves (e.g., bus trips, sleepovers, locker rooms, and clubs led by students). It is most helpful to write the phrases and steps one will use on a cue card to review prior to entering these situations.

Facilitated practice

This is a skill one hopes does not have to be practiced in real situations. One can schedule times to role-play with a student in preparation for possible teasing situations.

Review

Any aggressive or passive reactions to teasing should be discussed and the student can be redirected to respond more assertively using the skill steps described. As always, be careful not to shame students for a passive or aggressive response, but instead validate their feelings and suggest better alternatives.

 Showing good sportsmanship

Rationale

How you deal with others when you win or lose a game is more important than the outcome of the game. Losing a game without losing your temper can help you maintain friendships. Similarly, winning a game without bragging helps others gain respect for you.

Staying calm in the face of losing a game

The following thoughts may help you keep calm by giving you some perspective on losing a game.

- Think about what is more important to your future: friendship, or winning games. Success is not measured by how many games you win. Nobody will ask you how many games you won when you interview for a job or when others decide whether they want to be your friend. Others are more interested in whether you can control yourself so they can get along with you.

- Remember, there will always be other games and other chances to win.

- The game is not a reflection of your overall abilities. Think about the many other talents you have.

If you win a game

Do not brag. Say something positive about the others' performance, like, "You played well."

Activity Page: Showing good sportsmanship

Teaching

1. **Explain** the rationale and skill steps. Parents and teachers may need to temporarily exaggerate the idea that losing calmly is better than winning a game as it shows maturity and character.

2. **Model** and **role-play** the skill steps. Use quick games so that there are many oportunites for winning and losing (e.g., tic-tac-toe, a race, or a short board game).

    a. Showing good sportsmanship is important not only when you win or lose the game, but also for any perceived win or loss during the game (e.g., getting a hit versus striking out, making a shot versus missing a shot, etc.).

    b. It is crucial for the instructor to praise and applaud those who lose without getting mad even more than those who win. Handling setbacks must be valued more than winning the game.

Generalization

Priming

Parents, coaches and teachers should remind students just before they play a game that they are more interested in how the students deal with losing than whether or not they win the game. As the game is played, the adult can anticipate who is losing and remind them that if they do not get mad, they will win a friend and they may receive a reward for staying calm.

Facilitated practice

Those helping the student can try to practice with the student by trying to win a game. They can say, "If I beat you at this game, will you be able to stay calm? That's much harder than winning the game. Can we try this?" Then the adult should show little enthusiasm when someone wins, and show great enthusiasm when someone deals well with losing to reinforce that losing well can be better than winning for those working on controlling themselves.

Review

Try coaching students to be "good sports" if they get angry. If this does not work, then you may need to use a distraction (e.g., walk away and do something else until the student is calm again).

Getting attention in positive ways

Rationale

In an effort to be liked, many people mistakenly try to get attention from others in any way they can. This is not always a good way to be liked or make friends. In fact, getting attention in a negative way can push others away.

Definitions of positive and negative attention

- Positive attention involves doing or saying things that others like.

- Negative attention involves doing or saying things that make others annoyed with you.

Issue	Positive	Negative
1. Making others laugh	It is okay to try to make others laugh as long as all those listening think it is funny.	Trying to make others laugh at the wrong time (e.g. during a class or another serious occasion) or after someone says to stop usually annoys others.
2. Being the center of attention vs. showing interest in others.	Asking about others and listening to them makes others like you more. Ask about the past, present, future of their interests (see skill #23).	Doing all the talking and trying to be the center of attention can backfire and push others away.
3. Telling interesting stories.	Telling interesting stories related to the listener's interests may make people like you.	Trying to shock people with disturbing stories or touchy subjects may make others uncomfortable and dislike you.

Activity Page: Getting attention In positive ways

Teaching

1. **Explain** the rationale, definitions and the examples of positive and negative attention.

2. You can use a **game show approach** (such as *Who Wants to be a Millionaire*) to review and **role-play** the skill. Sample questions are detailed below:

   a. Will always being the center of attention help others to like you more? (No, always being the center of attention may push some people away).

   b. Is it okay to try to get others to laugh all the time? (No, if it is the wrong time to be funny, this may make others annoyed).

   c. What can you say to show your interest in others rather than be the center of attention? (Ask about their past, present, future, or interests).

   d. What should you not do to try to keep people's interests? (Do not tell shocking or disturbing stories).

   e. Show what you could do to get positive attention from your friend.

Generalization

Priming

Good times to prime students include prior to meeting new peers, getting together with people they want very much to impress, and before occasions requiring a serious demeanor (e.g., ceremonies, funerals, or presentations).

Facilitated practice

You can bait the skill asking students to stop when they are saying things that upset others, then prompt them to ask about others or be a good listener instead.

Review

Redirect negative ways to get attention to appropriate ways to maintain friendships. Some students may need a loss system where they will get warnings for inappropriate remarks until they lose a privilege or get a "time out."

 **Where to find a date and how and when to ask someone on a date**

Rationale

Although it would be wonderful if you did not need to do anything to find a date and that potential romantic partners would just come to you, this rarely happens. Most of us have to work a little to find a date.

What is a date?

Going out with someone in an identified setting such as a restaurant, cinema, or cultural event with the intent of getting to know them better to see if you both would be interested in developing a romantic relationship.

Where to find a date (see also Skill #32, "Where to find friends"):

1. High school, college, community college, adult schools often have clubs centered around certain interests.

2. Community youth group.

3. Local places of worship (Church, Temple, Synagogue). Often specialized activities and clubs are places to begin interacting with others around a common interest or mission.

4. Vocational training program.

5. College union/recreation center.

6. Family and friends. One of the best sources for meeting others is through mutual friends or family. Polls show that most married couples actually met each other through mutual friends.

7. Internet. The virtual world can be an easy way to find people with common interests and experiences through websites that allow you to converse about particular interests and online gaming that allows you to play games with others over the internet. Caution is advised for dealing with people you meet on the web, as you never know who they really are, and many predators use the internet to find people to steal from or potentially abuse. If you plan to meet someone in person that you met online, it would be wise to do that with a parent or another adult in a public place to insure your safety. In addition, do not divulge any financial

information (e.g., credit card or bank account numbers) to individuals you meet online as they may be trying to steal from you.

8. Singles events. Many organizations sponsor singles events to meet people. One program called "Speed Dating" may be especially helpful in that you are assured to talk with many new people as they break up the members into dyads for a series of brief conversations so that each person gets a chance to talk to many others.

9. Library, gym, dance clubs, and parties are also other possibilities.

What to do when you meet someone?

Use the skills listed under "Getting to know someone new" (Skill #24) to find out what you might have in common with the other person.

Activity Page: Where to find a date

Teaching

1. **Explain** the rationale and describe the places that students could meet potential dates.

2. Students should create an action plan that lists places that they frequent and the type of person that they want to ask for a date. Go through the list of places and help the student identify favorable scenarios.

3. Students should list their assets and challenges and identify what will increase their chances of success when meeting someone.

Generalization

Priming

Students can be primed prior to entering social situations that these are places that they might meet someone. The skill "Getting to know someone new" (#24) can be reviewed prior to entering these situations and a summary of the skill can be placed on a cue card to help remember the skill. It is also important to consider many of the nonverbal skills related to dress and hygiene prior to entering these situations to maximize the student's chances.

Facilitated practice

Speed dating is an activity that helps singles structure their socializing to meet many people in one outing. In this format, individuals have scheduled conversations with one other person, before rotating to another person. Usually there are a series of five-minute conversations with up to ten or more people. It would be helpful for high schools, colleges, or other organizations to use this format to help people meet each other rather than leaving it up to individuals to initiate conversations on their own.

Review

Students should review their progress and obstacles in these social settings. They may need to review hygiene and dress issues, conversational issues, and ways to overcome their fear of rejection to maximize their chances.

Asking someone out on a date

Rationale

As much as we wish others would ask us out, sometimes we have to do the work to arrange for a date. The most successful people in the dating game are those who are willing to take the risk and ask someone out. This skill maps out a safe approach to asking someone out.

Steps to asking someone out

1. Use the skill "Getting to know someone new" (Skill #24) to find out what you may have in common with the person. Do not seek personal information about past relationships. Focus on their interests and activities. They must be the center of attention!

2. If the person seems interested in talking with you (e.g., they ask about your interests and they do not make an excuse to stop talking with you), then you might ask if it would be okay to exchange phone numbers or email addresses so you could talk again sometime.

3. If they provide you with their phone number or email, contact them no more than twice in a week unless they tell you to call more often.

4. If they respond to your emails or phone calls or they initiate the call, then they might be interested in you. At this point you can suggest getting together with them in a place/activity that you will both enjoy (based on your common interests). Movies, restaurants, concerts, sports activities, and other special events are good choices.

5. If they say yes, offer to pick them up and to do it at a convenient time for them.

6. If they say no, you can ask if they might want to go out another time. If they say no, then do not ask them again, but rather say, "If you change your mind let me know." Asking too many times may upset and annoy the other person, so if you have asked twice, then let them ask you next time.

Dealing with Fear of Rejection

Everyone fears being rejected. If you let that stop you from asking someone out, you will never have a date. Remember:

- The other person probably fears being rejected as much as you do. The worst thing that can happen from asking is that they say no. Then you can ask someone else.

- For most people, it takes asking someone out many times before someone says yes. This does not mean that there is something unlikable about you, it just takes time for you to find someone you like who also like you.

Activity Page: Asking someone out on a date

Teaching

1. **Explain** the rationale and need to set reasonable expectations (i.e., that it is normal to get rejected most of the time because it is hard to find someone you like and who likes you). Explain that if they liked everybody that would be easy, but if most people are picky, then the chances of a match are rarer and thus it will take more tries before you find a match.

2. Students should create an action plan that lists people they might want to ask out based on those they have met.

3. Any fears of rejection should be challenged (e.g., see the Daily Record of Anxious Thoughts). Students should focus on their assets and what they have to offer others.

4. **Model** and **role-play** getting to know the other person and asking them out. Practice this when the other person seems interested and disinterested, reviewing the need to back off when the other person does not ask questions back, return calls or emails.

Generalization

Priming

Students may want to script out what they will say by phone, email or in person to ask someone out and role-play prior to contacting the person.

Facilitated practice

Speed dating is an activity that helps singles structure their socializing to meet many people in one outing. In this format, individuals have scheduled conversations with one other person, before rotating to another person. Usually there are a series of five-minute conversations with up to ten or more people. It would be helpful for high schools, colleges, or other organizations to use this format to help people meet each other rather than leaving it up to individuals to initiate conversations on their own.

Review

Students should review their progress and obstacles in these social settings. They may need to review hygiene and dress issues, conversational issues, and ways to overcome their fear of rejection to maximize their chances.

 Reading the signals—when to pursue a romantic relationship

Rationale

It is very important to identify the signals of when others want to be pursued for romance and when they do not. Misreading the signals can sometimes have major consequences. For example, trying to touch or kiss others who do not want to be can lead to legal actions.

What is a romantic or intimate relationship?

When two people find each other attractive, they sometimes pursue a romantic relationship. Such a relationship involves having a close friend with whom you share personal information with and with whom you may want to kiss, hold hands, or engage in sexual activity.

A sequence of intimacy

When you meet someone for the first time that you like and have some attraction to: **It is not okay to follow them around or try to touch them or suggest that they go out with you.** Before you can begin a romantic/physical relationship with someone, you must first:

1. Get to know them.

2. Ask them out on dates.

3. Make sure they enjoy the dates.

4. In the context of a date, make sure they want to be touched or to be physical with you before you try to touch them.

How to know whether to pursue dating the other person

This skill is very challenging as it is based upon your ability to reflect on the feedback that is provided by the other person. The following is a checklist to assist you in this process. If you have more than four "No" answers, then you may think about backing off from pursuing a romantic relationship with this person.

1. Do they seek you out for conversation?   Yes/No

2. Do they use sentences rather than one word answers when you are conversing with them. Yes/No

3. Do they inquire about your interests? Yes/No

4. Do they share the same interest? Yes/No

5. Do they seem excited rather than bored to see you? For example, do they smile when they see you? Yes/No

6. Do they get close or make physical contact when they see you? Yes/No

7. Do they call or email you? Yes/No

8. Do they return your calls or emails? Yes/No

9. Do they ask you to do things or activities that you both like? Yes/No

How to know whether to pursue being physically intimate with someone

1. The first rule is that physical intimacy should occur only after you get to know someone, and they agree to go on a date.

2. The second rule is that **you should ask before touching** them, to be sure it is okay. The following are some signs that the other person would be open to physical contact:

   a. While on a date, do they seek out touch with you (e.g., by holding your hand, kissing you, or inching closer to you, putting their arm around you or putting your arm around them).

   b. Do they suggest going somewhere more private?

   c. If you ask to touch them, offer a kiss on the cheek, or to hold their hand during the date, do they seem to accept that or do they turn away from you and say no?

Activity Page: Reading the signals— when to pursue a romantic relationship

Teaching

1. **Explain** the rationale and need to follow some steps before becoming romantically involved or trying to be physical with someone.

2. Students should discuss those whom they are romantically interested in and try to determine if they have gotten to know them and are receiving signals that suggest that they could go to the next step of asking the person out.

3. **Model** and **role-play** welcoming versus unwelcoming behaviors (see Skill #1). Instead of modeling and role-playing the signs of physical interest in others, which might be uncomfortable for the students and the teachers, it may be better to play clips from TV shows or movies depicting the different signals of physical interest and disinterest. Soap operas, the show "blind date" and some of the reality shows may be good sources for such clips.

Generalization

Priming

Students should be reminded of the need to sequence their approach to developing a romantic relationship rather than coming on too strong. Reminders to get to know others, ask someone out, and then ask before touching are key. Students may need others to remind them of another's interest or disinterest to help the student know who and who not to pursue.

Facilitated practice

It is not likely that a student will be coached by someone during potentially intimate moments or dating situations, unless their partner is willing to provide this feedback. Thus most students will rely on being primed prior to a date, and review after such interactions.

Review

Students should review their experiences on a date or in asking others out. The signals of interest and disinterest can be reviewed to help the student interpret their partner's thoughts and feelings.

 # Sexual harassment

Rationale

Sometimes students unknowingly engage in sexual harassment of others and as a result can suffer legal actions against them. It is important to know what constitutes sexual harassment and to avoid engaging in any such activity.

Definition

Sexual harassment is any unwanted words or actions of a sexual nature. This might include:

- Comments or teasing about one's body, sexual behavior, or sexual orientation.
- Touching, pinching, grabbing, or rubbing up against someone or rubbing yourself in front of others.
- Graffiti, pictures, cartoons, audio, or videos of a sexual nature.
- Threats to hurt someone or cause a problem for someone if they do not perform some act of a sexual nature.
- Bribes or rewards offered to someone in exchange for sexual favors.

What you should know

- Sexual harassment is illegal. Schools and employment settings have a policy forbidding sexual harassment.
- It is illegal for anyone to punish you for telling others, so you should tell.
- By telling others, you may prevent the person from harassing you and others.

What to do if you think you are being harassed

- Tell the person to stop. That is the only way they will know the behavior is unwanted.
- Tell a trusted adult, such as the principal, teacher, supervisor, human resources specialist or a parent.
- Keep a record of when and where the harassment took place.
- If the behavior does not stop, you can file criminal charges through the police department.

What to do if you were told that you were harassing others

Immediately stop the behavior. Explain that you did not realize that it upset others and apologize to all those involved. You may need to stay away from the people you harassed if they request that.

Activity Page: Sexual harassment

Teaching

1. **Explain** the significance of sexual harassment and possible social and civil penalties. Define what it is.

2. Have students help you identify examples of sexual harassment (they do not need to share personal information here but can tell us general examples).

3. **Model** and **role-play** what to do if you are a victim. Practice telling others to stop and reporting the activity. Also practice what to do if they are a bystander or if they inadvertently harassed someone and did not realize it.

Generalization

Priming

For students who have been targeted before, prime them on communicating that the others' behavior is unwanted and to report any incident. For those who have harassed before, prime them on what is not okay to do and what are better ways to interact and get to know others.

Facilitated practice

Students should be coached to communicate that they want something to stop if the harassment occurs in front of an adult. Similarly, students who did the harassing must be told that their behavior is unacceptable and could result in legal actions if they do not stop.

Review

Review with students any incident of sexual harassment and how they can respond as a victim or accidental perpetrator.

Do's and don'ts on a date

Rationale

Getting a date is great, but having a date go well is even better. The following lists things to do and not to do to maximize the success of your date.

What to do and not to do

Skill	Do	Don't
Dress, hygiene and grooming	Clean your hair, teeth and body. Wear clean clothes appropriate to where you are going.	Forget to wash. Wear dirty, torn clothes that tell the other person you do not care enough to look good for them.
Listening	Listen carefully to your date. Ask about their interests and their life.	Do all the talking. Tell about your life without ever asking about theirs.
Show caring for others' feelings	Show that you care if they are talking about something that upset them. Say you understand, share a similar experience or offer to help (See Skill #42 and 43).	Ignore signs of upset. Tell them that what upset them does not matter.
Compliment	Compliment them.	Insult or criticize them.
Arriving to the date	Be on time and offer to pick them up.	Be late and tell them to go way out of their way to get you.
Paying for things	Offer to pay for your date.	Tell them you have no money and expect them to pay.
Compromise	Find out what they want to do and offer to do some of what they like.	Insist on doing only what you want to do on the date.
Expectations (about activities, topics of discussions, and sex).	Follow their lead so they can feel some level of control.	Expect and demand that your date follow what you want to do when you want to do it.

Activity Page: Do's and don'ts on a date

Teaching

1. **Explain** the do's and don'ts on a date.

2. Using a game-show format, **model** and **role-play** the right and wrong ways for each skill in the Table.

   a. For example you can model a behavior from the Table and then offer prizes if they correctly answer the following questions: "Is this a DO or a DON'T? What skill is this?"

   b. You can also ask them to role-play a particular skill to get prizes.

3. Since the Table covers quite a lot of material, you may want to consider reviewing only those skills relevant to the students you are teaching. For example, if dress code is never a problem, but making small talk is, then focus on making small talk.

Generalization

Priming

Those skills relevant to the student's needs should be primed before going on a date. They can be written on a cue card for easy review.

Facilitated practice

If a student is double dating with an adult, the adult can coach them to use the skills; otherwise, the skills must be primed and role-played just before the date.

Review

The student can get feedback about how the date was by calling or emailing the person to ask how they are and whether they enjoyed the date. Asking the person out again and getting a yes indicates a positive response. If the person says no, then it may be helpful to ask the person for feedback about what they liked and disliked about the date to help learn from the experience.

Communicating clearly to meet each other's needs

Rationale

Everyone in the world would like their needs, wishes and wants to be met. The success of a romantic relationship depends in part on each person trying to meet the other's needs. To do this, it is important for the couple to be able to clearly communicate to each other about their needs. Often, instead of communicating what we want to begin with, we end up angrily complaining later about what we did not get. The focus of this skill is on helping couples make a plan of how they can please each other to avoid getting angry later.

First schedule a time to talk about ways to keep your relationship working

Ask your partner when might be a good time to talk privately. Explain that you want to make sure each knows the other's likes and dislikes so that you can continue to have a healthy, satisfying relationship.

Find out what your partner likes

1. Ask your partner about what they like and dislike when it comes to

   a. Talking with you (e.g., do you listen well enough for them? Do you show support when they are upset?).

   b. Going out (e.g., where do they like and not like to go?).

   c. Physical intimacy (e.g., what kind of touch do they like or not like and when?).

   d. What are their favorite foods, clothes, gifts, special activities?

   e. What makes them laugh?

   f. What makes them calm when upset?

2. Write down their responses to these questions as this will be your guide to what you can do to please your partner. Consider keeping this written guide with you at all times to refer to when your partner is upset, wants to talk, or might want to be intimate.

3. Try not to get angry or defensive if your partner complains about something you have not done for them. Instead, try to focus on what you can do for them.

Telling your partner what you want

1. Decide what you want to share with your partner about what you would like from him or her.

   a. State positively what you do like or want. For example, "I like it when you . . ." or "I would love it if you would . . ."

   b. Avoid complaining about what your partner does not do (e.g., "You never . . ."). This will decrease their desire to please you.

2. Rehearse what you want to share:

   a. Use a calm tone and speech pace.

   b. Stay on topic.

   c. Use short sentences.

3. Answer questions that are asked of you.

 **Activity Page: Communicating clearly to meet each other's needs**

Teaching

1. **Explain** the importance of clear communication of each other's needs and review the steps to talking about this with their partner.

2. On one piece of paper, create a list of the questions they will ask their partner about their wishes. On a separate piece of paper have them prepare a short list of wishes they want to request of their partner.

3. **Model** and **role-play** how to request their wishes positively and how to listen to their partner's wishes with getting angry or defensive.

Generalization

Priming

Whenever students complain of difficulties with their partners, prime them on how to communicate more clearly about what they and their partners want.

Facilitated practice

Students can practice this in any relationship, not just romantic ones. For example, you can bait them by complaining about something they have not done (when you never asked them to do it in the first place) or by not doing things that you know they want you to do. Then coach them to schedule a time to communicate more clearly about what you and the student want.

Review

Provide feedback to students when they complain about relationship difficulties with others (e.g., when they have not clearly expressed what they wanted or gotten information from others about what they wanted). Direct them to clearer communication.

Asking for reasonable modifications

Rationale

Individuals with a documented disability may be entitled to certain changes or modifications in schools or employment settings that help compensate for their difficulties. To receive those modifications, individuals must follow certain procedures, as teachers or employers will not automatically provide students with them.

What is a reasonable modification?

In public high school, students are entitled to a free and appropriate education. That means no matter what the student's ability, the public school must provide them with an appropriate program suited to their abilities. This means that the student may be able to receive many modifications including replacement classes if a student is unable to handle the work of a particular course. For example, if a student is unable to do the work in a foreign language class, that class can be waived and a replacement class can be provided. The consequence of waiving requirements in high school is that certain colleges will require students to have completed a certain course (e.g., foreign language) and thus the student who did not take that class may not be able to enter that college.

Colleges do not have to provide their students with a "free and appropriate education" that is suited to their abilities. **Students are only entitled to modifications that compensate for their disability, and are still required to complete the essential course work.** If they are unable to complete the course requirements, the college is not required to give them a replacement class and the student may simply not be able to get credit for that course. Similarly, in an employment setting, individuals may be entitled to certain modifications at the job, but they are still required to complete the essential duties of the job, otherwise they may not be fit for the job. The following are examples of reasonable and unreasonable modifications:

Examples of reasonable versus unreasonable modifications

Difficulty	Reasonable	Unreasonable
Problems staying focused	Extra time on a test or same amount of time with breaks allowed	Take a shorter test with easier problems that do not take as long to do.
Fine-motor or hand writing	Use of a laptop or alternative writing device	Requirement to write papers is waived
Social anxiety	Can work alone unless program goals require interacting with others. For example, in a clinical nursing program, an internship in which one must interact with clients is required because interacting with clients is a goal of getting a clinical nursing degree. One cannot waive this requirement and still pass the program.	Waive the need for any interaction when the program goals require it, or waive the need to complete a project because it involves group interaction.
Comprehension	Visual or written cues to support auditory material, extra help or tutoring (although in college students usually have to request this help themselves).	Requirement to complete class material that is hard to understand is waived or replaced with easier, different material. In high school, it is possible to replace class material or entire course requirements and still graduate from high school. But then the student may not have needed requirements to get into certain post-secondary settings.

How to ask for modifications

The need for any modifications **must first be documented by a professional** (e.g., learning consultant, mental health professional, medical doctor, speech and language therapist). To get this documentation, students may need to be evaluated by a competent professional. Public high schools are required to provide a free evaluation upon request to determine eligibility or need for modifications and support services. They are not required to repeat this evaluation if it has already been done. Colleges and employers are not required to provide these evaluations and thus it is the responsibility of students and their families to seek out such an evaluation on their own. When such documentation is in hand, one can then request reasonable modifications that help compensate for the student's disability. **Remember, students should "request" a modification, not demand a modification.** Respectful language and tone of voice will be met with more success than disrespectful demands.

- **In high school**, the student and/or a parent/guardian can request the modifications from their special services case manager (if the child is classified and eligible for special education services) or from a designated administrative staff member in the school who coordinates "504 plans" (if the student is not a classified student and does not receive special education services). The term "504" refers to a special section of the law that allows for students to receive modifications even if they are neither classified nor eligible for special education services.

- **In college**, the student him or herself must request the modifications from the offices of special services and show documentation that provides a rationale for receiving those modifications. Students are entitled to either receive those modifications or to receive, in writing, an explanation as to why they are not eligible for those modifications with suggestions for alternatives to those modifications.

- **In a work setting**, it is sometimes preferable to inform an employer of any special needs after receiving the job, although in all fairness, employers should be told during the application process. Request for any modifications should be addressed to the office of human resources at the employment site and/or to your direct supervisor. Although federal law forbids employers to fire individuals because of a disability, one can be fired for failure to competently perform the duties of the job. Thus modifications should support the individual in a job task, but not allow the individual to avoid the essential duties of their job.

- Whether in high school, college, or a work site, students should make sure their teachers or supervisors are aware of their modifications, and to **ask for those modifications well in advance** of when they will need them. For example, if students are entitled to extra time on a test, they should ask the teacher for this days before the test if possible so the professor can make the arrangements. If they do not use the extra time that is okay, but they may have trouble if they ask for extra time during the test without reminding the professor before the test.

 Activity Page: Asking for reasonable modifications

Teaching

1. **Explain** the definition of reasonable modifications and the steps to ask for those modifications.

2. Have students list those modifications they have used in the past and those they might need for upcoming school or work settings. This information is typically derived from meetings with special education specialists, support staff, parents and the student to review recent evaluations and make recommendations about programming (see Chapters 2 and 3).

3. Have students create a plan for how they will request these modifications (e.g., do they have documentation, where can they get documentation, from whom will they request the modifications).

4. **Model** and **role-play** asking a teacher, employer, or college student support services for modifications. (Be sure to model and role-play what to do if the modifications are denied: like asking for an explanation and possible alternative modifications).

Generalization

Priming

Students should be reminded prior to tests, classes or employment situations to request any of the modifications they might need. Cue cards can be utilized to review just prior to meeting with a teacher, employer or special service support staff.

Facilitated practice

Students can regularly role-play asking for these modifications in preparation for when they will need to do so.

Review

Provide feedback to students if they needed a modification and did not request it or they asked too late or in a disrespectful way.

Dealing with frustrating work

Rationale

If we only approached work that was easy and familiar, we would rarely be able to grow and learn new things. The only way to develop new skills is to occasionally challenge ourselves with difficult work. Getting mad or refusing to do such work is not helpful. The following skill suggests positive ways to cope with difficult or frustrating work.

How to cope with frustrating work

1. **Check it out** before you get mad or refuse to do it. Often we think work will be difficult and do not even try it. It is important to attempt to do the work before we pass judgment on how hard it is.

2. Don't be afraid to **ask for help** if you do not understand something. The most successful people in the world all received help and benefited from others' ideas. Help does not mean someone does the work for you; help means someone will explain the work so you can do it for yourself.

3. Part of getting help might involve **asking to watch someone else** do the work first to get the idea of how it is done.

4. **Negotiate or break up the work** into smaller parts rather than refuse to do the work. Even after getting help, the work may still feel to challenging or too lengthy to complete in a timely way. It is preferable to ask to do a smaller portion of the work rather than refuse to do it all together.

5. If you find yourself becoming increasingly frustrated, it is wise to **take a short break**. It is difficult to think when one is angry. After a break, you may feel calm enough to return to the work with a fresh attitude and willingness to try again.

What not to do

Don't try get out of the work by making an excuse or by trying to get in trouble. This will only make you feel bad and stop you from growing. Instead, be brave and tell someone you do not know how to do the work.

Activity Page: Dealing with frustrating work

Prior To Teaching This Skill

Students often refuse to try work because it really is too hard or they have developed a "learned helplessness" attitude in which they think they cannot do it because they had trouble in the past. In addition to working on the skill steps for dealing with hard work, teachers and parents must *first* address the following two issues:

- If the work is too hard, it must be **modified** by changing the quality of the work (e.g., breaking down abstract tasks into simpler steps) or changing the quantity of work. Sometimes just asking them to do smaller amounts at a time, followed by a break or reward, can get them started.

- For students who have developed a "learned helplessness" attitude, helping them to do the work is about building their confidence in their ability. You must prove to them that they are able to do the work by starting with work they definitely can do and showing tremendous encouragement and praise as they do it.

Teaching

1. **Explain** the rationale and skills steps.

2. **Model** the right way and wrong way to handle frustrating work. In modeling the wrong way, you may want to demonstrate ways that the students have avoided their work (e.g., pretending to be sick, getting too silly, getting mad and complaining about the work). Discuss with students why someone might do it the wrong way (e.g., they are embarrassed to ask for help, they fear others will laugh at them). Counter such self-defeating thoughts reminding them that the smartest people are those who ask and get help and those who don't may not really be doing the work right.

3. **Role-play** the skill steps. Note: when role-playing, set a limit on how long a break can be and how many breaks you are allowed. Allowing one five-minute break per subject or period may be a good idea. It is not okay to keep taking breaks so you never do any work, but it is

preferable to ask for one break than to have a tantrum when overly frustrated. Suggested role-plays:

a.   Give the student some work that is moderately challenging (i.e., they can do some, but not all of it).

b.   Ask the student to perform a physical activity (e.g., catching a ball or jumping rope) that is moderately challenging (i.e., they can do some, but not all of it).

Generalization

Priming

This is the most crucial aspect of preventing frustration and angry outbursts. Remind students before any new or challenging work how to cope with frustrating work. This can be especially helpful if a teacher reminds all students that it is okay to ask for help so that no one student feels singled out.

Facilitated practice

Working and going to school will entail numerous opportunities each day to deal with frustrating work. It is crucial for support staff to prime students several times per day to use these skills to avoid extreme frustrations. Counselors and parents can bait the skill to help students practice by telling students they will be testing their memory of the skill from time to time. Then purposely give students something moderately difficult to do (i.e., they can do some, but not all of it). Prompt or wait for him or her to try it, ask for help, negotiate or break it into smaller parts, or ask for a break.

Review

After difficulties handling frustrating work, provide students with feedback about positive ways to cope with such work next time.

 # Accepting no or waiting for what you want

Rationale

Sometimes parents, teachers, employers, friends and romantic partners say no or make you wait when you ask them for something. Sometimes they ask you to stop an activity you are enjoying. If you get angry in these situations because you did not get what you wanted, then others may be angry and less likely to give you what you want. The following skill explains how best to get the things you want.

If you do not get mad when you do not get what you want, others will be pleased

As a result they may:

- give you more of what you want later, or

- if they can't give you exactly what you wanted, they may give you something else later.

What to say

Tell the person, "Okay, I can wait" or "If I can't have that, that's okay. Would it be okay to get something else?"

Stopping a favored activity

When you have to stop doing something you like (e.g., using the computer) to do something that you do not like as much (e.g., a writing task), realize that if you accept this, others may be pleased enough to let you do the favored activity again sometime. If you do not accept this, others may not trust that they can let you do the favored activity because you cannot stop when told.

 **Activity Page: Accepting no or waiting for what you want**

Teaching

1. **Explain** the rationale and what is in it for them if they can accept no or wait for what they want. Give examples of the values of waiting (e.g., the longer you go to school, the better the job you can get, or the more you save your money, the more you can let your money work for you and the more you can buy).

2. **Model** and **role-play** the skill steps.

   a. A parent asks a student to stop playing video games and do their homework instead. Show how the parent might let the student return to the game if the student accepts the interruption.

   b. A student asks his parents for a costly item or special privilege (e.g., to stay out late) and is told no. Show the parent giving something else to the student if the student accepted no.

   c. A teacher tells a student to stop one activity, like using the computer, and go to another less desired activity, like tedious writing work.

Generalization

Priming

Remind students of the rewards and opportunities that await them if they can accept no or wait for what they want. Particularly do this prior to going somewhere where they will ask for something (e.g., a store, or a classroom that has desired activities). For example, offer to get them double of what they want later if they can accept no, or offer to get something else they want if they can accept no. Challenge the students to see how long they can wait before getting what they want. Offer better rewards for longer waiting.

Facilitated practice

Bait the skill by telling them you will test their ability to wait and accept no. Then show them something they want and wait for them to ask for it. Then say that they can not have it. If they accept no, then offer them the item or something else because they were able to wait.

Review

If students got angry and did not wait, remind them of the rewards of waiting or accepting no. Try to focus on the positive rewards of waiting rather than the negative consequences of getting angry.

Asking nicely for what you want

Rationale

You are more likely to get what you want by asking nicely. This skill explains an approach that is most likely to help you get more of what you want. Making demands in a way that bothers others is likely to annoy them and make them less likely to give you what you want.

1. Ask nicely (requests versus demands).

When you want something from a parent, teacher, or employer, it is best to request it rather than demand it.

- Requests begin with works like "May I . . ." or "Would it be possible to . . ." Demands start with words like "Give me . . ." or "Do this . . ."

- Also use a nice tone of voice rather than an angry, demanding tone.

2. Compromise when asking nicely does not work.

If they will not give you what you want, you can ask nicely for something else. This is called compromising, where you get some of what you want and the other person gets some of what they want. You might suggest:

- Meeting the person halfway and just getting some of what you asked for

- Doing something for them so they will give you something you want.

3. Accept no when compromising does not work.

Sometimes parents, teachers or employers cannot compromise and cannot give you any of what you want. Then it is best to accept no for an answer so they will be happy and more likely to give you something else you want another time.

 **Activity Page: Asking nicely for what you want**

Teaching

1. **Explain** the rationale and skill steps.

2. **Model** and **role-play** the steps using real examples from the students' own lives or the following examples. Be sure to **model** request words and tone, and how to compromise or accept no when necessary.

    a. A student asks a teacher if they can get a one week extension on a paper.

    b. A student asks a parent if they can get a really expensive video game.

    c. A worker asks the boss if he can get a couple of hours off that afternoon because he has to study for a test.

Generalization

Priming

Students should be reminded whenever they will be in positions where they will want to request something (e.g., when they are in a store with their parents, or when they need something from a teacher or employer).

Facilitated practice

Adults can help students practice by baiting the skill. Students should be told first that they will be tested on this skill. Then adults can talk about or show students desired items or activities, wait for them to request one and coach students to do it nicely, compromise and accept no if necessary.

Review

Students should be given feedback to use the skill steps if they demand something or persist in asking when already told no.

Working cooperatively in groups

Rationale

Most high schools, colleges, and work settings will occasionally require that individuals work together in groups. It is important to know how to do this to advance in school and in work environments.

Getting along with others is more important than the particular project you are working on

Being able to get along with others will help you to be a valued member of a group, school or employment setting. If instead you care more about the project than the people you are working with, others may resent you, and you may not be able to get the project done. If everyone argues, work cannot get completed.

How to make decisions when working on a group project

1. **Allow each person to say their idea** for the project.

   a. Say what you want to do.

   b. Don't insult others' ideas. If you do not like someone's idea, say "That's an interesting idea, but I think this is better because . . ."

2. **Discuss** which ideas you like and be willing to compromise. Remember it is more important to get along than to make everyone select your idea. In order to get along you might:

   a. Combine each person's ideas together

   b. Come up with a new and different idea than any other individual's idea

   c. Try to convince others of your idea by being positive, "I like your idea, but I think this is even better because . . ."

3. **Take a vote** on what idea(s) to select and go with the group If the majority wants one idea, but you want something else, then go with the majority unless their idea is dangerous.

Roles you might select as you work with others

In a group, each person must play a particular role for the group to function. The following lists some of the roles you might play when participating in a group. There can be more than one person for each role, but all roles must be filled for the group to function.

- **Leaders**: The leaders don't decide what idea to do, the leaders only keep everyone working on the task.

- **Idea contributors**: Everyone should be an idea contributor, telling others their thoughts and ideas.

- **Record keepers**: Keep notes of ideas so group can come back to the work at a later time.

58 | Activity Page: Working cooperatively in groups

Teaching

1. **Explain** the rationale and skill steps for making decisions in a group. Then explain the roles one can play as a group member.

2. **Model** the process of making decisions in group. As an example, pretend that the group must come up with a name for a pizza restaurant. Using yourself and other adults or students, model how each person will come up with a name, then compromise about what name to use (perhaps by combining portions of each person's idea) and then voting on what the final name will be.

3. Break up students into groups of two or three. **Role-play** the process of making group decisions by using the following activities. In each activity make sure students identify who will be a record keeper and keep track of everyone's ideas as well as combined ideas, and the final selected idea. **Each activity can take several sessions to complete, so it is advised that students do only a portion of each activity in each session.**

   a. Come up with an advertisement for a new pizza restaurant.

      i. Start by deciding what the name of the restaurant will be.

      ii. Then come up with what is special about the restaurant, which will determine the words in the advertisement.

      iii. Then decide who will read the advertisement to others.

   b. Come up with a commercial for a new imaginary invention. (3-session project)

      i. Come up with the name.

      ii. Decide what it does.

      iii. Create a story board for the commercial. For example, first an announcer introduces the product and explains what it does, then customers demonstrate how it works, then another announcer tells how and where to get the product.

      iv. Decide on who will act out which parts.

      v. Perform the commercial.

    c. Create a short film or movie.

        i. Come up with the idea for the movie.

        ii. Come up with a story board.

        iii. Decide who will play what part.

        iv. Rehearse and perform for the camera.

Generalization

Priming

Students should be primed to use these steps before all group projects. In schools, this means teachers should be informed of these skill steps to describe to their students before assigning them group projects. It is especially important to stress "getting along" more than "getting your way." Teachers may want to consider giving extra credit to groups that show cooperation instead of extra credit for the content of the work.

Facilitated practice

Group projects in schools and work settings are perfect opportunities to practice as long as students get primed on the skill steps prior to any group project and coached during the process. Students can receive additional practice by participating in group therapy or recreation groups designed specifically to practice this skill. Groups can make a series of films, new games, write music or poetry, or any other creative group project.

Review

Students should be redirected to the skill steps whenever they begin to argue, insult other students, or refuse to work with others.

59 Dealing with mistakes and correction

Rationale

All of us make mistakes and need to be corrected at times. If we can tolerate this, we can learn new things and succeed in school and at work. If we cannot tolerate making mistakes or being corrected, it is harder to learn anything new and succeed.

What to think about mistakes

Mistakes are actually good events because they help us learn. When we get things right we often do not think about it again, but when we make a mistake, we often think about it and learn something new.

- If you think mistakes mean you are not smart, you are wrong. Mistakes are a sign that you are taking a risk to learn new things. The smartest most innovative people in the world make tons of mistakes; that is what it takes to learn something new.

- Being perfect is not realistic. It is more impressive to handle mistakes well than to get something right the first time.

What to think about being corrected

Corrections can be helpful or hurtful. When someone just tells you that you are wrong, offers no way to do it better and insults you, that is hurtful and you need not listen. But if others offer you a way to improve what you did, they are trying to help and you should listen. Consider the advantages of correcting your work:

- You will learn more and do better work

- You will get your work done sooner by making the correction rather than arguing about it, which only prolongs how long you have to work.

What to do if you make a mistake or get corrected

- Correct your mistake, or ask for help if you are not sure how to make the correction.

- If your mistake hurt someone, then apologize.

 Activity Page: Dealing with mistakes and correction

Teaching

1. **Explain** the rationale and how to think about mistakes and correction. Describe the steps to take when you make a mistake or get corrected.

2. **Model** and **role-play** the right and wrong ways to handle mistakes and corrections using real life examples from the students or the following examples:

   a. Give students a task to spell a very challenging word, or do a very challenging math problem. When they make a mistake, guide them through the skill steps and praise them for handling the mistake well rather than for getting the problem right.

   b. A teacher indicates that a student did not write a paper on the right topic and asks that the student redo the paper to match the original assignment.

   c. A parent tells a student that they put the dishes in the wrong place after clearing out the dishwasher.

   d. An employer tells an employee that he did not file papers where they should be filed and to redo the job.

Generalization

Priming

Students should be reminded about this skill prior to challenging work that will likely result in mistakes. It should be stressed that it is more important to be able to handle mistakes well and accept correction than to be able to get the job done perfectly the first time, as perfection is not a realistic expectation.

Facilitated practice

Tell students you are purposely going to give them work that is hard to do so that they make a mistake. Remind them that you are more interested in how they handle a mistake than getting things right. Then give them something near impossible to do and coach them through the steps. Many students will benefit from a behavior chart where they get more points for handling mistakes and correction than for getting work right the first time. This chart can help "perfectionistic" students overcome their overvaluing of perfection and help them focus instead on how they handle imperfection.

Review

Provide feedback to students after they make mistakes or are corrected, praising them for handling it well, or if they got upset, reminding them that handling the mistake is more important than getting the work done right the first time.

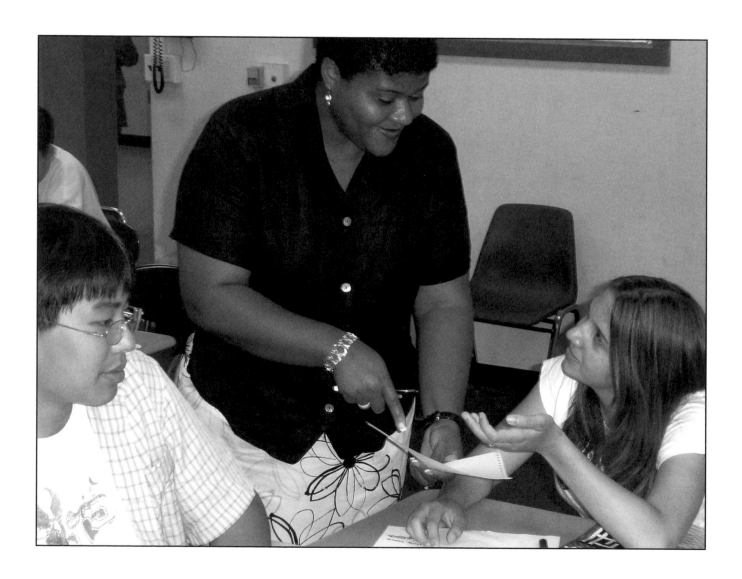

 How to respectfully disagree with teachers, parents, or supervisors

Rationale

Sometimes the decisions of those in charge are wrong. How you communicate with them about their decisions is crucial. If you argue with them, they may get angry, which could cause trouble for you. If you say nothing, then something may be done incorrectly. This skill is about how to tell someone they may be wrong in a way that they will not be angry.

Do I need to say anything?

If someone in charge makes a decision that you think is wrong, but it will not hurt you or anyone else, then it may not be worth bringing it up at all since no one likes to be criticized. **If the decision is bad for you or others then you might want to tell them.** The following are situations that might be bad for you or others:

- A teacher may provide false information to the class.

- A parent may decide to do something that will negatively affect someone in the family.

- An employer is not following a procedure, which could cause harm to others. (You do not need to say anything if the departure from the procedure will not result in any harm to others).

How should I tell the person in charge?

First, try to say what you have to say privately so as not to embarrass the other person. Instead of directly saying they are wrong, you can pose it as a question to alert them to the situation.

- **Right way**:

  1. Find a private area. "Can I talk to you for a moment?"

  2. "Is this the way to do it because I thought . . .?" or "Can you explain this to me because I thought we were supposed to . . .?"

- **Wrong way**: In front of everyone say "You are wrong; the right way to do it is . . ."

Activity Page: How to respectfully disagree with parents, teachers or supervisors

Teaching

1. **Explain** the consequences for arguing with those in charge. Review when it is and is not okay to tell others they are wrong. Then review how to tell them.

2. **Model** and **role-play** telling others they are wrong using real life examples from the students or the following situations. Make sure you model and provide feedback about tone of voice and facial expressions.

   a. A parent incorrectly tells you that you are supposed to go to your piano lessons today.

   b. A teacher tells everyone something false, for example, that humans are not mammals.

   c. An employer breaks usual procedure and lets his coworkers go early one day before vacation (and there are no immediate needs at the job). Note the right response here is to do nothing.

   d. An employer decides to cut corners at his restaurant and just rinse off plates with cold water rather than clean with hot water and soap.

Generalization

Priming

Students who have a tendency to argue with adults because they think the adults are wrong (i.e., not because they just like to argue) should be primed regularly on this skill. Prior to going to school or work, then again after school or work, they should be reminded about how to talk with others if they think they are wrong.

Facilitated practice

For students who have this difficulty, there will be many opportunities each day to coach them to respectfully suggest that the other person may be wrong.

Review

Provide feedback after a student has had difficulty expressing their opinion to someone in charge. Remind them how to respectfully pose a question rather than state someone is wrong.

Dealing with stressful living situations

Rationale

All of us at times experience stress in our living situations due to conflicts with parents, siblings, or roommates, or separation from significant people in our life. Sometimes we may try to deal with the problem directly and other times we may prefer to try to get our minds off the problem. Both strategies can be okay if handled positively. This skill maps out positive and negative ways of handling stressful living situations.

Facing the stressful situations; trying to solve the problem

Facing the problems directly mean trying to deal with the source of the stress so you can deal with the problem. There are positive and negative ways to do this (see table):

POSITIVE	NEGATIVE
Respectfully confronting the person who is contributing to the problem. Use and "I" message to assert yourself: "I feel_____, when you _____. I want _____ _____."	Aggressively arguing with the person who is contributing to the problem.
Talking about the problem with a trusted friend or adult who can try to help you find ways to deal with the problem.	Acting out your feelings on innocent others who are not contributing to the problem by teasing or criticizing.

Ways to get your mind off the problem.

These strategies involve trying to get away from the problem rather than trying to solve the problem. Some problems cannot be easily changed and thus you will have to find ways to get a break from the stress. For example, an untreatable chronic illness in the family can be stressful, and while there may be no way to "solve" the problem, there are ways to get a break from thinking about it.

POSITIVE	NEGATIVE
Doing something fun with friends or by yourself, like exercise, listening to music, watching TV or other pleasant activities to get your mind off things.	Threatening to hurt or kill your self. This will create more problems and solve nothing. There are other ways to give your self a break from the stress or to solve the problem directly.
Walking away from the stressful situation, but telling others where you will be and when you will return.	Running away. This can cause more problems. You may be able to walk out if you let others know where you will be and when you will return.

Activity Page: Dealing with stressful living situations

Teaching

1. **Explain** that there are two general strategies for handling stress: dealing with problems directly or escaping problems. Map out for students the positive and negative ways to try to solve and avoid problems.

2. Have students **identify** what problems they might be dealing with, **develop a plan** to deal with it, then **role-play** parts of their plan. Follow these steps below:

   a. Have students write on a piece of paper some of the stressful problems they are experiencing.

   b. On a separate piece of paper, have students write ways to directly deal with the problem.

   c. Next, have students write positive ways to get their mind off of the problem.

   d. Have the students role-play some parts of their plan, especially those that require students to respectfully confront others.

Generalization

Priming

Whenever students are going to return to a stressful living situation, they can be reminded about their plan for how to deal with it.

Facilitated practice

Students can be coached by parents and others to use their plan when they are under stress. Putting the plan in a prominent location (e.g., the refrigerator, their room) may help to remind students when the situation arises).

Review

Students should be encouraged to review with others (e.g., in counseling) how they are doing with their plans to handle the stress. Any negative behaviors can be responded to with exploration of more positive ways they might handle the situation.

Choosing job/career directions

Rationale

Finding a suitable career can be an overwhelming task for anyone. Careful planning is necessary to find a career that one likes, one is capable of, and that can help sustain a living. This skill provides a path to help find such a career so that one can make plans to get the appropriate training and experience to pursue it.

Career exploration should begin at least by age 14

If you receive special educational services in high school, your school must have an Individualized Educational Plan (IEP) that maps out your course of study and any special services. The following is a sample timeline of what career exploration activities should be in your IEP for each year in school:

1. By freshman year, or by age 14, your IEP should contain plans for career exploration and vocational preparation.

2. By the end of sophomore year your IEP should contain plans for conducting a Functional Vocational Assessment.

3. By the end of sophomore year, ensure that your IEP includes plans for career exploration including such activities as job shadowing, job sampling and/or internships.

4. At the beginning of junior year, apply for Vocational Rehabilitation services, and if you are eligible, request a technical consultation with a VR counselor.

5. By senior year, ensure that your IEP has specific employment goals, including part-time employment during senior year, vocational training, internships, employment development and/or job search activities.

If you are not receiving special education services, you may want to make sure you also receive the services listed above (particularly a functional vocational assessment), yet your school is not required to provide them as they would be if you had an IEP. Thus you may have to contract with private agencies to receive a functional vocational assessment and job training.

Conducting a Functional Vocational Assessment

- The purpose of this assessment is to identify your interests, preferences, abilities, and aptitudes. Functional vocational assessments involve both written and hands-on assessments. Written assessments may help determine students' interests, job preferences, and to some extent abilities, yet they cannot provide the kind of information that can be obtained by actually performing a job. Thus it is important to also have "hands-on" assessments of your performance while trying out a job to see what you need help with and what parts you do and do not like about the job.

- Many schools have personnel trained to do Functional Vocational Assessments, but if they do not, you or your parents should request that the school contract with an individual or agency that is qualified to conduct the assessment.

Activities that may be part of a functional vocational assessment and help you explore career options

- **Vocational testing:** You may fill out pencil and paper questionnaires to help determine your interests, preferences, and abilities. Information from such measures may point you in the direction of certain job and career paths. A vocational counselor at your school or a private agency can supply these measures.

- **Career fairs and job tours:** Many high schools conduct annual career fairs that provide opportunities for students to become aware of employment and career opportunities in their community. Local community colleges also sponsor career days/fairs. Job tours are another way for you to explore work and career opportunities. These are typically less formal opportunities for individuals or small groups of students to visit local industries and businesses to observe what is done there, and to talk with employers and workers about particular jobs.

- **Community Asset Mapping:** This is a useful activity that can be conducted as a classroom activity or homework assignment. To complete a community asset map, a student makes a list of employers in their community, and the types of jobs available. This can be done by consulting the yellow pages, newspapers and conducting web searches. Family members, friends and church members are also good sources for this information. The community asset map can serve as a resource for identifying opportunities for job shadowing and internships.

- **Job shadowing and internships:** Job shadowing involves a student spending some time with a person who does a job that the young person has some interest in. Job shadowing is usually a short-term activity, from one to a few visits. Internships are a more formal and long-term activity, typically involving a student working part time in an employment setting each week for a semester or school year. Job shadowing should occur in freshman and/ or sophomore years, and internships in the junior and senior years.

- **Supported Employment:** Is an approach that involves providing supports (like a job coach or teacher) to help young people get and maintain competitive employment. Many schools provide supported employment services, or contract with an adult service agency to provide them. Depending on the needs of a student, supported employment services may be provided as early as the sophomore year as part of a student's Individual Education Program. Supported Employment services may involve:

  — Group model: a full-time instructor working with a small group of students in one or many employment settings, or a full-time instructor working with a small group of students in multiple work sites in various community settings. This approach enables students to sample a variety of jobs with instructor support.

  — Entrepreneurial business model: A private business, typically retail or manufacturing, employs students with disabilities. Many schools have developed their own small businesses in order to provide such experiences for students.

  — Individual Placement Model: In this approach, students are assisted to obtain competitive employment in an integrated setting. Initial training and on-going support are provided by an instructor or job coach. Natural supports, such as co-worker support, are utilized.

Other places to obtain help in exploring career options

- **Department of Vocational Rehabilitation:** Vocational Rehabilitation (VR) is a nationwide, federal and state funded program to assist eligible individuals to identify employment goals, and to obtain education, training and other supports needed to become employed. Each state has a central VR agency with local offices. You must apply for Vocational Rehabilitation services and you must be found eligible based upon documentation of your disability. You should apply for VR services no later than the beginning of your junior year of high school.

If you are found eligible and become a client of VR, rehabilitation counselors will provide technical consultation to you, so that appropriate services may begin following graduation.

- **One-Stop Career Centers:** The federal Department of Labor, in partnership with the states, has created a network of local One-Stop Career Centers. These Centers provide a variety of employment related services, including career counseling, job listings, and referrals to job training programs. To learn more about One-Stop Career Centers: 1-877-348-050 www.careeronestop.org

Career options that students with autism spectrum disorders have found helpful and not helpful

To help you consider what type of employment appeals to you, consider the recommendations below presented by Temple Grandin, Ph.D. (1999). She is probably the most well known autistic adult who writes and lectures about autism. Here is a list she created of some career options that students with autism spectrum disorders have found helpful and not helpful, along with her comments:

- "Bad Jobs for People with High Functioning Autism or Asperger's Syndrome: Jobs that require high demands on short-term working memory

  — Cashier—making change quickly puts too much demand on short-term working memory

  — Short order cook—Have to keep track of many orders and cook many different things at the same time

  — Waitress—Especially difficult if you have to keep track of many different tables

  — Casino dealer—Too many things to keep track of

  — Taxi dispatcher—Too many things to keep track of

  — Taking oral dictation—Difficult due to auditory processing problems

  — Airline ticket agent—Deal with angry people when flights are cancelled

  — Futures market trader—Totally impossible

  — Air traffic controller—Information overload and stress

  — Receptionist and telephone operator—Would have problems when the switchboard got busy

- Good Jobs for Visual Thinkers

  — Computer programming—Wide-open field with many jobs available especially in industrial automation, software design, business computers, communications and network systems

  — Drafting—Engineering drawings and computer aided drafting. This job can offer many opportunities. Drafting is an excellent portal of entry for many interesting technical jobs. I know people who started out at a company doing drafting and then moved into designing and laying out entire factories. To become really skilled at drafting, one needs to learn how to draw by hand first. I have observed that most of the people who make beautiful drawings on a computer learned to draw by hand first. People who never learn to draw by hand first tend to leave important details out of their drawings.

  — Commercial art—Advertising and magazine layout can be done as freelance work

  — Photography—Still and video, TV cameraman can be done as freelance work

  — Equipment designing—Many industries, often a person starts as a draftsman and then moves into designing factory equipment

  — Animal trainer or veterinary technician—Dog obedience trainer, behavior problem consultant

  — Automobile mechanic—Can visualize how the entire car works

  — Computer-troubleshooter and repair—Can visualize problems in computers and networks

  — Small appliance and lawnmower repair—Can make a nice local business

  — Handcrafts of many different types such as wood carving, jewelry making, ceramics, etc.

  — Laboratory technician—Who modifies and builds specialized lab equipment

  — Web page design—Find a good niche market; can be done as freelance work

  — Building trades—Carpenter or welder. These jobs make good use of visual skills but some people will not be able to do them well due to motor and coordination problems.

  — Video game designer—Stay out of this field. Jobs are scarce and the field is overcrowded. There are many more jobs in industrial, communications business and software design and computer programming. Another bad thing about this job is exposure to violent images.

— Computer animation—Visual thinkers would be very good at this field, but there is more competition in this field than in business or industrial computer programming. Businesses are recruiting immigrants from overseas because there is a shortage of good programmers in business and industrial fields.

— Building maintenance—Fixes broken pipes, windows and other things in an apartment complex, hotel or office building

— Factory maintenance—Repairs and fixes factory equipment

- Good Jobs for Non-Visual Thinkers: Those who are good at math, music or fact

  — Accounting—Get very good in a specialized field such as income taxes

  — Library science—Reference librarian. Help people find information in the library or on the Internet.

  — Computer programming—Less visual types can be done as freelance work

  — Engineering—Electrical, electronic and chemical engineering

  — Journalist—Very accurate facts, can be done as freelance

  — Copy editor—Corrects manuscripts. Many people freelance for larger publishers

  — Taxi driver—Knows where every street is

  — Inventory control—Keeps track of merchandise stocked in a store

  — Tuning pianos and other musical instruments—Can be done as freelance work

  — Laboratory technician—Running laboratory equipment

  — Bank Teller—Very accurate money counting, much less demand on short-term working memory than a busy cashier who mostly makes change quickly

  — Clerk and filing jobs—Knows where every file is

  — Telemarketing—Get to repeat the same thing over and over, selling on the telephone. Noisy environment may be a problem. Telephone sales avoid many social problems.

  — Statistician—Work in many different fields such as research, census bureau, industrial quality control, U.S. Dept. of Agriculture, etc.

— Physicist or mathematician—There are very few jobs in these fields. Only the very brilliant can get and keep jobs. Jobs are much more plentiful in computer programming and accounting.

- Jobs for Nonverbal People with Autism or People with Poor Verbal Skills

    — Reshelving library books—Can memorize the entire numbering system and shelf locations

    — Factory assembly work—Especially if the environment is quiet

    — Copy shop—Running photocopies. Printing jobs should be lined up by somebody else

    — Janitor jobs—Cleaning floors, toilets, windows and offices

    — Restocking shelves—In many types of stores

    — Recycling plant—Sorting jobs

    — Warehouse—Loading trucks, stacking boxes

    — Lawn and garden work—Mowing lawns and landscaping work

    — Data entry—If the person has fine motor problems, this would be a bad job

    — Fast food restaurant—Cleaning and cooking jobs with little demand on short-term memory

    — Plant care—Water plants in a large office building."

Grandin (1999)

Activity Page: Choosing job/career directions

Teaching

1. **Explain** the rationale for planning a career. Review the schedule of planning that should be in place starting by age 14 if you are receiving special education services. Discuss what other options exist if you are not eligible for special education services (e.g., seeking vocational counseling and job training from community or private agencies).

2. Have students **create an action plan** based on what grade they are in (see Exploring Career Path action plan). For example, freshmen may want to check their IEPs to make sure there is a general plan that outlines an exploration of career opportunities. Those who do not have IEPs (i.e., they are not receiving special education services) should begin to map out a general plan that may include seeking services from outside vocational counseling and job placement agencies. Sophomores should plan when they will begin a Functional Vocational Assessment to assess their interests, preferences, and abilities and what activities will be part of that. Juniors, seniors and beyond may want to plan what kinds of jobs they want to sample and how to do that.

Generalization

Priming

Students may need reminders to follow their action plans. Any resistance can be explored as this may be a sign of anxiety. Many older high school students often fear graduation and work life. This fear may need to be discussed and students may need to be assured that they will be supported throughout and reminded of their past successes.

Facilitated practice

All the job-sampling activities are opportunities to get coaching on the job as they explore different worksites. Attending job fairs and working with a vocational counselor are also ways of coaching students in career exploration.

Review

Students may need feedback about the way they are exploring career options. Some students may not do enough and their anxieties may need to be discussed, while other students may be doing too much and need help focusing their efforts.

Exploring Career Path action plan

What plans are in your IEP to explore careers? No IEP? What plans can you make with outside agencies to explore career options? Name particular activities and when you might do these activities. Use the ideas listed and fill in your own ideas.

WHEN	ACTIVITIES
Sophomore year	Check my IEP for career plans and course work to support that? Make arrangements with outside agencies if I do not have an IEP or make use of the school's career exploration activities?
Sophomore year	Schedule a Functional Vocational Assessment? This may include interest inventories, other paper and pencil measures, job sampling, other activities?
Junior Year	Explore jobs through supported employment, internships, job shadowing, volunteer work, and plan coursework?
Senior Year	Explore jobs through supported employment, internships, job shadowing, volunteer work, or other activities? Plan coursework.
After Graduation	Explore jobs through supported employment, internships, job shadowing, volunteer work, or other activities? Plan coursework.

Conducting a job search

Rationale

Although it would be nice for people to just offer us a job, most of us have to actively work to get a job. This skill describes an overview of specific things you can do to get a job. The skill lessons that follow will help you gather the materials needed to start your job search.

At what stage of a job opening do people get jobs?

Many people still get jobs before the job is actually advertised. That means we should not wait until a job is advertised to apply for a job because there will be a lot fewer jobs to choose from. Many jobs come when an applicant sends information to an employer before there is an opening or when the applicant hears that someone may be leaving a job but the job has not yet been posted.

Ways to look for a job

Since many people get jobs before a job is advertised, it is wise to seek out jobs before they are advertised as well as apply to jobs that are posted. The following lists ways to search for posted and unadvertised jobs and what you will need to do to apply for a job:

RESOURCES	HOW TO BEGIN	WHAT YOU NEED
1. Build a network of friends, relatives, and acquaintances who can tell you of possible job leads or who will agree to be professional or personal references for you (i.e., people who can attest to your good qualities).	You can begin with all your current friends and relatives and neighbors. To track down former friends and acquaintances, try the following websites that track addresses and telephone numbers: www.theultimates.com. To track previous business colleagues, try Elyon.com which is a data base of names associated with different employers. To reach a former classmate or roommate, check the alumni association of your former school or university (those alumni associations can be searched for through Google.com or Yahoo.com).	1. A script to talk with these people to inquire about jobs and ask if they would be a reference for you. 2. A resume to send to those employers even before they post any jobs. 3. Thank you notes to thank those who agreed to give you a job lead or be a reference for you

RESOURCES	HOW TO BEGIN	WHAT YOU NEED
2. Research companies that might have the kind of job you want.	Look up in a business directory, ask your friends and relatives, and search the internet for companies that offer the kind of employment you want. For company summaries, try the following internet sites: www.hoovers.com and www.wetfeet.com. For information about compensation and benefits in your profession or industry visit the website of your professional association or trade organization (which can be found at www.weddles.com).	1. A script to talk with potential employers, 2. A cover letter 3. Resume sending to those employers.
3. Use the internet and newspapers to search for advertised jobs.	Some excellent websites to search for jobs are: monster.com, headhunter.com, joboptions.com, hotjobs.com, nationjob.com, careerbuilder.com, careermosaic.com, careerpath.com, careers.wsj.com	1. A script to talk with potential employers, 2. A cover letter 3. Resume sending to those employers.
4. Attend job fairs.	Inquire at your high school, local universities, or community agencies about upcoming job fairs in your area.	1. A script to inquire about the jobs they offer and 2. A resume to give them.
5. Use community agencies that may have connections with employers	Consider contacting the Department of Vocational Rehabilitation (DVR), a nationwide, federal and state funded program to assist eligible individuals to obtain education, training and other supports needed to become employed. Each state has a central VR agency with local offices. One-Stop Career Centers are federal and state funded Centers that provide a variety of employment related services, including career counseling, job listings, and referrals to job training programs. To learn more call: 1-877-348-050 www.careeronestop.org	To use DVR, you must apply for Vocational Rehabilitation services and be found eligible based upon documentation of your disability. Apply for VR services no later than the beginning of your junior year of high school. If you are found eligible, rehabilitation counselors will provide technical consultation to you, so that appropriate services may begin following graduation.
6. Door to door search	Scan your neighborhood for help wanted signs or simply ask in businesses whether they are hiring.	1. Script. 2 Knowledge of how to fill out applications 3. Resume.

Activity Page: Conducting a job search

Teaching

1. Discuss the importance of seeking out jobs that are not even advertised yet. Review some of the job search strategies and what materials and skills you may need to be able to pursue each strategy.

2. Each student should create an action plan and schedule of their job search activities (see attached **Job Search action plan**). This requires students to create self-imposed deadlines for when they will have certain materials ready to conduct a job search activity (e.g., scripts to talk with others, cover letters, resumes, and thank you notes) and when they plan to engage in job search activities. It is recommended that students who are not currently working or in school plan to devote 4-5 hours a day to a job search strategy every day and treat the search as a job itself. For those who are in school fulltime or working, then 1-2 hours every day may be a more realistic goal.

Generalization

Priming

Students may need reminders to follow through on their self-imposed deadlines. Any resistance may be a sign of anxiety as many older high school students often fear graduation and work life. This fear may need to be discussed and students may need to be assured that they will be supported throughout and reminded of their past successes.

Facilitated practice

Students may benefit from coaching as they create their scripts, resumes, letters and other materials. They may also benefit from coaching as they use the internet or review newspaper advertisements.

Review

Students may need feedback about the way they are planning their job search. Some students may not do enough and their anxieties may need to be discussed, while other students may be doing too much and need help focusing their efforts.

Job Search action plan

In order to really make use of the job search strategies, it is crucial to schedule your time. The following table asks you to indicate when you will have certain materials ready to begin your job search, and when you will use these strategies.

Strategy	Materials I will need	When I will have materials ready (Specific date)	When I will use the strategy (Days and Times)
Build a network of friends, relatives, and acquaintances	Script to call or contact them A resume to send them Thank you notes		
Research companies that might have the kind of job you want	Script to call or contact them A cover letter A resume to send them		
Use the internet and newspapers to search for advertised jobs	Script to call or contact them A cover letter A resume to send them		
Attend job fairs.	Script to tell them about your interests A resume to give them		
Use community agencies that may have connections with employers	Application and documentation of disability if needed Phone numbers of local agencies		
Door to door search	Script Application knowledge Resume		

 Writing a resume and cover letters

Rationale

Although you may talk with prospective employers, do not expect them to remember all you said. A resume is a written summary of your relevant training, job experience, and skills. Sending your resume to others allows them to have a convenient reminder of you and your interest in their organization. Cover letters sent along with your resume help communicate directly what your interest is and why you may be right for the job.

Getting started

To write a resume, you want to gather information about your education and training, work or volunteer experience, any special awards or special organizations you are in, and references (i.e., people who you know personally or professionally who are willing to recommend you to an employer). Use the **Resume Information Sheet** to summarize this relevant information.

Putting your resume together

Resumes can be organized in **chronological order**, or according to **functional skills**, or a mix of the two (see sample resumes). The choice of how to organize your resume depends on what you want to highlight to an employer.

- If you have very few job experiences, you may want to highlight your functional skills rather than list your work experiences.

- If, on the other hand, you have very extensive job experiences but a limited set of different skills, than you may want to highlight those different job positions rather than your functional skills.

- If you have both relevant job or training experiences and relevant skills for a job, than you may want to list both a chronological order of job experiences and list different skills. See the three sample resumes provided as a guide for making your own.

Finishing touches

- Before sending out your resume, ask a mentor or trusted friend to look it over and help you edit it to get it just right.

- Keep it on a computer file so you can email it to others and easily make changes as necessary.

- Select an easy-to-read font on good quality paper to print out and mail to employers.

Writing a cover letter

When you send your resume out to a prospective employer, it is helpful to send out a letter that explains what you are looking for or what job you are applying for. Use the **cover letter worksheet** to guide what you write for your own cover letters. See the samples provided to help you organize your letter. **Sample 1** is a cover letter sent to an employer before a job is posted. **Sample 2** is a cover letter sent out in response to a job posting.

Activity Page: Writing a resume and cover letters

Teaching

1. **Explain** the rationale for writing resumes and cover letters.

2. Students should **set a deadline** indicating when they will complete their resume and have cover letters ready to send out.

3. Have students fill out the **Resume Information Sheet**.

4. Then students should **choose a style** for their resume (chronological order, functional skills, or a mix) according to what they want to highlight.

5. Have them assemble the resume on the computer and **ask others to help** them edit before printing on high quality paper.

6. Have them **write a cover letter** for at least one prospective employer using the cover letter worksheet and sample cover letters to help guide what they say. They should ask someone to edit the cover letter before sending it out.

Generalization

Priming

Students may need reminders to stick to their deadline to complete their resumes and cover letters. Any fears of actually getting a job may need to be discussed if the student seems very resistant. Students should be reminded that they do not have to take a job just because they get an offer.

Facilitated practice

Students may need coaching on assembling their resumes and cover letters and choosing the right words.

Review

Provide constructive feedback to help students highlight their skills and experience in a positive way.

Resume Information Sheet

Contact information

Name and address:

Phone number and email address:

Type of position desired:

Education and training

Specialized training or courses

Name of Institution/School:

City and State:

Dates attended:

Certificate or degree earned:

Graduate Training

Name of Institution/School:

City and State:

Dates attended:

Major:

Certificate or degree earned:

College

Name of Institution/School:

City and State:

Dates attended:

Major:

Certificate or degree earned:

High School

Name of Institution/School:

City and State:

Dates attended:

Special courses:

Certificate or degree earned:

Work and/or volunteer experience

Name of business/company:

Address and phone number:

Supervisor:

Job title and duties:

Start and end dates of experience:

Skills utilized (i.e., use of machinery or equipment, computer programs, communication skills required):

Name of organization:

Address and phone number:

Supervisor:

Job title and duties:

Start and end dates of experience:

Skills utilized (i.e., use of machinery or equipment, computer programs, communication skills required):

Associations or clubs

Name:

Address:

Member status:

Awards or recognition:

References

Name:

Address:

Phone and email:

Relationship to you:

Name:

Address:

Phone and email:

Relationship to you:

Cover Letter Worksheet

Your name

Your Address

Your phone number

Their address

Date

Dear _____,

"I am seeking a position as _____." Or "I am applying for the

position as _____." Say something complimentary about the

organization like "I have always been impressed by your organization and look forward to any

opportunity to work with you.

_____

_____. Say something about your experience:

_____

_____.

"I have enclosed my resume along with references for your consideration. I look forward to

meeting with you if possible to discuss any job positions that are or may become available. Thank

you for your time and consideration."

Sincerely,

Your name

Sample Cover Letter 1

John Smith

35 Maple Avenue

Coletown, New York 12082

Tel: (845) 682-9898

New York Tigers

1245 Roseland Boulevard

Redding, New York, 13445

February 1, 2006

Dear General Manager,

I am seeking a position with a professional athletic organization. I have been a great fan of the New York Tigers all my life and would look forward to any opportunity to be part of your organization. Previously, I was equipment manager for a top-rated college football team until my graduation and developed skills in managing their practices, arranging travel plans, and insuring that all their equipment was ready when needed.

I have enclosed my resume along with references for your consideration. I look forward to meeting with you if possible to discuss any job positions that are or may become available. Thank you for your time and consideration.

Sincerely,

John Smith

Sample Cover Letter 2

John Smith

35 Maple Avenue

Coletown, New York 12082

Tel: (845) 682-9898

New York Tigers

1245 Roseland Boulevard

Redding, New York, 13445

February 1, 2006

Dear General Manager,

I am applying to the advertised position of assistant to the general manager. I was the equipment manager for a top-rated college football team for three years and developed skills in managing their practices, arranging travel plans, and insuring all their equipment was ready when needed. I have enclosed my resume along with references for your consideration.

I have been a great fan of the New York Tigers all my life and would look forward to any opportunity to be part of your organization. I am eager to meet with you at your earliest convenience to discuss the position. Thank you for your time and consideration.

Sincerely,

John Smith

Sample Resume (Highlighting Functional Skills)

Robert Smith
343 Oak Road
Mapletown, NJ 07044
Tel: (973) 555-8282
Robertsmith@netmail.com

Position Desired
Graphic Designer

Graphic Design Skills
- Web Page Design
- Book and Magazine Cover Design
- Poster Layout
- Brochures
- Business Cards
- Slide Show Presentation

Business Skills
- Work well with deadlines
- Customer centered approach
- Work well with colleagues
- Open to feedback
- Detail-oriented, well organized

Software Skills
- Quark Express
- Photoshop
- Pagemaker
- Type Styler
- Illustrator
- Macwrite
- Microsoft Word
- Microsoft Powerpoint
- Microsoft Excel
- Microsoft Publisher

Education
Drew University, Madison, New Jersey
B.A. degree in Art, May, 2004

Relevant Experience
College coursework, September 2002-May 2004
Design of web pages, business cards &, brochures, poster ads, slide show presentations, and book covers.

Own graphic design business, May 2004 - present
Offering clients brochures, business cards, poster ads, and web page design.

References
Anton Smith, M.A., Drew University, Madison, New Jersey. College Advisor, Tel: (908) 555-4444
Jed Baker, Ph.D., Social Skills Training Project, Somerset, New Jersey. Customer. Tel: (732) 214-1200.

Sample Resume (Highlighting Chronological Experience)

Robert Smith
343 Oak Road
Mapletown, NJ 07044
Tel: (973) 555-8282
Robertsmith@netmail.com

Position Desired
Graphic Designer

Education
Drew University, Madison, New Jersey
B.A. degree in Graphic Design, May, 2005

Work Experience
Own graphic design business, May 2004 - present
- Offering clients brochures, business cards, poster ads, and web page design.

R & B Printers, South Orange, New Jersey. September 2004 – Present
- Assist in layout and design of brochures, posters, business cards, and all print requests from customers.
- Use of multiple software programs including Quark Express, Photoshop,Pagemaker, Type Styler, Illustrator, Macwrite, Microsoft Word, Microsoft Powerpoint, Microsoft Excel, and Microsoft Publisher.
- Able to work under deadlines in a customer-oriented work environment. Detail oriented and well-organized.

Dan's Designs, Montville, New Jersey. January 2005 – May 2005. Internship.
- Contributed to all aspects of a cutting edge design firm.
- Assisted with creation of logos and layout for advertisements for local businesses.
- Work well with colleagues under a deadline and open to all feedback.

Art Warehouse, Springfield, New Jersey. June 2001- August 2003
- Assisted customers, stocked shelves, ordered supplies, answered phones, and opened and closed store.

References
Anton Smith, M.A., Drew University, Madison, New Jersey. College Advisor, Tel: (908) 555-4444
Jed Baker, Ph.D., Social Skills Training Project, Somerset, New Jersey. Customer. Tel: (732) 214-1200.

Sample Resume (Mixed: Functional Skills and Chronological Experience)

Robert Smith
343 Oak Road
Mapletown, NJ 07044
Tel: (973) 555-8282
Robertsmith@netmail.com

Position Desired
Graphic Designer

Education
Drew University, Madison, New Jersey
B.A. degree in Graphic Design, May, 2005

Skills
Graphic Design Skills

- Web Page Design
- Book and Magazine Cover Design
- Poster Layout
- Brochures
- Business Cards
- Slide Show Presentation

Business Skills

- Work well with deadlines
- Customer centered approach
- Work well with colleagues
- Open to feedback
- Detail-oriented, well organize

Work Experience
Own graphic design business, May 2004 - present

- Offering clients brochures, business cards, poster ads, and web page design.

R & B Printers, South Orange, New Jersey. September 2004 – Present

- Assist in layout and design of brochures, posters, business cards, and all print requests from customers.
- Use of multiple software programs including Quark Express, Photoshop, Pagemaker, Type Styler, Illustrator, Macwrite, Microsoft Word, Microsoft Powerpoint, Microsoft Excel, and Microsoft Publisher.
- Able to work under deadlines in a customer-oriented work environment. Detail oriented and well-organized.

Dan's Designs, Montville, New Jersey. January 2005 – May 2005. Internship.

- Contributed to all aspects of a cutting edge design firm.
- Assisted with creation of logos and layout for advertisements for local businesses.
- Work well with colleagues under a deadline and open to all feedback.

Art Warehouse, Springfield, New Jersey. June 2001- August 2003

- Assisted customers, stocked shelves, ordered supplies, answered phones, and opened and closed store.

References
Anton Smith, M.A., Drew University, Madison, New Jersey. College Advisor, Tel: (908) 555-4444

Jed Baker, Ph.D., Social Skills Training Project, Somerset, New Jersey. Customer. Tel: (732) 214-1200.

 Scripts for networking with friends, relatives, and potential employers

Rationale

Most people still get jobs through people they know. New employers may have greater trust in you when they know someone who knows you. The larger your network of friends and acquaintances, the more job possibilities you will find.

Whom should you contact? How do you build a network of contacts?

Networking means to ask friends, relatives, old employers, and anyone you meet if they know of any job possibilities and if they know other people you can contact to ask about job openings. Thus for each person you already know, you can get two or more new contacts until your network grows. Use the Network Worksheet to start planning who to talk with:

- **List all the friends you can contact** (do not forget friends and acquaintances from previous experiences (schools, clubs, universities). www.theultimates.com is a website that can help you track down telephone numbers and addresses of people you once knew.

- **List all the relatives** you can contact.

- **List former employers**, teachers and supervisors.

- Consider **people you see on a daily basis** but have not previously considered to be friends like people in stores, banks, restaurants, worksites or schools you attend.

- From each person on these lists, try to get two more contacts.

Script for calling a friend, relative, current or former employer, teacher or supervisor:

1. Hi, this is _____. I am looking for job as a _____ and I was hoping you could help. Is this an okay time to talk?

2. Do you know anyone who may need someone who can _____?

3. Do you know anyone else who might know of any job openings?

4. Would you be willing to be a reference for me? Would you be comfortable telling others about my skills in _____ and some positive personality traits such as _____? If so, can I get your address and how an employer could contact you?

5. Thank you very much for your time.

Script for calling someone who has been referred to you by others:

1. Hello, this is _____. I am a friend (or relative or acquaintance) of _____. I am looking for job as a _____ and he/she said that you might be able to help. Is this an okay time to talk?

2. Do you know anyone who may need someone who can _____?

3. Do you know anyone else who might know of any job openings?

4. Thank you very much for your time.

Send a thank you note after calling someone

This will increase your chance of getting a good recommendation and helps remind the person you are still looking for work. See sample thank you notes.

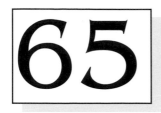

Activity Page: Scripts for networking

Teaching

1. **Explain** the need for networking and the steps involved.

2. Have students fill out the Networking Worksheet with those they know (remind them to return to the sheet as they get new referrals).

3. **Model** talking with friends, relatives, former teachers, prospective employers and those they do not know whom they have been referred to. Show a respectful, grateful approach as well as a self-centered approach in which the student does not ask if it is okay to talk and does not thank the person.

4. Have the students **role-play** the scripts.

5. Have students create a deadline for when they will begin contacting the people on their list.

Generalization

Priming

Remind students whenever they will be around others that they can tell them they are looking for work and try to get some job leads. Role-play to prepare with different people they may interact with.

Facilitated practice

Adults can coach students (with permission from the student) when they are around others to help them ask about job leads.

Review

Provide feedback for students about how to talk respectfully, articulate what kind of job they want, and show appreciation to others for their help.

Networking Worksheet

For each person on this list, find out two more people who they can suggest you contact.

List your friends	Additional contact	Additional contact
1.	1.	2.
2.	1.	2.
3.	1.	2.
4.	1.	2.
5.	1.	2.
6.	1.	2.
7.	1.	2.
8.	1.	2.
9.	1.	2.
10.	1.	2.
11.	1.	2.
12.	1.	2.
13.	1.	2.
14.	1.	2.
15.	1.	2.

List your relatives	Additional contact	Additional contact
1.	1.	2.
2.	1.	2.
3.	1.	2.
4.	1.	2.
5.	1.	2.
6.	1.	2.
7.	1.	2.
8.	1.	2.
9.	1.	2.
10.	1.	2.
11.	1.	2.
12.	1.	2.
13.	1.	2.
14.	1.	2.
15.	1.	2.

Former employers or supervisors	Additional contact	Additional contact
1.	1.	2.
2.	1.	2.
3.	1.	2.
4.	1.	2.
5.	1.	2.
6.	1.	2.
7.	1.	2.
8.	1.	2.
9.	1.	2.
10.	1.	2.
11.	1.	2.
12.	1.	2.
13.	1.	2.
14.	1.	2.
15.	1.	2.

List the people you see each day at work, school or in the community	Additional contact	Additional contact
1.	1.	2.
2.	1.	2.
3.	1.	2.
4.	1.	2.
5.	1.	2.
6.	1.	2.
7.	1.	2.
8.	1.	2.
9.	1.	2.
10.	1.	2.
11.	1.	2.
12.	1.	2.
13.	1.	2.
14.	1.	2.
15.	1.	2.

Sample Thank You Note

(when you have spoken with an employer about a job they advertised)

John Smith

35 Maple Avenue

Coletown, New York 12082

Tel: (845) 682-9898

New York Tigers

1245 Roseland Boulevard

Redding, New York, 13445

October 10, 2005

Dear General Manager,

Thank you for taking the time to speak with me about the job position in your organization. This is precisely the kind of job I have been looking for and I believe my skills and experience would be a good match for the position. Please do not hesitate to call me if you have and further questions. Thank you again for considering me for the job.

Sincerely,

John Smith

Sample Thank You Note
(when you have spoken with someone who does not have a job opening but gave you some leads or agreed to be a reference for you)

John Smith

35 Maple Avenue

Coletown, New York 12082

Tel: (845) 682-9898

Mrs. Mary Johnson

342 Rose Lane

Cedars, New York, 13091

October 10, 2005

Dear Mrs. Johnson,

Thank you for taking the time to speak with me and giving me some leads on jobs. I plan to call the people you suggested immediately. I am also very grateful to you for agreeing to be a reference for me. Your words have always meant a lot to me and I am sure your recommendation will be a huge help in my finding employment.

As you know, I am eager to find a position as a _____. Please let me know if you hear of any other openings in this area. Thank you again for all your help.

Sincerely,

John Smith

Interview skills (and whether to disclose a disability)

Rationale

Employers often consider a face-to-face or phone interview as critical to hiring someone since this interaction provides some information about what it will be like to interact with that person on an ongoing basis. Thus it is crucial to develop a plan for having a successful interview.

Should you disclose information about a disability?

Many adults with Autism Spectrum Disorders (ASD) indicate great difficulty with interviewing because of their difficulties with social interaction.

- **If social difficulties are readily apparent** during an interview (e.g., difficulties with eye contact, flow of conversation, or idiosyncratic movements) it is often helpful to disclose to the employer that you have a disability while explaining that although it may be noticeable, it will not in any way interfere with performing the duties of the job. In fact, you may want to point out how many aspects of autism spectrum disorders make someone an excellent employee (e.g., the desire for rules and consistency often make ASD individuals more honest, hardworking and reliable than those without autistic disorders). See **"Disclosing a disability worksheet."**

- **If your disability will interfere with the job** duties (e.g., social skills are key to sales positions), then the job position may not be right for you.

- **If your disability is not at all noticeable** and will not interfere with your job, then there may be no need to disclose information about a disability.

Preparing for the interview

- **Research the position** to find out exactly what the job duties are, what skills they are looking for and what the company does. This way you can prepare answers that will match what the employer is looking for. Study the job posting to find out more about the position to be filled. To find out more about the company try one of the following websites: www.interbiznet.com/hunt/, www.joboptions.com, wetfeet.com. corptech.com, google.com (then insert company name). Companiesonline.com prnewswire.com, hoovers.com, and vault.com (this contains an employee message board of what employees say about their company).

- **Create a portfolio of your work** to show the employer. This might include: Samples of writing, drawings, music, pictures of projects you completed, machines you have maintained, crafts, computer programs, or lists of satisfied clients.

- **Rehearse a 1-minute commercial** about yourself (see "Tell me about yourself worksheet").

- Rehearse what you might say, if anything, **about a disability** (See **"Disclosing a disability worksheet"**).

- **Rehearse answers to common interview questions**, questions for you to ask them, and how to close the interview (see **"Answers to Common Interview Questions"**).

- **Rehearse how to get to the interview** (take a trial run of your travel plans).

Dressing for the interview

For men and women: Dress one step above what might be expected dress code for the job.

- **Men**: Shaved, hair groomed neatly, pressed suit or dress pants and dress shirt, shoes with dark socks (no white socks), matching belt and shoes, clean looking brief case.

- **Women**: Business dress suit or outfit, nothing too revealing, shoes not sandals, hair is neat (no "big" hair or elaborate styles), not too much make-up, neat portfolio or briefcase.

Nonverbal skills during the interview

Nonverbal skills are crucial, although any information you provide about a disability (see above) may help offset any difficulties here. But it still makes sense to try to present yourself as well as possible. Use the **Nonverbal Behavior Checklist** as a guide for how to conduct yourself in the interview.

After the interview is over

- Write a thank you note (see sample thank you note).

- Call to check on the progress of their search for an employee. Say, "This is _____ calling for _____. He or she interviewed me for the position of _____ (job position) last _____ (day of interview). I was calling to thank him or her and to check on the progress of their search for an appropriate candidate. I would like to express my continued interest in the job and any opportunity to work with him/her. If he/she has any questions, I can be reached at _____ (phone number and email). Thanks again."

Activity Page: Interview skills

Teaching

1. **Explain** rationale for the importance of the interview and need to prepare.

2. Have students decide whether they need to disclose something about their disability and if so, to prepare a statement about their disability using the "Disclosing a disability" worksheet.

3. Have students write up a brief commercial about themselves to answer the "tell me about yourself" question using the "Tell me about yourself" worksheet.

4. Have students write up sample answers to common interview questions and a closing statement using the "Common interview questions" worksheet.

5. **Model** and **role-play** the interview stressing the nonverbal cues (see nonverbal behavior checklist) as well as the content of their answers to questions.

Generalization

Priming

Preparation is everything when it comes to the interview. Students need to prepare their material and role-play many times, especially the night prior to the interview. They can commit some of the answers to a cue card to review just prior to the interview.

Facilitated practice

Others can coach students during role-plays to refine their nonverbal and verbal responses.

Review

Provide feedback to students after their role-plays, stressing the positive to build their confidence, then adding areas to improve.

Tell me about yourself worksheet

I have always been interested in _____(the type of career you are trying to get) because _____ (list why it has meaning to you- but do not list money as a reason). I am eager to _____ and willing to do the hard work to be successful at (list job position). I am currently _____ (list current year in school or current job) and will graduate from _____ (school) with _____ (degree/honors). I have _____ (list experience, training, job experiences). Through these experiences, I have learned to _____ (list specific skills), which I see as important for a career in _____ (career related to job position).

Sample Answer to "Tell me about yourself"

(for a college student seeking a job as assistant to a research librarian)

I have always been interested in library science because I love researching and cataloguing information. My memory for factual information is probably my greatest strength. I am eager to gain experience in a library environment and I am willing to do the hard work to be successful as an assistant to the research librarian. I am currently in my first year of college at Rutgers University and plan to major in library sciences. I have volunteered at my high school's library for two years helping the librarians restack shelves and catalogue books, as well as assisting teachers and students to locate books and other information resources. Through these experiences, I have developed excellent organizational skills, learned to follow multiple directions and take initiative, and meet the needs of library patrons, which I see as important for a career in library science.

Disclosing a disability worksheet

"I think it is important for you to know that I have _____

(Asperger's Syndrome, Autism, another disorder), which describes people with

_____ (often above average intellectual ability and some

difficulties socializing). In no way will this interfere with performing the duties of my job. It may

be helpful for you to contact my references to hear about my very positive past job performance.

What you may notice about me is that I _____

_____ (do not socialize that much and do not often make perfect eye

contact), but I am usually _____ _____ (more

productive than most because I am not socializing, and always honest and reliable). I hope this will

not dissuade you from considering me for the position."

Note: If the position requires extensive socializing (e.g., a sales position), you may want to explain

how you get around social difficulties, or you may not want to consider applying for that job.

Sample answers to common interview questions
(see also Kennedy, 2000; Grandin, 2004)

1. What kind of experience do you have for the job?

    a. Ask what the duties of the job are and what kind of experiences they are looking for and then try to match your answer to what they want.

    b. Do not say that you do not have any experience! Remember, many skills are transferable to many jobs, so you do not need to have the exact experience in this kind of job. Consider volunteer, paid work, experiences in clubs, classes and other training that have given you skills at:

        i. Problem solving

        ii. Organizing and prioritizing work tasks, time management

        iii. Working well with others

        iv. Skills specific to a particular job like: computer skills, typing, filing, answering phones, mechanical abilities, and artistic abilities.

    c. If you are shy, consider showing them a portfolio of your work such as samples of writing, drawings, pictures of what you have accomplished, machines you have maintained, projects you have created, crafts, computer programs, lists of satisfied clients, etc.

2. What are your strengths?

    a. Write 3-5 examples or stories that detail your abilities. Consider these positive abilities:

    b. Specific job-related skills: computer, mechanical skills, writing, artistic ability, crafts, typing, filing, etc.

    c. Transferable skills:

        i. Leadership and working well with others

        ii. Organization and time management

        iii. Hardworking, dedicated, willing to go the extra mile

        iv. Open to learning and feedback

        v. Self-starter, highly motivated, fast learner.

3. What are your weaknesses? Or what would you change about yourself?

a. Focus on improving things you already to well rather than sharing a genuine weakness. "I would like to continue to learn more computer program languages so I can do more kinds of programming jobs."

b. Admit to weaknesses that are really strengths. For example, "I can be a bit of a perfectionist as I like to do things right."

4. Where do you see yourself in five years?

Answer should be consistent with where you could advance in that company (but do not mention that you want the interviewer's job).

5. Do you prefer to work with people or alone?

Although you may prefer to work alone, if the job requires working with people, it is better to say you are flexible and can work well alone or with others.

6. What are your outside interests?

Be enthusiastic in talking about any special interests, but do not share interests that raise others' concerns, such as interests in weapons, horror films, or sexual material).

7. How do you deal with stressful situations

Describe an example that shows how you stay calm to try to solve problems by:

a. Collecting more information about the situation

b. Considering the various options

c. Seeking others' opinions or advice

d. Taking action

8. Why should I hire you?

Give three reasons covering your:

a. Experience and training relevant to the job

b. Positive traits

c. Your interest and desire to work for their company.

9. What kind of hours would you want to work? Do you want to work full-time or part-time?

Express your desire to work whatever hours the job calls for.

10. If you were fired or changed jobs a lot, here are some reasonable explanations:

a. The previous employer was downsizing.

b. The previous jobs were just temp jobs to increase my skill. I was waiting to get a more permanent position in the area I like.

c. If you were fired for misconduct and the person can look this up in a public record or call a previous employer and find out, then tell the truth and stress how you learned from your mistake and are very different now than you were then.

d. Do not lie. You can withhold certain information, but do not make up untrue events.

11. Why do you have many years between jobs?

   Explain that you were more selective, waiting for the kind of job opening that you really want, such as what you are now applying for.

12. Questions for you to ask them:

   a. What are the main responsibilities of the job?

   b. Who will I report to?

   c. Can you describe a typical day?

   d. Are there any opportunities for further training?

   e. Is there any travel expected?

   f. What are the hours of the job?

   g. Do not ask about money until they offer you the job. Do your research to find out how much people make at such a job and then ask for just above the average salary for such a job (see www.weddles.com for salary information about various professions).

13. Closing the interview:

   a. Listen for clues that the interviewer wants to end the interview (e.g., he or she may stand up, say "okay then," or begin to shuffle papers and look away at other things).

   b. Thank him or her. Say, "Thank you so much for meeting with me."

   c. Check if there are any concerns the interviewer has about your skills. Say, "Based on what I've told you, do you have any concerns about my ability to perform successfully at the job?" If they have any concerns, try to remind them of your skills and commitment to do all it takes to be successful at the job.

   d. Ask if it is okay to follow up with them. Say, "I know you will be busy interviewing others, but would it be okay to call you to check on the progress of your search?"

Sample Thank You Note for the Interview

John Smith

35 Maple Avenue

Coletown, New York 12082

Tel: (845) 682-9898

New York Tigers

1245 Roseland Boulevard

Redding, New York, 13445

February 1, 2006

Dear General Manager,

Thank you for meeting with me yesterday to discuss the equipment manager position. I was very impressed with your knowledge of the team and its history and the excellent way in which you have managed the organization. This is precisely the kind of job I have been looking for and I believe my organizational skills and past experience as equipment manager at Sentinel University make me a good match for the position. I am eager to take the next step and will follow up this letter with a phone call to see how you are doing with the search. Please do not hesitate to call me if you have any further questions. Thank you again for considering me for the job.

Sincerely,

John Smith

The structure of the letter includes:

1. A thank you for meeting with you.

2. A reminder of when and what you interviewed for.

3. A reminder of your skills and experience as they relate to the job.

4. An expression of your continued interest and desire to follow up with a call.

Nonverbal Behavior Checklist

Grooming: Are you showered, hair washed and neat, shaved if a man, the right amount of makeup if a woman?

Dress: Are you dressed one step up from what is expected at the job? Clothes are neat and pressed?

Greet the interviewer with eye-contact and a smile and say, "Hello, nice to meet you."

Establish a positive beginning by complimenting the interviewer on their office, pictures, the company or something else you see.

Take your cue from the interviewer: Wait for them to extend their hand for a handshake (some people do not like to shake hands). Wait for them to indicate where to sit (do not just sit before being told where to sit).

Show a good listening position during the interview: leaning towards the interviewer, facing the interviewer with eye-contact (it is okay to occasionally look away and then come back), quiet hands and feet rather than fidgeting, try to smile and nod as you listen to them.

Read the interviewer's interest in what you are saying. If they seem disinterested, ask them what they would prefer to hear about. For example, say "would you like to hear about my training or relevant experience?" or "What would you most like to hear about?"

Handling rejection

Rationale

It is inevitable that we will not get every job we apply for since their may be many people applying for one job. The most successful job seekers are those who do not give up, learn from their experience, and continue to pursue employment.

What to think if you do not get the job

If unemployment is high and jobs are scarce, it means you will not get most jobs. This has little to do with you and more to do with the high number of applicants for each job. For most people, it takes many attempts to get a job. Expect many rejections before getting a job. Don't let rejection discourage you from trying, because the more you try the more likely you will be to get a job!

Consider what you can learn from the experience

- Ask the employer if they are willing to share their thoughts about why you did not get the job to help you refine your application skills.

- If you lacked the required experience for the job, consider what kind of training or volunteer experience you could do to gain the needed experience. Or consider whether you need to apply for a different kind of job.

- If the reason for the rejection had to do with nonverbal/social interaction skills at the interview, consider the need to create a better disclosure statement about your disability that explains these difficulties but points out how they will not interfere with the job. Also consider adding more references who can attest to your high level of job performance or adding to your portfolio to show employers sample of your excellent work.

Activity Page: Handling rejection

Teaching

1. **Explain** need to expect rejection without being discouraged.

2. Discuss past job rejections and review ways to explain why you did not get the job.

3. Create an action plan to improve your chances at the next interview, including ways to get more training, better ways to explain your disability, add references who can attest to your excellent abilities, or improve your portfolio of sample work.

Generalization

Priming

Before applying and interviewing for a job, discuss the possibility that the student might not get the job (to offset any great disappointment that otherwise may occur) and remind them that they must keep applying to be successful.

Facilitated practice

Coach students through a recent job rejection, helping them to come up with constructive explanations for not getting the job and how to learn from the experience.

Review

Provide feedback to students about any overly negative thinking after a rejection that is interfering with their job search. Help them alter their approach to interviews and the job searching approach when necessary.

Do's and don'ts to maintain a job

Rationale

Although it is hard to get a job, keeping a job can be even more difficult as you are being evaluated every day. How you act on the job determines whether you can maintain employment or even get a raise or job promotion.

Things to do and not to do to at your job.

Skill	DO	DON'T
Dress Code and Grooming	Dress as formally as your boss and coworkers do. Keep your body, hair and teeth clean each day, shave as necessary.	Dress as uniquely as you desire, even if it differs radically from all the other workers. Disregard hygiene.
Arriving and leaving each day	Be on time to your job and consider staying late to complete assignments (this shows your boss you are committed to doing a good job).	Show up late and leave early.
Learning about your job responsibilities.	Ask what your specific duties are when you begin the job. Write down what to do so you will not forget and have to keep asking the boss.	Avoid asking what to do. Just relax and do what you want until someone tells you to do something.
Listening and taking instruction	Always demonstrate a good listening position with your boss or co-workers. Consider taking notes on what they say so you do not forget any instructions.	Show a poor listening position (no eye contact, turn away) and do not bother to try to remember what they say.
When you do not know what to do	Ask for help or clarification if you do not understand what to do (this is okay as long as you are not asking the same questions over and over again).	Pretend you understand and then don't do anything because you really do not understand what to do.
Taking initiative	Keep busy, particularly in front of your boss. When there is down time, try to find another task that needs to be completed based on notes you have taken about your job duties.	Sit with nothing to do, especially in front of your boss so he or she sees they are paying you for nothing today.

Things to do and not to do to at your job (cont.)

Skill	DO	DON'T
Responding to criticism, accusations or complaints (see Skill #69)	Listen to the feedback without getting angry. If what they are saying is true, then agree with them and pledge to improve in that area. If it is a false accusation then express your confusion about why they accused you of doing something wrong and ask for an explanation.	Get mad and deny anything your boss says that might be negative about you.
Respectfully disagreeing with others (see Skill #60)	Calmly express that you do not understand the direction, criticism or complaint. In a questioning tone of voice say "I thought . . . (and express your opinion or understanding).	In an angry tone, tell the other person that they are wrong and you are right.
Work Cooperatively with others (see Skill #58)	Discuss ideas openly, be willing to compromise or go with the majority vote.	Insult others' ideas, be unwilling to compromise, refuse to participate unless they do things your way.
Make small talk with others	Greet the boss and coworkers. If they ask you how you are doing, respond and then ask them back how they are doing. Say goodbye when you are leaving for the day.	Ignore others greetings or attempts to ask how you are doing.

68 | Activity Page: Do's and don'ts to maintain a job

Teaching

1. **Explain** keys to maintaining employment by reviewing the information in the table. Give some examples of the different skill issues such as:

   a. For dress code: How wearing sweat pants to an office job might create a problem.

   b. For when you do not understand: Imagine the boss explains that an important sales call is coming in and you do not understand the directions, so you do not answer the phone. This causes the boss to lose an important client and then you get fired.

2. **Model** and **role-play** the right and wrong ways for each skill in the Table. Because accepting criticism and respectfully disagreeing with others are important and involved skills, they appear in separate skill lessons (see Skill #69 and #60) so you can allocate more time to practicing those skills. Use a game-show format to model and role-play the skills.

   a. For example, you can model a behavior from the Table and then offer prizes if they correctly answer the following questions: "Is this a DO or a DON'T? What skill is this?"

   b. You can also ask them to role-play a particular skill to get prizes.

3. Since the table covers quite a lot of material, you may want to consider only reviewing those skills relevant to the students you are teaching. For example, if dress code is never a problem, but making small talk is, then focus on making small talk.

Generalization

Priming

Those skills relevant to the student's needs should be primed before going to work every day. They can be written on a cue card for easy review.

Facilitated practice

Job coaches and teachers who support students at a worksite can actively coach those students on the skills.

Review

Getting regular feedback from employers is key to being able to make the necessary adjustments to maintain good job performance. If students do not have a job coach, they might want to consider asking the employer on a periodic basis for a review of their job performance so they can improve. Most employers would welcome such an opportunity from a motivated employee wanting to improve their performance.

 # Responding to criticisms, accusations or complaints on the job

Rationale

The ability to respond well to criticism on the job can help you maintain your job. Responding with anger and rejecting all criticism makes it hard for others to get along with you and may lead employers to fire you.

Keep calm—it is okay to make a mistake

Stop and remind yourself to keep calm. Everyone makes mistakes. It is the process of correcting mistakes that allows us to learn. If you get mad, it makes others not want to interact with you and you could lose your job.

Decide what kind of criticism it is

There are three types of criticism: **true constructive** criticisms (what they are saying about you is true and they offer a way to improve), **false accusations** (what they are saying is false), or *insulting criticism* (they are name-calling with insulting words).

- **If it is true constructive criticism**, say, "You're right. I am sorry. Let me try to fix that. " Then offer a plan or discuss making plans to improve. You may ask the employer what you can do to improve. If you are asked to correct work, it is often best to do it rather than argue because then you will sooner be able to put it behind you.

- **If it is a false accusation**, criticism or complaint, don't get angry. Be open to the possibility that you may have done something wrong from another's perspective. Calmly express your confusion about such an accusation and ask for them to explain what and why they think you did something wrong. You can say::

  — "I am confused. I did not . . ."

  — "I am confused, I thought I was supposed to . . ."

  — "Can you explain what was supposed to have been done?"

- **If it is insulting criticism**, using demeaning name calling, use an "I" statement to express your feelings and ask for them to stop talking to you that way. For example:

  "I feel _____ (offended, upset)

  when you _____ (call me names or scream).

  I would like you to _____ (tell me what I did wrong without insulting me)."

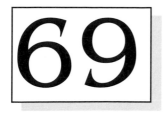

Activity Page: Responding to criticisms, accusations or complaints on the job

Teaching

1. **Explain** the rationale that how you respond to criticism from an employer can help you to keep or lose your job.

2. **Model** and **role-play** situations in which the student feels the criticism is accurate and when the student believes they have been falsely accused. Use actual situations that have occurred or the following suggested situations:

   a. An employer says that the student did not file some papers according to the instructions they were given. If this is correct, then the student can agree, apologize and ask to correct the problem. The student may want to write down the instructions so that they will remember for next time.

   b. A student is falsely accused of leaving a work space dirty, but the student was never in the work space. Show how the student can calmly express his/her confusion since he/she was not at the work space.

   c. A student is being insulted by a coworker for working too slowly. The co-worker says the student is "stupid" or some other insulting remark. Show how the student can respond with an "I" statement.

Generalization

Priming

Prior to getting feedback from employers on scheduled evaluations or after the student has completed a project at work, students can be reminded about how to handle different kinds of criticism.

Facilitated practice

Anytime one has to provide feedback to students is an opportunity to practice. It may be best to preface feedback with reminders about why and how to accept constructive criticism. Then ask if they are ready for such feedback so they have time to prepare themselves.

Review

Redirect negative reactions to criticism. Ask them if they perceived it as a true criticism, false, or insulting and remind them how to deal with each kind of criticism.

Exiting a job

Rationale

There are many reasons one might leave a job. Sometimes one might want to leave and other times one is told to leave. In either case, it is important to try to leave a job without creating bad feelings so you can:

- Get a recommendation from the employer for another job
- Avoid negative gossip about you that might interfere with you getting another job

When you want to leave a job

- **Give advance notice** (usually at least two weeks before you leave). You may want to do this verbally to your boss and in writing to make it official.

- **Explain why** in a way that does not insult others

  — Need more challenge – looking for more advancement

  — Interested in pursuing a different career

  — Need to focus on studies or family issues so no time for work

- **Thank the employer** for giving you the opportunity to work

- Consider asking them for a **recommendation** for a future job

- If you had to leave the job for health or other personal reasons (other than that you did not like the job), you may be eligible for unemployment benefits. Contact your local **unemployment agency** to apply (www.workforcesecurity.doleta.gov/map.asp for local agencies in your area).

When asked to leave a job

- If you were fired from a job, you may also be eligible for unemployment benefits. Contact your local unemployment agency at the website listed above.

- Most employers have policies to provide feedback to you of any problems and make plans to correct those difficulties prior to firing you. You may want to request that they follow any such procedures and allow you to correct any problems rather than firing you.

- Contacting an attorney?

  — If you believe you were fired only because you have a disability and the disability did not affect   your job performance, then you may want to contact an attorney.

  — Similarly, you may want contact an attorney if you were fired because of some criminal behavior on your part. You may want to insure that nothing incriminating is put on your employment record or discussed with the general public to avoid problems getting other jobs.

  — **A word of caution** on bringing legal action against employers: there are websites that keep track of people who sue or bring legal action against employers and other employers check those websites and try to avoid hiring people on that list. So unless you are sure you were discriminated against or that they may spread by rumors about you to others, you may not want to hire an attorney.

- Consider what you can learn from the experience. What will you do or not do at the next job?

Activity Page: Exiting a job

Teaching

1. **Explain** the importance of minimizing negative perceptions of you by the former employer when leaving a job. Go over the steps involved when leaving because you want to or because you were fired.

2. **Model** and **role-play** the right and wrong way to explain why you are leaving a job to an employer.

Generalization

Priming

Remind students about the steps to exit a job effectively when they voice their intentions to do so.

Facilitated practice

Help students draft a letter and role-play how to leave a job. Help them apply for unemployment benefits if appropriate. If they were fired, coach them on how to assess whether they need to consult an attorney to limit any public statements the former employer can make or whether they might have been discriminated against.

Review

Provide students with feedback about what they said to employers about leaving a job. If they were fired, provide feedback about why they were fired and what to do to protect their image and learn from what happened.

Managing money

Rationale

Although there is more to life than money, having a comfortable amount of money can improve the quality of your life by allowing you to make more choices about what to do for work and recreation and where to live. The more money you have, the more freedom you have to choose what you do and where you live.

The key to having money is to:

- **Know how to make it.** This requires developing a career and job interest that can actually provide a paycheck. See Skill #62, "Choosing job/career directions," for ideas about jobs that pay.

- **Know how to save money.** This skill is essentially about learning to delay your immediate pleasures and not buy certain things so that you can save money. Saved money can be invested to make you more money even when you are not working.

As a first step, consider what your financial goals are (what do you need the money for?):

- **Invest in your future.** Consider goals that will help you to eventually make more money and be able to make more choices in life. Paying for college, job training, a car, a wardrobe for work, or your own place to live are often investments in your own future as they may help you to be able to get a higher paying job and make more choices about your life.

- **Short-term pleasures.** Do you just want to buy something for your immediate pleasure? Entertainment, toys, and other amusements are okay, but buying too many of these things may interfere with saving money for things that help you to grow and have more money in the future.

Create a budget that will allow you to save the money you will need

- Consider how much money you will need to reach your goals (e.g., to pay for school, training, transportation, clothes, a place to live) and when you want to have this money. Use the **"Create-a-budget" worksheet** to help you calculate how much you need to save each month to reach your goals.

- Adjust your expenses to stay in your budget by

  — Lowering unnecessary expenses (entertainment, gifts).

  — Consider living with parents longer to save money

- Consider ways to boost your income by extra work, chores, jobs around the house or in the neighborhood, or selling old items.

Avoid debt and late fees

- If you have credit cards, always pay off the balance in total each month. Otherwise you will be paying more than you owe in interest to the credit card companies.

- Consider using electronic/automatic billing through a checking account that you set up at a local bank. If your bills are paid automatically from your account, you will avoid late fees if you forget to pay. You must of course keep enough money in the account to cover the bills.

Learn to invest saved money

Consider seeking advice from a financial consultant to invest money in interest-bearing bank accounts, stocks, bonds, and mutual funds, or other investment vehicles. Your money can be making you money when properly invested.

Become a savvy shopper

Most items you want to purchase (cars, food, entertainment, clothes) can be found at varying prices. It pays to compare to see who has the lowest price for what you want. The internet is an excellent source for comparison shopping of many items. You may want to go to www.google.com and search for the item you want. You will get a list of stores that sell the item along with a list of websites that show many prices for different stores. Remember to check the actual price and shipping costs. Don't fall for advertisers promising that something is on sale, just search for the lowest price.

Activity Page: Managing money

Teaching

1. **Explain** the need to save money to increase the quality of one's life and ability to choose one's lifestyle. Review the steps to developing financial goals, and creating a budget.

2. Have students identify some of their concrete financial goals (i.e., what they want to be able to afford) and when they would like to achieve them.

3. Have students fill out the **Create-a-budget worksheet.**

4. As they discover the difficulty of creating a balanced budget, have them consider what expenses to lower and what ways to boost their income.

5. Consider referring them to free financial advisors through local agencies or investment houses to help them make plans to invest their savings.

6. For those students in debt, help them develop a plan to get out of debt.

Generalization

Priming

Remind students of their budget and goals prior to going shopping or wherever they may be tempted to make impulsive purchases.

Facilitated practice

Coach students to make wise buying and savings decisions as they get paid and tempted to buy items.

Review

Review with students their progress in keeping to their budgets and reaching their goals. Help them make adjustments as necessary.

Create-a-budget worksheet

Financial Goals

I need _____ amount of money by _____ amount of time to be able to pay for

_____ .

Monthly Savings Goal

In order to have this money I need to start saving _____ amount of money each month.

Create a Monthly Budget

Fill in monthly income and monthly expenses so that monthly income minus monthly expenses will add up to your monthly savings goal.

INCOME SOURCES (amount)	EXPENSES (amount)
Job	Housing
Governmental supports	Food
Parental supports	Phone
Gifts	Electric
Other	Cable, internet
	Clothes
	Transportation costs
	School/work materials
	Healthcare
	Entertainment
	Gifts
	Other

Total Income_____ - Total Expenses _____ = Monthly Savings goal _____

If income minus expenses does not equal your monthly savings goal, then you must consider ways to increase your income or lower your expenses.

- **Consider lowering expenses**:

   — Lower unnecessary expenses (e.g., entertainment, gifts).

   — Consider living with parents longer to save money.

- **Consider other ways to make money** by extra work, chores, jobs around the house, or in the neighborhood, or selling old items.

Dealing with emergencies and emergency workers (such as police or hospital workers)

Rationale

It is important to be prepared for emergencies and know who and how to reach out for help when needed. It is equally important for emergency workers to understand you to best be able to help you in an emergency situation. Many students on the autism spectrum have mistakenly been perceived as being on drugs, under the influence of alcohol, or resisting authority when in a crisis because of some eccentric behaviors that were expressed when highly stressed. It is helpful to have a statement that explains any odd behaviors that may appear when under high levels of stress.

If you are lost or in a crisis situation and do not know what to do

Consider keeping a cell phone and a list of emergency contacts (including emergency services) with you at all times so you can call a trusted friend when in a dangerous or confusing situation such as:

- Getting lost

- Running out of money and not knowing how to pay to get somewhere

- If you were robbed or assaulted. Call the police as well as your personal contacts. If your phone was taken, go to the nearest phone booth and call 911 and make a collect call to your personal contacts.

- If you see a dangerous fire, call 911.

If stopped by a police officer or another authorized agent

Consider handing them a prepared statement about your disability in case the officer thinks you are acting oddly. Having a prepared statement can help explain any odd behaviors to the officer and help them treat you in a way that will reduce problems (see the Emergency Information Sheet).

 **Activity Page: Dealing with emergencies and emergency workers (such as police or hospital workers)**

Teaching

1. **Explain** the need to be prepared for emergencies.

2. Have them create a list of emergency service numbers and personal contacts to keep with them at all times (at home and on their person). Consider putting this information on a card and laminating it.

3. Have them create a prepared statement about their disability using the sample statement as a model. This can also be put into card form and laminated to keep with them at all times.

4. Consider **modeling** and **role-playing** the use of the emergency cards if:

    a. They see a dangerous fire.

    b. They are stopped for speeding while driving.

    c. They are questioned by a security officer for talking to themselves loudly in a mall.

    d. They are lost.

Generalization

Priming

Remind students to carry their emergency cards with them.

Facilitated practice

Coach students to use their cards if you are with them during an emergency.

Review

Provide feedback to students of what they could have said, whom they could have called after an emergency situation.

Sample Emergency Information Sheet
(give to police or other authorized individuals during a crisis)

I have Asperger's Syndrome (AS),

a neurobiological disorder on the autism spectrum. AS affects my ability to communicate and interact sometimes, especially in times of stress or crisis. Individuals with AS may:

- Lack eye contact

- Be overly sensitive to sounds, touch or light

- May not always answer questions in a way that relates to the topic

In case of an emergency, please contact:

_____   _____

Please note the following suggestions for assisting individuals with AS:

- Be patient and calming. Individuals with AS who feel attacked may become agitated and not think about what they are saying or doing.

- If an individual is very agitated, try to distract him or her by talking about another topic until they are calm.

- Avoid abstract language, slang, or idioms as some individuals with AS may not understand.

Negotiating transportation

Rationale

To be able to use transportation effectively allows you greater choice in what jobs you can get, where you live, and where you want to shop or enjoy recreational activities.

Gather information about public transportation

- The internet is a great source of information about local public transportation services and opportunities to carpool with others. Try the following websites:

    — www.local.com

    — www.commuterresource.com

    — www.roadbuddies.com

- Consider state and federal agencies that may fund transportation to and from jobs, healthcare appointments, and other activities. Medicaid may provide free transportation to healthcare appointments, and other agencies may provide free transportation to jobs. You may want to contact the following website for more information about programs that fund transportation: www.ctaa.org.

- When using public transportation, consider the following unwritten rules:

    — Never sit right next to a stranger if there are other seats available.

    — Let others off a bus or train before getting on.

    — Don't eat or drink if you are sitting very close to someone and your food or drink could spill on them.

    — Don't stare at strangers or start long conversations with them. It is okay to say hello to strangers, but they do not expect you to ask many questions or tell them much about yourself.

    — Try not to talk out loud to yourself or engage in odd motor mannerisms. If you cannot help talking, then be ready to explain to others that you were just thinking out loud if they stare at you. For motor movements, you may want to explain that you just get restless and this lets out some energy.

Gather information about obtaining a driver's license

- Contact your local Department of Motor Vehicles (DMV) to find out the steps to obtaining a driver's license (see www.DMV.org).

- Consider taking driver's education while in high school or private driving lessons from a driving school if out of high school.

Practice your transportation routes

Prior to driving or taking public transportation alone, practice with a coach or friend to help you get used to the route.

Have a crisis plan

- Consider keeping a cell phone and a list of emergency contacts with you at all times in case you get lost and need help getting somewhere (see Skill #72).

- If stopped by a police officer or another by authorized agent when driving , consider handing them a prepared statement about your disability in case the officer thinks you are acting oddly (see the Emergency Information Sheet in Skill #72).

 **Activity Page: Negotiating transportation**

Teaching

1. **Explain** the rationale for knowing how to use transportation, public or private. Review the ways to get information about their preferred use of transportation and detail the "unwritten rules" of using public transportation.

2. Have them create an action plan about what transportation routes they will investigate, when they will try them, with whom, and when they plan to try it on their own, if appropriate.

3. Students should create a crisis plan, including contacts and a prepared statement (see Skill #72).

4. **Model** and **role-play** appropriate transportation behaviors including

   a. Where to sit

   b. Letting people off prior to entering

   c. Appropriate greetings and limiting conversation

   d. How to explain talking to oneself or odd motor movements

Generalization

Priming

Remind students to explore their transportation needs when considering plans to go somewhere like work, recreational activities, or to visit others. Have students practice the route before they might need to use it if the upcoming event is important and they need to be on time.

Facilitated practice

Practice with the student until they can navigate the route themselves. Coach them on appropriate behaviors while using transportation.

Review

Provide feedback to students about their travel decisions and behaviors while on route.

References

Baker, J. E. (2001). *Social Skills Picture Book*. Arlington, TX: Future Horizons, Inc.

Baker, J. E. (2003). *Social Skills Training for Students with Asperger's Syndrome and Related Social Communication Disorders*. Shawnee Mission, KS: Autism Asperger's Publishing Company.

Baker, J.E. (in press). *Social Skills Picture Book for High School and Beyond*. Arlington, TX: Future Horizons, Inc.

Baron-Cohen, S. (1995). *Mindblindness*. Cambridge, MA: The MIT Press.

Baron-Cohen, S. (2002). *Mind Reading: The Interactive Guide to Emotions*. DVD-ROM set. University of Cambridge.

Beck, A. (1979). *Cognitive Therapy and the Emotional Disorders*. New York, NY: Plume.

Benson, H. (1976). *The Relaxation Response*. New York, NY: Avon.

Burns, D.D. (1990). *The Feeling Good Handbook*. New York, NY: Plume.

Canter, L. (1987). *Assertive Discipline*. New York, NY: Harper and Row.

Dunn, M. (2005*). S.O.S. Social Skills in our Schools: A Social Skill Program for Children with Pervasive Developmental Disorders, including High-functioning Autism and Asperger's Syndrome, and their Typical Peers*. Shawnee Mission, KS: Autism Aspergers Publishing Company.

Ehlers, S., & Gillberg, C. (1993). "The Epidemiology of Asperger's Syndrome - A Total Population Study." *Journal of Child Psychology and Psychiatry, 34* (8), 1327-1350.

Frith, U. (1989). *Autism: Explaining the Enigma*. Oxford, England: Blackwell.

Grandin, T. (1999). "Choosing the Right Job for People with Autism or Asperger's Syndrome." Fort Collins, CO: Colorado State University.

Grandin, T. & Duffy, K. (2004). *Developing Talents: Careers for Individuals with Asperger Syndrome and High-Functioning Autism*. Shawnee Mission, KS: Autism Asperger's Publishing Company.

Gray, C. (1996). *The Sixth Sense*. Unpublished manuscript.

Gresham, F.M., Sugai, G., & Horner, R. H. (2001). "Interpreting Outcomes of Social Skills Training for Students with High-incidence Disabilities." *Exceptional Children, 67*, 331-344.

Haring, T. & Breen, C. (1992). "A Peer Mediated Social Network Intervention to Enhance the Social Integration of Persons with Moderate and Severe Disabilities." *Journal of Applied Behavior Analysis, 25*, 319-333.

Hobson, R.P. (1996). *Autism and the Development of the Mind.* Mahwah, NJ: Lawrence Erlbaum Associates.

Hunsberger, M.B. (2001). "Transitioning At Its Best." In *Families: The Family Support Magazine, Volume10, Number 2*, pages 1-4. Published by the New Jersey Developmental Disabilities Council.

Kennedy, J. L. (2000). *Job Interviews for Dummies* (2nd ed.). New York: Hungry Minds, Inc.

Kim, J. A., Szatmari, P., Bryson, S. E., Streiner, D. L., & Wilson, F. J. (2000). "The Prevalence of Anxiety and Mood Problems Among Children with Autism and Asperger Syndrome." *Autism, 4,* 117-132.

Klin, A., Volkmar, F. R., & Sparrow, S. S. (2000). *Asperger's Syndrome.* New York, NY: The Guilford Press.

Ledgin, N. (2002). *Asperger's and Self-Esteem: Insight and Hope through Famous Role Models.* Arlington, TX: Future Horizons, Inc.

McAfee, J., & Mann, L. (1982). "The Prognosis for Mildly Handicapped Students." In T.L. Miller & E. Davis (Eds.), *The Mildly Handicapped Student* (pp. 461-496). New York, NY: Grune and Stratton.

McGinnis, E., & Goldstein, A. (1997*). Skillstreaming the Elementary School Child: New Strategies and Perspectives for Teaching Prosocial Skills.* Champaign, IL: Research Press.

Myles, B. S., & Southwick, J. (1999). *Asperger's Syndrome and Difficult Moments: Practical Solutions for Tantrums, Rage, and Meltdowns.* Shawnee Mission, KS: Autism Asperger's Publishing Company.

Odom, S.L., & Strain, P.S. (1984). "Peer-mediated Approaches to Promoting Children's Social Interaction: A Review." *American Journal of Orthopsychiatry, 54,* 544-557.

Odom, S.L., & Watts, E. (1991). "Reducing Teacher Prompts in Peer-mediated Interventions for Young Children with Autism." *Journal of Special Education, 25*, 26-43.

References

Patton, J., & Dunn, C. (1998). *Transition from School to Adulthood: Basic Concepts and Recommended Practices*. Austin, TX: Pro-Ed.

Twemlow, S. W., Fonagy, P., Sacco, F.C. Gies, M.L., Evans, R. & Ewbank, R. (2001). "Creating a Peaceful School Learning Environment: A Controlled Study of Elementary School Intervention to Reduce Violence." *American Journal of Psychiatry, 158*, 808-810.

Wagner, M., Blackorby, J., Cameto, R., Hebbeler, K. & Newman, L. (1993). *The Transition Experiences of Young People with Disabilities: A Summary of the Findings from the National Longitudinal Transition Study of Special Education Students*. Melo Park, CA: SRI International.

Wagner, S. (1998). *Inclusive Programming for Elementary Students with Autism*. Arlington, TX: Future Horizons, Inc.